TRUE RAIDERS

Τrue Raiders

THE UNTOLD STORY OF THE 1909 EXPEDITION TO FIND THE LEGENDARY ARK OF THE COVENANT

Brad Ricca

THORNDIKE PRESS
A part of Gale, a Cengage Company

Copyright © 2021 by Brad Ricca.
Thorndike Press, a part of Gale, a Cengage Company.

ALL RIGHTS RESERVED
Thorndike Press® Large Print Biography and Memoir.
The text of this Large Print edition is unabridged.
Other aspects of the book may vary from the original edition.
Set in 16 pt. Plantin.

LIBRARY OF CONGRESS CIP DATA ON FILE.
CATALOGUING IN PUBLICATION FOR THIS BOOK
IS AVAILABLE FROM THE LIBRARY OF CONGRESS.

ISBN-13: 978-1-4328-9441-2 (hardcover alk. paper)

Published in 2022 by arrangement with St. Martin's Publishing Group

Printed in Mexico
Print Number: 01   Print Year: 2022

For my brother, Chris

And I will lead the blind
in a way that they know not,
in paths that they have not known
I will guide them
I will turn the darkness
before them into light,
the rough places into level ground.
These are the things I will do,
and I will not forsake them.
— Isaiah 42: 16

All men dream, but not equally. Those who dream by night in the dusty recesses of their minds, wake in the day to find that it was vanity: but the dreamers of the day are dangerous men, for they may act on their dreams with open eyes, to make them possible.

— T. E. Lawrence,
Seven Pillars of Wisdom, 1926

CONTENTS

PERSONS IN THEIR ORDER OF APPEARANCE

Sir Charles Warren: A longtime servant of the British Empire, Sir Charles made significant archaeological finds in Palestine, was appointed to a civil administration post in London, and served as a general in the Second Boer War in South Africa.

Monty Parker: The second son of the Earl of Morley, Monty served as a captain in the First Boer War with the Grenadier Guards. After a tour in India, a shadowy group called the Syndicate approached him about a secret project they wished him to lead.

Johan Millen: A Swedish engineer who was part of the Syndicate.

Ava Astor: The wife of American business magnate John Jacob Astor, Ava was a socialite and fashion icon in New York and London. She was known as "The Most Beautiful Woman in the World."

Dr. Valter Juvelius: A Finnish poet, translator, and surveyor with a doctorate degree who was a friend of Johan Millen, Dr. Juvelius claimed to have uncovered a secret code — a cipher — in the Book of Ezekiel that revealed the location of the lost Ark of the Covenant.

Cyril Foley: An Eton and Cambridge man, Cyril was a professional cricket player who served his country during the infamous Jameson Raid in the First Boer War.

Natalie Maurice: An American tourist to the Holy Land.

Father Louis-Hugues Vincent: French by birth, Father Vincent joined the Dominican order at the École Biblique of St. Stephen's Basilica in Jerusalem, where he studied biblical archaeology.

Bertha Vester: The leader of the American Colony in Jerusalem, a collective Christian community devoted to philanthropic and commercial concerns.

The Baron Edmond de Rothschild: The leader of the French branch of the famous Jewish banking family and collector of rare antiquities.

The Friend: ???

THE KEY

And now he told me some of his strange experiences and actions from the Eastern countries he had been. I didn't know what to think . . . but it's hard to claim him a liar without a doubt. His speech was calm and orderly, like an educated man . . . He talked like he knew things, like they were ordinary, everyday events.

I wondered if he was hiding the main thing itself.

I can usually tell when someone is telling a story where the truth ends and the lie begins. The sound gets a new tone, the language suddenly sneaks in, just like a foot in soft clay . . . and the teller's gaze wanders for a moment.

But not this! He spoke with moderation. He looked in my eyes the whole time.

I have to think he either found me boring and it was a trap for me, from start to finish, or his reports, with their descriptions, even in the most bizarre passages, were sheer truth.

He told me of his time in Jerusalem, of all places.

And a treasure that lay there.

— Heikki Kenttä,
pseudonym of Dr. Valter Juvelius,
*Valkoinen kameeli ja
muita kertomuksia itämailta,*
(*The White Camel*), 1916

■ ■ ■ ■

PART ONE:
THE CIPHER

■ ■ ■ ■

ONE

Jerusalem, 1867

From the valley, the mountain that rose in the half-light before them seemed to be getting closer; but sometimes, it looked as if it had only been painted there, in the background of things, by some artist's brush. The hour was late and the sky was still blue, though the entire slope of the mountain was already cast in shadow. Like so many things around Jerusalem — the places, the people, the stories — the hill was something ancient yet real, a physical anchor to an unfathomable past that extended all the way back to the very times of God. As the sun began to slowly pass from sight, the sky and the sharp peak began to form a single dark image, its outline flecked with light.

Three sets of boots splashed in a line through the shallow pool on the ground, uncaring of where they stepped. Like the mountain, it too was swallowed in darkness.

Only the contrast of stacked rocks here, a tuft of shrubbery there, gave it any definition. As the three men stopped and looked into the empty stone basin, they saw a tunnel descending downward.

They lit their candles one by one. Sergeant Birtles went first into the empty pool. He was large and strong, with a full brown beard that seemed to move with every breath like some great snoring bear. His heavy white shirt was tucked into his steel blue pants, with two broad red stripes running down the legs. Behind him was a local fellah with a large black beard, dressed in robes and a turban that had not been white for some time. As they entered the low tunnel, Birtles pulled out his brown canister and began running his measuring tape along the stone walls. He fixed it with the thumb of his leather glove as his candle flickered over the tiny printed numbers. They walked down rather easily, even as the hard edges of the stairs crumbled like bits of crusty bread.

Behind them, standing at the tunnel's opening, was a man, though he was little more than a silhouette in a pith helmet. He followed them down and came into view, with his compass and field book clutched to his chest. He crammed his equipment under his arm and held his candle up. Captain Charles Warren looked young for his age, with dark eyes and a handsome face under close-cropped hair and a beard. His pencil held firmly in his teeth, he was sweating like a butcher, but he looked perfectly composed. There was a look in his eye not of madness, not entirely, but of a marked enthusiasm. Warren looked at his companions. The romance of the moment was not lost on any of them, but enough was enough. It was time to get on with things.

They walked slowly, with their backs almost parallel to the cool walls. As they made their way in, the strange midnight of the tunnel devoured all but the pooling circles of light from their candles. The ground had a thin crust to it. Warren pressed the toe of his boot onto it to make sure it would hold. There was a little water on the ground, but certainly nothing to be worried about. They proceeded slowly down through the tunnel. They walked, plain sailing, for about three hundred feet.

Captain Warren stopped the fellah's torch with his hand and slowly directed it toward the left wall. There, under the wavering light, were rough marks gouged into the stone. Warren looked at Birtles, who understood his thoughts immediately. These scrapes had been made by a chisel a long time ago. Birtles pulled at his open collar. Warren could see the sweat dripping from his forehead. The deeper they got, the more stifling it became. Warren gave the ceiling a wary look. As if the heat was not enough, the tunnel seemed to be getting smaller. Jagged crags in the walls were prodding into their backs.

They moved forward even more slowly, hunching over further. Birtles kept unrolling his never-ending tape. Soon, they were reduced to a single file. Captain Warren ran his own tape from ceiling to floor. He took his pencil from his mouth and began scratching numbers into the small notebook. The ceiling, which was sixteen feet at the great entrance, was now down to four feet, four inches. Warren then measured the width of the tunnel. He focused on the small black number on the tape. It was now a mere two feet across. Captain Warren took the candle and pushed it forward into the blackness. If this tunnel was what he thought it was, then it made sense that it did not always have to be tall enough for walking. But that was not going to make it easy. Warren looked ahead. The tunnel continued in a wavy line to the east. Birtles crouched forward first, unwinding his tape, and they moved on.

When they reached four hundred and fifty feet in, the passage was only three feet, nine inches tall. Warren again marked it into his notebook with his little pencil.

"Wait," he said.

Warren moved to the front. He moved his candle higher in the air, but where it should have met the ceiling, it continued even higher. The tunnel seemed to be growing again. Warren stepped forward and looked upward. The low ceiling gave way to a shaft that led upward at a steep angle. He looked for a handhold or ridge, but there was none. He stretched out his arm. The candle fought against the darkness, but its power was limited. The tunnel went up, but to where? Warren looked down at his old black boots. The small stream at their feet seemed to be growing. Warren made a note of the shaft, and they continued.

Several minutes later, Birtles stopped in his tracks, bumping his head in the process. He cursed in the half darkness. Warren edged his way to the front and saw the reason: they had run into a wall. Birtles grunted. They would have to turn back. Warren could hear the fellah breathe a sigh of relief. But Warren again reached forward, and this time lowered his candle. The soft glow fell down the side of the wall to reveal more darkness. The tunnel had not stopped; it had only gotten smaller. Warren made a quick measurement: it was only two feet, six inches high. He heard another long sigh.

They dropped to all fours and moved forward, crawling in the skinny rivulet of water. Warren tried not to think of the sheer weight of rock and dirt above them, just outside the city of Jerusalem. He knew there were farms and houses up there in the village of Silwan filled with people who slept, oblivious to their night crawling.

Warren looked down. The water seemed to have risen again, now reaching their hips, but it was still only about four inches deep. In the stale air, its iciness was refreshing. Warren washed some over his face and shook it off. When he opened his eyes, he saw Birtles once again stopped, his face frozen in fear. Warren felt something brush against his arm.

There was something in the water.

Warren plunged his arm in with a splash, grabbed the slippery monster with his bare hand, and pulled it into the air.

They pushed their lights closer in. In Warren's hands was something wet, long, and bright green.

He opened his hand.

It was a drooping stalk of cabbage.

"Hrm," he grumbled. Warren looked down. More bits of cabbage floated by them. He looked at his wet sleeve. The waters were unquestionably higher.

Warren knew that the fountain was sometimes used by the nearby villagers as a kind of scullery. But while Warren understood the cabbage, he had no theory as to why the water was getting higher. The waters of the fountain came intermittently at best and had risen only two hours before their entrance; they had timed their approach accordingly.

"How far?" growled Warren, his eyes glowing. Birtles checked his tape, which was now up around his head.

"Eight hundred and . . . fifty feet."

The Englishmen and their companion dropped to their stomachs and inched forward like woodland animals. The channel was now less than two feet high. The water was running about a foot high itself, which still gave them room to breathe, but not very much, and the water seemed to be flowing through them at a faster pace. Warren caught a look at the fellah's face, soaked and scared. They were just heads now, floating beneath the surface of the earth.

As they advanced through the tunnel, the

water began rushing by them with greater speed, splashing up even higher. Birtles's great beard was already reduced to a black slick. Warren bit hard on his pencil. The only dry item on his person was his hat.

Warren slowly shifted his notebook and tape around and somehow maneuvered his lit candle to his mouth. They crawled another fifty feet — the ceiling was now just above one foot high. They had to twist their necks to gulp at the thin layer of air between the water and the rocky ceiling. The air was hot and tasted old and sour. Warren knew that their situation was dire indeed. If they turned to go back, the surge of water would probably drown them, pushing their bodies out, perhaps in time to meet someone coming to the fountain to do their morning wash. But if they went forward, and the water rose even two more inches, they would still drown and end up in the same place. Warren closed his eyes for a moment and tried to think, gritting his teeth. He opened his eyes. There was no choice.

"Follow me," he said, moving forward.

At about nine hundred feet, Warren saw something dark wavering in the water beneath them.

"Stop," he said.

Warren took off his hat and tried to shift

everything again, including his candle, to his free left hand. The flame held still for moment, slanted in the air, but then plunked into the water. There was a soft hiss as the candle was carried away by the fast current. Warren took a deep breath, put his pencil back between his teeth, and plunged his head under. As he held his compass, field book, and hat only marginally above the water, Warren looked through the murkiness beneath. Blinking his eyes, he saw two passageways — one on either side — that branched off from the main tunnel. He pushed his fist forward into the tunnels, but they only went in about two feet each. Were these openings false cuttings or were they actual tunnels, stopped up with debris? Did they go farther? He stared at their gloomy openings, quivering under the water. He felt chilled and alone. Warren floated there for a moment. One of the openings seemed to have a darker aspect to it. Out of the corner of his eye, Warren thought he perhaps saw something, but he could not be sure of anything.

Warren pushed his head up, took out his pencil, and gasped at the air. He tried to take in another breath, but it stopped in his throat. His eyes opened wide. Something was wrong. He opened his mouth to shout, but no sound came out. He looked at his pencil: the tip was missing. He could feel the sharp piece of lead stuck back in his throat.

Warren tried to cough but felt only a stabbing pain. He sucked in air that went nowhere, dropping his hat, which went floating off in the stream behind him. The fellah stared at him, not sure what was happening. Warren looked at his hat, then pointed to his mouth.

His face was turning blue.

"He's choking!" shouted Birtles.

Warren's eyes began to bulge. He thought of that dark tunnel beneath him.

Birtles clapped him on the back and the piece of lead went flying through the air like a bullet, landing in the rushing water. Warren spat and took a gulp of water. He put his hand to his neck and swallowed, looking relieved. He looked at the sorry remains of his favorite pencil with anger. He shoved it back in his mouth. He looked at Birtles, nodded, and they continued.

They crawled in a zigzag direction through the rushing water, still running the tape, when the height of the tunnel miraculously increased to a palatial four feet, six inches, which buoyed their spirits. They finally had some room to breathe. But at over one thousand feet, the tunnel tightened again to a paltry two feet, and in another hundred feet went down to one foot, ten inches. Warren again feared a dark end in these ancient caves.

The fellah, who had seemed utterly defeated a few hundred feet before, suddenly clenched his fists and made his way to the front, plunging and puffing through the water like a young grampus. Warren was impressed. The passage rose again to above two feet, and Warren heard something.

"Halt," he said.

It was a faraway sound, but because of the echo, he could not be sure. He moved forward, then backward, then forward again. There it was.

Drip. Drip. Drip.

They were fourteen hundred feet in and had finally heard the dripping water that might signal the source of the spring. Warren moved to the front and began running his dirty hands over every surface of the rock.

There.

Warren's fingers found a fault in the stone, and he began feeling out its edges. He pushed his ear to it. He heard a loud gurgling. He listened more intently. Somewhere in the rock, from that close, it was almost a roar.

Warren examined the area and measured it. He took out his pencil, bit at it to expose some more lead, and wrote down his findings. They had found the location of the spring. Warren nodded, and they continued, following the tunnel as it wound to the east. The ceiling rose to six feet, and they finally could stand again, slow but triumphant, their soaked joints cold and rheumy. At 1,658 feet, Birtles finally stopped his tape, and Warren wrote down the final numbers. They managed smiles as they looked upon the passage leading past another shaft. After about fifty more feet, they walked up a short set of stone steps into a large, cracked cave. They could feel the cool air of an exit.

When they finally emerged, under an ornate arch and up a long set of stairs, it was dark outside. They stood shivering for some minutes before their awaiting attendants realized they had arrived and rushed to cover them with blankets. They had been in the wet, cold cavern for nearly four hours. Now that they were back on the solid ground of Palestine proper, just a fair bit from the walls of Jerusalem, the stars were shining and a fire had been started. There were different degrees of darkness, thought Warren, but none so deep as underground.

Later, sitting in front of the fire with his recovered hat drying next to him, Warren looked into his notebooks. They had successfully traveled underground from the Pool of Siloam all the way to the Gihon Spring. But it was the discovery of a shaft and some possible other openings that threw considerable light on their adventure. The existence of those dark tunnels — which had appeared on no map but were mentioned in the Scripture — suggested that there were areas of this maze that yet lay beyond their sight. Warren shivered and drew his knees together.

He looked out toward the wall of the city. Under the bright starlight, he could see the glint of the Dome of the Rock, the Haram al-Sharif, the sacred shrine built by the Arabs on the site of the original Jewish Temple, built by King Solomon, the son of David. Dipping his gaze downward, Warren pictured the tunnel they had just struggled through and how it stretched up toward the Temple Mount itself. There was a labyrinth under their feet, and there was no telling where it might lead to.

Or to what.

Warren pushed his boot against the fire

until the embers glowed orange. There were many old stories about the gleaming forbidden treasures of Solomon that still might be hidden under the mountain. Things were always out of sight here, thought Warren. That was the whole point. He shivered, though he was not sure if he did so because of the lingering chill of the water or something that, in the brisk and holy silence of the Jerusalem night, he couldn't quite bring himself to say.

Thirteen Years Later, 1880

The midday June sun glittered off the surface of the Pool of Siloam like flowing handfuls of stars. A barefoot sixteen-year-old Jacob Eliahu walked backward, slowly, on the hot rocks. He stopped, wiggled his toes, and, with a shout, ran forward and leaped into the air, splashing magnificently into the water. Sitting on the edge of the basin, Sampson, his friend, laughed out loud. When he stopped, Sampson looked down to the pool. Jacob was nowhere to be seen.

The waters were perfectly still.

"Jacob? Jacob!" he said, with increasing alarm.

Jacob finally surfaced with a great splash, his dark hair wet, long with curls. As he breathed in, he was laughing himself.

"I told you," said Jacob, "much better than school!"

Jacob took a few lazy turns around the basin as his friend scolded him for being cruel. The water was cold and refreshing. It was worth any trouble they might be in for skipping class at the Boys' School of the London Mission to the Jews, Jacob thought, as he enjoyed the perfect peace between water and sun. In the distance he could see the city of Jerusalem and the golden dome, peeking over the wall. Jacob stopped and looked down. He seemed to be looking into the water itself, as if it were some faraway picture.

"You want to swim down the tunnel?" Jacob asked.

Sampson took on a frightened look.

"Not this again," he said. "No! A dragon lives there!"

Jacob splashed at him and laughed. "Come on," he said. "I have some candles."

The two friends fixed the candles to some pieces of wood and tied them around their necks with strings. "You go in over at the Gihon Spring," said Jacob. "I will go in here, and we will meet in the middle!" His friend did not look too excited but nodded and left to run the short distance to the fountain. Jacob was left alone in the Pool of Siloam.

Jacob lit his candle and gently set it onto the water. He slowly made his way to the opening, pushing himself along with his arms. The tunnel before him, half in water, seemed like the inside of a long, meandering snake. Jacob yelled out to his friend but heard only an echo that sounded like some other version of him. He had probably run off, Jacob thought, as he moved farther in. Soon, he was in almost total darkness.

Though he was missing school, Jacob knew the story of this tunnel by chapter and verse. It had always fascinated him. The tunnel dated back to when Sennacherib, the king of Assyria, invaded Judea and trapped King Hezekiah inside Jerusalem. After consulting the prophet Isaiah, Hezekiah convened his royal engineers and tasked them with a secret project: they would build tunnels under the countryside so that water from Gihon Spring could be diverted to the Pool of Siloam, which was at the time inside the city walls. They could then survive the siege.

Jacob ran his fingers along the rock. Did he feel chisel marks? He also knew the stories that these tunnels, in addition to securing water, could have been used to secret away the golden treasures of the Temple. But there were other rumors, too: that these relics were protected by something else, something ancient and evil.

Jacob's candle went out, and he was immediately lost in the greatest, largest darkness he had ever known. It smashed away the walls of rock and seemed to suspend him in black space. He lifted his hands from the rock. There was no up or down or back or forth. He felt warm and cold, alone and somehow not. He could feel the water and the air in the tips of his fingers and in his lungs. He could visualize the place he was in, but he could not see it.

Jacob fumbled with his matches and somehow got one to flash. A cloud of light billowed around him. He steadied himself on the rock again and felt something strange. The chisel marks were going the opposite way. He felt along the wall some more. He raised his light and stared.

He was looking at something he had never seen before.

When Jacob emerged from the other end of the tunnel at the spring, he was sopping wet with a wild look in his eye. He could see shapes of people around him. Someone was directly in front of him.

"Sampson!" shouted Jacob, running to

embrace his friend. But it was only a peasant boy, who thought that Jacob was a genie and fainted.

Sampson, as Jacob finally realized, was long gone. When Jacob crookedly got to his feet, the village women from Silwan who were filling their jars with water shrieked and cursed. Some moved to attack him. In a flurry of splashing laundry, Jacob somehow managed to escape. He stumbled his way along the ridge back to school. He thought about what he saw, which had seemed almost as if it were following him. When he finally plodded in, his classmates stared at his wet curls. Sampson sank down in his seat. Jacob breathlessly told the teacher, Mr. Schick, what happened.

His discovery made its way through his school, and to Jerusalem itself, where it caused a sensation in the Jewish quarter. The scholars came in their tall dark hats. They called forth the young Jacob, who told them what it was that he had seen. The old men said it was a discovery of significant archaeological importance. Jacob felt proud and brave, but also humbled. He had not found a golden treasure, or a fierce dragon, but an ancient inscription set into the wall. The find was important because, for the first time, those stories about Hezekiah's old tunnel might be proven true after all. Jacob was surprised that people thought they were not.

When they attempted the tunnel, they confirmed the discovery, but the tablet was so old and covered with deposits that it could not be read. What parts were visible were so archaic that they would require a specialist to decipher. In 1881, the Englishman Henry Sayce arrived and went into the tunnel, holding a flashlight in his mouth. After some very awkward positioning, he made a rubbing of the tablet. He attempted to translate the first line of the inscription. Although not at first sight filled with holy wisdom, its mysteries were great.

It read, simply:
Behold.

Two

MONTY PARKER

London, Spring 1908
28 Years Later

The man in the white captain's hat moved down the sidewalk to the left, then the right. He had a thin pipe in his mouth. He stopped and closed his eyes halfway, bracing himself for impact as the horde of schoolchildren running toward him finally reached his position. As they tumbled by, two of them bumped into his legs, causing his pipe to jar loose from his mouth. When the children looked up to apologize, they saw the man was already putting it back to his lips. They stared at him, terrified that he was going to box their ears. The man looked angry, until he saw a woman making her way behind the children.

"Don't be late for school," he said, with a slightly overexaggerated smile.

As the children rolled on, the man picked up his own pace. He made the turn onto

Princelet Street, and though it was only about three hundred feet long, he kept to the sidewalk. He passed the synagogue, a three-story brick building with heavy-looking brown doors underneath an impressive stone arch. The windows were shuttered; he could see nothing of what was inside. A Jewish man, tall and thin and dressed in black, walked to the right door, opened it just enough to squeeze through, and closed it behind him with a thud.

The man with the pipe crossed and made his way up the right side of the street, his face feeling the warmth of the springtime sun. The stores and buildings were made of sooty black brick. On the corner was an infamous lodging house, known as the Beehive. The man walked by, past slouchy travelers and fast-walking ladies. Every time he came to the East End, he wondered who in their right mind would open a solicitor's office here. He walked past the dark passageways and tight warrens that connected to the neighboring streets in Spitalfields and Whitechapel. It had been many years now, but not many enough. As people walked these old streets, many still avoided the alleyways, even in the daytime.

The man walked over a coal-hole cover. He turned into building number 8 and walked through the door. He could hear a viola being played — beautifully — in one of the rooms. In the hallway was seated the old, familiar rabbi who also had offices there. The rabbi, with his curling hair and pudgy frame, was supposedly the best mohel in the quarter. The man took out his pipe and nodded hello before walking to the door with the sign MARTINEAU & REID, SOLICITORS stenciled on the thin glass. He opened the door to see a man, finely dressed with slight spectacles, standing before him.

"Monty!" said Mr. Martineau, "I was just about to check on you. Where were you? Come in."

Monty put his pipe back in and cracked another smile under his mustache. He was lean and handsome, with a thin face and tanned skin. He had few wrinkles and a very easy smile that was echoed in his eyes. Monty shook his lawyer's hand.

"How are you doing?" asked Martineau, with a softness to his voice. Monty looked away quickly, dismissing the question.

"Fine. Sorry for my lateness," he said to the rest, in a more charming tone. He stepped forward, surveying the room. The office was modestly furnished with a great walnut table near the window. An oil painting, a hunting scene of green and yellow,

40

hung on the wall. Around the table were three men, who then stood to greet him. Monty recognized one of them.

"Gentlemen," said Martineau, turning around. "I give you Captain Montague Parker, brother of the Earl of Morley, nephew of Earl Grey, and hero of the Second Boer War."

Monty shook his head in an almost angry denial of the last statement — and somewhat tired of everything that had preceded it. Monty had taken this meeting mostly as a favor to Martineau, whose brother-in-law was George Fort, the serious-looking businessman standing up before him.

"George, you know. And this is Captain Frederick Vaughn."

"Resigned from service, thank you" said Vaughn, with a wink.

Monty shook the hands of these earnest men. He hoped this was not about some real estate opportunity, because he certainly did not have the interest for it. Monty did not want to tell Fort that, but it would be bad form not to at least entertain him. As Monty was thinking, the third man was given a quick name, but he missed it. The man looked European, with a rumpled gray suit and frazzled whiskers; he smiled in excess and nodded several times. Martineau sat at the table and motioned for Monty to join them.

Because Martineau was the Parker family lawyer, Monty knew him well, especially of late. When Monty's father, Albert, a very popular politician, died three years ago, Martineau had dealt mostly with Edmund, Monty's older brother, who inherited not only the title of Earl of Morley and its seat in upper Parliament, but also stately Saltram House in the green Plymouth countryside. Saltram was a magnificent estate, covering eight thousand acres filled with high, corniced rooms and servants to spare. Monty could feel its dreamy atmosphere even now, its leveled staircase passing up past masterful paintings. And it had a library unlike any in Devonshire.

Edmund, the new Lord Morley, was just one year older than Monty. Their father's will was explicit: with the exception of the London house and its furniture, which had gone to their mother, everything went to Edmund.

"Let's get down to business, shall we?" said Martineau.

"Well, Captain Parker," said Vaughn, "we have quite the proposition for you."

Of course, sighed Monty to himself. Real estate.

The third man was now meekly staring down into his lap. He held a sheaf of heavy papers close to him. They were obviously valuable, at least to him.

"I told them about your service, Monty," Fort said, wagging his finger. "Lieutenant in the war. One of the youngest officers in his regiment, if I recall."

Monty shifted again. He knew he shouldn't have come. He should be at the Turf Club, like every other day.

"Monty is also very well versed in antiquities. His family has quite the art collection. He is now with the Grenadier Guards and has recently returned to us from India," said Fort. Monty thought it wise to keep quiet, as all he really did in India was drink gin and tonic.

"You need a soldier?" asked Monty, in a low, sarcastic tone.

"Actually," said Vaughn, "no."

Monty looked at the third man again.

"What's this all about?" he asked.

"Do you know of General Sir Charles Warren?" asked Vaughn.

Monty paused. Warren was the general at Spion Kop. Monty looked like he wanted to close his eyes, if just for a moment. Everyone knew what had happened there.

"Of course," said Monty, in a low voice.

"Are you aware of his archaeological work?" asked Vaughn quickly, making it clear that he had no wish to dwell on bad subjects. Monty's puzzled look served as his answer. Vaughn and Fort exchanged a disappointed glance.

"Thirty years or so ago, before the war, Warren worked in Palestine, doing some mapping of the tunnels there," said Vaughn. "He actually accomplished quite a bit." Vaughn unrolled a map and placed it flat on the table. The markings were light, but it appeared to be a side view of a long, curving tunnel. Vaughn put on his glasses and blinked as if the sun had just come out.

Monty looked at the cracked paper before him. He saw names he was unfamiliar with: Pool of Siloam, Hezekiah's Tunnel, the Virgin's Fountain.

"When Warren began work near Jerusalem as a Royal Engineer, it was some of the first done by the Palestine Exploration Fund, at the behest of Her Majesty, Queen Victoria, herself. His work was quite extraordinary, and, though he didn't find anything per se, it was really his . . ."

"We are looking to mount a similar excavation to look for something we think he missed," said Fort, obviously exasperated by Vaughn's long-windedness.

"This is delicate," said Vaughn. He looked at Fort, who nodded. He then turned to the third man.

"This is Mr. Johan Millen," said Vaughn. Hearing his name, the third man looked up. He was smiling again.

"He is here from Sweden and is an engineer," said Vaughn. "He represents a man who is . . . well . . . Mr. Millen, if you will?"

Millen rose and bowed. Not only did the man obviously know English but he clearly made Vaughn uncomfortable. Perhaps this would not be a waste of time after all, thought Monty. Millen took one of the papers he was holding and placed it on top of the map. Monty drew closer. The document looked somewhat similar to the first map, but not entirely so. There were strange drawings, symbols, and mysterious words scribbled all over it.

"Another map?"

"Yes and no, Captain Parker," said Millen, with an accent that dipped up and down. "It is like a key, but something more." Millen crossed his hands behind his back.

"The man I represent is a Finnish scholar named Dr. Valter Juvelius. He is a friend of mine, I should say. He is, also, quite brilliant. In addition to being a surveyor and an educator, he has been studying the Scripture in its most ancient form for a great many years.

"And he has found something extraordinary."

Monty gave him a look that said it was time to spit it out.

"Dr. Juvelius has discovered that the Old Testament," said Vaughn measuredly, "especially the Book of Ezekiel, contains a hidden code that provides a guide to these lost tunnels, the very same ones that Warren tried to explore."

"How?" asked Monty, looking up at Millen.

Millen pointed to a series of numbers on one of the pages. They were shakily written in black ink. "Very simple, actually, just an exchange of characters. The cipher is based on the holy number 7. From the initial letters of the words in a sentence, a stretch of sentences is picked out. Then, take out two letters according to the scheme 1, 2, 3, 4, 5, 6, 7, 1, 2, 3, 4, 5, 6, 7, 1, 2, 5, 8, in such a manner that one first takes out the initial letter 1, then the initial letter 2, and so on." He was speaking very quickly.

"These, placed together in writing, form new words and sentences. Look here." Monty leaned over as Millen took out another page and pointed to a long sentence. "This is Ezekiel 42." As he read it, he traced his finger along the verse, as if he were feeling for a vein in an arm. He ended on a passage that sounded like directions.

Then he brought me forth into the utter court, the way toward the north: and he brought me into the chamber that was over against the separate place, and which was before the building toward the north. Before the length of a hundred cubits was the north door, and the breadth was fifty cubits.

Monty looked at the text he was reading; it was filled with red marks. "Now," Millen said, "if we apply the cipher to the passage, this is what we get":

Six / under ways, / whoever / a measuring rod's length Goes down / here to / Five spear's lengths
The water
Six = the number of the evil one
Spearlengths cubits

Monty watched as Millen then pointed to the map.

"Spear lengths correspond to meters. Watch." His finger pushed along one of the several divided passageways springing from the main shaft tunnels, slowly down to a separate chamber that seemed to exist all on its own. There, someone had drawn a small pool with something suspended above it. It looked like a box. Straight, heavy lines radiated from its top.

"What is that?" Monty said, pointing to the strange drawing. Vaughn and Fort looked at each other.

"This is what the cipher leads to, Captain Parker, and what it has tried to protect for thousands of years. This is why Dr. Juvelius, and we, seek to go to Palestine."

Monty looked at the picture, at the box.

"The Ark of the Covenant," said Millen, placing his finger on the page.

Monty looked up and stared at the man. He looked at his lawyer, who appeared similarly dumbfounded. It was like staring into a mirror. For the first time since the war, Monty Parker, the easygoing soldier, the gentleman with a reputation for sport and conquest in all areas of life, seemed unable to form a thought.

"Like in Tara?" asked Monty, stumbling for a reference point. A few years earlier, a significant excavation was undertaken in Ireland to unearth the Ark, which some believed had been carried there ages ago by Israelites who had emigrated to Britain after their captivity in Assyria. It was a highly publicized affair and had garnered its share of loud protest. The incident at Tara was also a colossal failure; the diggers found nothing but damp Irish soil, with its distinct air of sulfur.

"No, no," said Millen. "This is the true Ark. The legendary vessel that held the remains of the Ten Commandments themselves! The means to communicate with God!"

There was a pause in the room, as the moment — and its impossible volume — began to necessarily dissipate, like sand through their hands.

"A story," Monty mumbled, or something probably like it.

Millen looked him in the eyes. "For over two thousand years, the whereabouts of the Ark of the Covenant have been one of the world's greatest mysteries. The question of whether it has remained safely concealed somewhere under Solomon's Temple or was taken away by one of the many besiegers of Jerusalem has never been truly answered.

"There is no objective in the world," said Millen, with great seriousness, "that can be compared with the quest for the Ark of the Covenant."

There was silence in the room again. The

noises out on the street seemed sharp.

"How much might it be worth?" asked Martineau, clearing his throat, but also unable to help himself.

"We estimate somewhere around one hundred million," said Vaughn, looking over his spectacles. Martineau stifled a gasp. Fort nodded.

"So, what do you think, old man?" asked Vaughn, looking at Monty.

"No," said Monty, his teeth clamped down on his pipe.

"What do you mean?" asked Vaughn, exasperation in his voice.

"No."

"Well, I have to say that is awfully sudden of you. We certainly hope that you will at least give us a chance to convince . . ."

"I didn't mean that," interrupted Monty. "The Ark. It's not worth one hundred million." He paused. "Double it. Two hundred million, easy." Silence covered the room again.

"We would form a Syndicate," said Vaughn, quietly. "Just us founders. We would retain equal ownership and all decision-making capabilities."

"You will need money," Monty said.

"We think we can raise that through subscriptions. Keep it private, you know."

Monty had to agree. Something like this would bring out all the deep pockets from their billiard rooms. They would probably have to turn many away.

"We want you to lead it," said Vaughn. "Dr. Juvelius will join us. We have another man in mind, a Swedish military man who has done some work in the Congo. You would have to negotiate for the land rights with the Turks. If we can get that accomplished, the locals should be much easier to deal with. Your . . . ah, charisma and discretion, as well as your reputation, should be of great help."

Mr. Martineau looked at Monty, almost pleadingly. Monty knew what they really wanted him for. They didn't have to say it. He looked at the map again.

"It would have to be a secret, of course," said Vaughn. "We've been talking about claiming we are a construction concern or something, building something nice for the locals."

"What's this?" Monty asked. He used his pipe to point to the straight lines coming out of the box on the map. They looked like a child's drawing of the sun.

Millen leaned over. His accent heightened the feeling of each word. "Dr. Juvelius thinks the Ark is protected by traps and guardians. He thinks that these lines represent a type of deterrent, perhaps radium, which is very dangerous. He thinks this is why, when the Israelites carried the Ark before them in battle, they were unstoppable." Monty stared at the drawing.

"The power of God," said Millen.

"I think you could raise the money," Monty said, sitting up in his chair. "Quite easily. But you'd first have to send a team to Jerusalem to make sure this cipher of yours actually works." He eyed Millen suspiciously.

"What are you saying, Monty? You'll do it?" asked Vaughn.

Monty looked at him.

When Monty left Martineau's office, he shut the door evenly and was only half surprised to see the same rabbi still seated in the hallway, slouched into a position of impressive repose. Monty nodded a goodbye anyway, which looked much like his hello, all the while wondering if the holy man had heard any of what had been said or had slept through it all.

Monty put his pipe to his mouth and walked out onto the East End streets.

THREE

MONTY PARKER

Ascot, England, June 1908

Racehorses thundered by as Monty adjusted the cuff of his right sleeve. He shut his eyes at the familiar pounding it made in his chest, but it lasted only a moment. He turned his head back toward the wrought iron staircase. There on the second stand he saw the royal family, perfectly seated in their white high-backed chairs like a set of finely decorated cakes. On the table near King Edward, with his salt-and-pepper beard, were the day's three prizes: the Gold Vase, the Royal Hunt Cup, and the magnificent Gold Cup, all under glass and guarded by constables. Monty saluted their box, filled with pink Dorothy Perkins and white roses. The royal family had been lately rare to the races. The Prince and Princess of Wales were also there with some of their children. Queen Alexandra smiled as the barrel-chested Edward looked out over his loud subjects.

Spread out before him in a sea of chatter and laughter, the area was packed to the seams with over two thousand people. Heavy rains had soaked everything to puddles the night before, but the sun had come out and saved the day. The women in their dresses strung their arms between the elbows of wealthy men with toppers and canes. Monty squinted at an acquaintance or two, nodding and smiling. Though many were wondering if White Knight, last year's winner, could hold off Lord Rothschild's Radium, the horses were only the secondary attraction. People did not come all the way to East Berkshire for the races, not really; they sought to be in the company of the king and queen. Monty was not interested in either. He was at the Royal Ascot this year for something else.

The Most Beautiful Woman in the World.

Monty laughed to himself. That is what the press had called her, repeatedly, complete with a lush image of her, posed in a shiny, snakelike dress. Monty showed his badge to the porter, who nodded approvingly. The small disc was stamped ascot royal enclosure over gold with a court of arms and the Royal Crown. For most, this small but powerful trinket, which permitted him into the most exclusive section of the track, was completely unattainable. For Monty, it was just one of the many advantages of being the brother of the Earl of Morley.

The current race ended to shouts and cheers. Monty continued to look around, trying, rather badly, to disguise his reconnaissance. Beds of rhododendrons bloomed in beds of scarlet, pink, and white. There was a good chance that she was not even here. Since her divorce had been announced, there had been some question about whether she had lost favor with the royal family. The papers had noted that this might prohibit an invitation this year. Though the rule was an unwritten one, it was tantamount to the Magna Carta: no one who had known so-called "domestic difficulties" shall be admitted to the royal enclosure at the race. It was the opinion of the writer, Charles P. Norcross, that she should "certainly not" be invited, though "perhaps" there was some chance she might. Norcross wryly remarked that all Ava's problems would disappear if she simply married an Englishman. Monty had smiled at that. Of all her suitors, the newspaper said that "Captain Montague Parker was generally accorded the position of favorite."

The writer wrote, in fact, that "Parker's recent attentions to Mrs. Astor were indefatigable."

Of course she would be here, thought Monty. Ava Lowle Willing Astor had crossed the Atlantic and had struck British society like a bolt of lightning. Ava was beautiful, almost supernaturally so, and she was utterly and completely rich. Or at least she was going to be when her divorce from John Jacob Astor was complete. The current rumors set her eventual settlement at ten million U.S. dollars. She had children: her sixteen-year-old son, Vincent, had sailing adventures with his father, while her five-year-old daughter, Alice, had a governess. Regardless, Ava's hand, once free, would be the greatest treasure in England. It was no wonder that Monty, who was nearly thirty, was one of her interests. It would be a fine match for him. His older brother had not yet married either, meaning Monty might — might — someday take his place as earl, though he of course hoped not. But Ava knew that he might. English society was, as always, a labyrinth of guessing and aim.

He saw her before he heard her. Up by the stairs, there was a flash of that dark hair, but it was really her voice, loudly saying hello to someone she had probably just met.

Monty grabbed another drink, quite possibly not his own, and stood behind a woman in an especially palatial dress who was lost in a pair of bronze binoculars.

Monty watched as every set of eyes — man and woman — tried not to stare at Ava. He could hear her. She spoke in a very practiced way, but he could pick out her accent anywhere. He moved his head to see her. He saw a flash of white. Ava always wore the type of dress that the English seemed, on the whole, not quite yet ready for. Today's seemed to have the usual absences that Monty knew would be written about in the newspapers. When she turned, he could nearly see her entire bare back. This was her calling card, for her followers and enemies alike.

Monty knew that while Ava was overjoyed to soon be rid of her boor of a husband, she had been apart from him for some time. Her own social adventures aside, everyone knew that her husband's attentions had also been elsewhere, and not just in the luxury hotel business. Their marriage had been one of American royalty, not of blood, but of cash. Its end would be long, drawn out, and transactional. She was a complicated and fascinating woman, thought Monty. He looked again; she turned and caught his glance just as she was speaking to someone else. It was her eyes: like smoke, soft and dark, that were deathly. Monty turned away and cursed himself. The Grenadier Guard, trained to be as still and solid as a block of stone, had caved. Monty shook his head. There was nothing "certainly not" about her. There was nothing remotely "perhaps."

Monty turned his attention to the horses. They were getting ready to scrimmage. His mother drew horses, seated in the great library at Saltram. As a child, Monty would stand next to her, in her white dress and blue jacket watching her pencil pull out the curves and lines. This was before Jack, his younger brother, came along. She loved horses. He heard Ava again and knew he would have to wait his turn among her many admirers. Or more likely, she might just leave without talking to him at all, especially since she knew he had seen her. The next horses were gathering in the stalls, getting ready for the race. Their riders adjusted their thick saddles and buckles to make sure everything was safe and sure.

"Captain Parker, I presume."

Her voice. Monty turned and took his hat off.

"My dear Mrs. Astor," he said, bowing his head and kissing her hand.

"Stop with that," she said.

"Ava," he said. She closed her eyes and smiled, taking in the sound of her own name. She greatly preferred his British pronunciation: *Ah-va.* Monty found it hard sometimes to know what was real and what was artifice with her, but he very much knew what she liked.

"I had read that you weren't invited," said Monty.

"Rubbish. I'm still married, aren't I?"

"You could have fooled me."

"Scandalous."

The papers also noted that Monty was one of the only people in the world who seemed capable of making the soon-to-be-former Mrs. Astor smile, just as she was doing at that moment. Those who knew her well thought such a power impossible. As the gossip columns had reported, Ava and Monty had indeed been "talking" for months, as they put it. She looked up at him, squinting her eyes in the sun, smiling. There is that moment when the idea of the thing and the very thing itself become real, when doubt becomes flooded with light and vanishes.

It was then that Monty thought he saw something flash across her face. Something new. She saw his recognition and moved to disguise it. Ava looked up at his captain's hat.

"Well, I daresay it's better than the dead bear," she said, pushing the lid up. He laughed. Monty knew that she positively loathed his guard helmet — four feet tall and made of Canadian bearskin, meant to terrify enemies on the battlefield. Monty wondered if she did not like him being in the guard at all, even though his duties at the present were completely ceremonial. It was a respectful post, though not perhaps respected. It depended on who you asked, like anything.

The gun sounded, and Monty jumped. He could not help it. Ava touched his arm.

The crowd gasped, then screamed. Monty turned to see a rider sailing through the open air. He hit the ground with a hard jolt as another horse rode by, kicking him in the head. The dirt that immediately rose into the air confused everything. The other horses scrambled and took off in different directions. The rider's blue cap could be seen several feet away from the haze. Once it cleared, the downed rider, dressed in cerise with gold sleeves, could finally be seen lying in a heap. He was not moving. Ava grabbed Monty's arm.

The empty horse trotted around, confused, with a wild, bulging eye. Monty could not tell if it was injured. A man in white ran onto the track at full speed as the entire crowd watched.

The medic finally reached the rider, who was still unmoving. The rider then began to stir in a crooked manner and Monty heard Ava exhale. After a few moments, the rider got to his feet, shaking his head. The crowd clapped. The rider's horse came over and he patted him on his black nose.

Monty turned back to Ava. She had her head turned back to the crowd. Monty was used to this; she was an inveterate creature of the social world. Still, Monty couldn't help following her line of sight. He recognized the man across the enclosure, who doffed his hat and smiled back at her.

Him.

Lord Curzon was handsome, with a dark complexion and slick black hair. He had medals pinned to his breast and seemed to stand at attention. He had been viceroy of India for a time when Monty was stationed with the guard there. Though Curzon had restored the Taj Mahal to its milky glory and had pressed some new territories for the empire, he was seen by many as another smooth-faced Eton boy playing at government, most notably because of the way he completely mishandled the great Indian famine. Nearly one million people died. This man was looking at Ava.

And she was looking back.

Monty had read in the same newspaper article about Ava that Curzon was another one of her potential suitors, but Monty had thought it a ludicrous fabrication meant only to sell more papers. Curzon had recently lost his wife, an American heiress to a department-store fortune. It was then that Monty Parker realized that it did not matter what the London papers wrote or how little he thought of him. Monty had gone to Eton, too.

"It was nice to see you again, Monty. I must . . ."

"Ava," he said.

"Oh, Monty, don't be like that. I'll be back."

"Him?"

She smiled, stopped, and turned back to Monty. She ran her hands over his coat, her hand pausing at his sleeve. She shook her head.

"Maybe if you got out of that dreary uniform once in a while." She looked up and smiled again, with the same look he had seen earlier. Only this time he knew what it was. It was a fleeting sort of sympathy, and it felt like being grazed by a bullet.

"Oh, cheer up," she said, "I'll be back."

As she pushed away, Monty saw the Gold Cup flash again in the sunlight.

"I'm going to be going away for a bit myself, actually," he said.

"Oh no, will you come back?" Her mind and eyes were elsewhere.

"You know I will. I'm going on an expedition," he said, in a much lower tone. "To find something."

"Oh really? How exciting! Tell me! I'll keep it secret." He had her full attention now.

"The Ark of the Covenant," he said, and though the words sounded like strange music coming from his mouth, they felt good to say in her presence, in the open air, though they seemed a pitch off from the very place he was standing. He had not yet told Vaughn that he would lead them when they had asked weeks ago, but now he supposed he just had.

Monty saw her eyes, deep and used to American mansions and millions. She looked at him in pure seriousness. There was an inside to the moment — quiet and still — but there was an immeasurable outside that Monty knew he would be entering soon. He stayed.

And then Ava laughed, again. She pulled at his lapels.

"OK then, Captain Parker," she said, stepping away, the old look in her eye once more. "Bring me back the Ark of the Covenant . . . and perhaps we'll talk again."

As Monty watched her make her way from him, he knew she did not believe him. He was not sure if he believed himself. But he felt that he would see her again.

Later, when Ava was deep in conversation with Lord Curzon (who indeed did seem a bit stiff), she looked over her shoulder to find Monty.

But he was already gone.

Of course, she did not believe him. She was used to impossible promises from impossible men. She looked over to the king and saw the Gold Cup. Even though it was under glass, it gleamed in the sunshine. One of the guards looked at her. Ava knew that it was being protected because last year someone had stolen it. Such a thing had seemed impossible.

Ava stifled a laugh and dismissed the thought in her mind.

FOUR

MONTY PARKER

Fall 1908

Over the next few months, Monty Parker traveled on trains and boats that moved with smooth purpose across the map of the world. After resigning from the Grenadier Guards in August, Monty went to America to help find backers for the expedition. In hotel lobbies along the East Coast, Monty smiled, uncrossed his legs and stood, shook hands, told this and that important financier about the enterprise over a drink or two — only enough to get them interested — and did it all over again an hour or so later. Sometimes it felt ridiculous to say — "my associates have made a monumental find in Palestine based on a mathematical code" — but Monty would just say it and most people believed it. Some did not, of course, but Monty would sit on the richly upholstered chairs and wait for the next appointment. He had a drink in his hand and ate the chops, St. Hilaire at the Waldorf-Astoria.

By the time Monty's trip was nearly over, it was clear that funding was not going to be an issue. By the end of the day, when a particularly rich industrial magnate offered up his checkbook, Monty was heard to say, "I'm sorry we're full up." After all, the more people who invested, the more people they would have to share with once they found the Ark.

Monty returned to London in October. They assembled their secret group of Vaughn, Fort, and Millen, along with their newest hire, Captain Axel Werner Hoppenrath, a Swede with narrow eyes and a flamboyantly curled mustache. His military background was undisguised in his bearing and uniform. When Monty shook his hand, he noticed that behind him was another man, rail thin, in his early forties with black hair and a Vandyke beard. He wore a forgettable wool suit and slight glasses, and his face seemed sunken. He had an air of intelligence about him.

"This is Dr. Juvelius," said Millen, stepping forward.

"A pleasure," said Juvelius. Monty shook his hand. Millen could read the surprise on Monty's face. "Dr. Juvelius can speak

English in spots, but his writing requires great aid," he said. "I will serve as his translator today. Captain Hoppenrath can help as well."

Monty nodded, and they sat down. Monty had paid for Juvelius to come to England. Anyone could flash some numbers and claim they had cracked a biblical prophecy; Monty wanted to look this man in the eye.

"The cipher, then?" asked Monty.

Millen said something in Swedish, and Juvelius produced a leather bag. He took out some messy papers, which he opened on their table. Juvelius said something else. To Monty, it sounded like there were fish sliding around in his mouth. Juvelius pointed to the page.

"This is the original text in Ezekiel," said Millen. "The prophet, you know."

Monty gave him a stare.

"Right," said Millen.

Juvelius began speaking. Millen nodded, kept nodding, and when Juvelius had stopped, he offered his translation. It was awkward at first, but eventually they found a rhythm among the three of them as ideas became words, looping through the air between them like a ribbon. It was then that Monty realized that Juvelius was showing him the same example that Millen had at their first meeting.

"No, no," said Monty. "Show me how it works."

Juvelius listened to the translation, then said something animatedly to Millen. He looked offended.

"You will understand, Mr. Parker, this is very difficult. Dr. Juvelius reads the Bible in the ancient Hebrew before translating it to Swedish. I could try to translate into English, but it takes a knowledge of all three to keep the cipher pure."

Monty stared Juvelius down.

"Show me," he said.

Millen and Juvelius spoke for a moment.

"There is an example here in the cipher — I will translate that, but I warn you it may be imperfect." Monty nodded.

Millen spread the cipher out and began copying something from the first page onto a blank sheet of paper. He scratched some things out, conferred with Juvelius, and then motioned for Monty to look. Monty smelled pencil on paper.

"Here is the paragraph," said Millen. "There is some loss due to translation."

Here discovered peculiar cipher writing has always been deciphered perfectly mechanically the scheme. That the bible-text has not been corrupted afterwards, but evidently only revised in regards to orthography. And certain uncertain separate sounds is particular as the interesting. The cycle itself with its seven numbers has a holy significance and is by no means unknown. The number is generally used as a factor during the Talmudic period in mystic cabalistic formulas obeying complicated rules.

Monty winced. "Now, if we apply the cipher . . ." and here Millen took a pencil and began crossing out single letters, then underlining others, all the while counting from one to seven. When he stopped, he rechecked his work. Juvelius kept nodding in agreement.

"Now observe," said Millen said. He began circling some of the letters he marked and reproduced them at the bottom of the page. Letters became words, then became two, became three. Monty looked. Using letters obtained from the cipher, the hidden message of the paragraph was laid bare at the bottom of the page.

It read: "Hesekiel's chiffer."

"Hezekiel," said Millen. "The great king of Jerusalem whose tunnels we will soon be entering."

Monty looked closely. Millen had clearly followed a process that looked methodical, but card sharps did the same thing. But it seemed to have worked. Monty looked up. Juvelius was staring at him.

Juvelius proceeded to speak very quickly, his eyes almost closing; Millen followed with his translation a few moments behind. Juvelius explained that the great secret that had been revealed by the cipher was that the Ark had remained in its original place where King David had first placed it, one thousand years before Christ. Juvelius quoted Isaiah: the Lord promised David that, because of the Ark, his lineage would be secure, "as a nail in a sure place!" Juvelius said that this verse "may be taken perfectly literally and must not be considered as symbolical," that the Ark was indeed in a fixed place. Juvelius then read from the cipher again, in a passage he had decoded from Ezekiel:

Hurriedly seek "the gold," resplendent, embellished, the "enclosed," and the entrance emptied (of water); and in the division(?) spacious occur with delight return!

There was a moment, or perhaps a great many of them that slowly blended into one, where Monty either began to believe in what he was being told or, perhaps more likely, wanted to believe what it might get him.

"How did you come by this?" asked Monty. Millen answered immediately.

"A man named Melander began work on it many years ago, but Dr. Juvelius has perfected it. He has unlocked the key."

Juvelius sat down again and began working more numbers from his pencil to the paper. Monty could tell that it was an obsession to him. That meant he was either an expert they should listen to, or he had been utterly consumed by his work.

"Now what?" asked Vaughn.

They agreed to draw up the papers to form the official J.M.P.V.F. Syndicate, named after their last initials. Though they would have to announce it in the newspapers for legal reasons, Monty urged everyone to keep things as secret as possible. Their success depended on it.

"If everything goes well, we will need some more men," said Monty, looking around. "No offense. Soldiers. Gentlemen," he said, nodding to the Syndicate, "you can take care of that." Vaughn nodded.

"And one more thing," said Monty. "Dr. Juvelius and Captain Hoppenrath are going on a trip with me."

"Where?" said Millen.

"We're going to test it," said Monty. "In Jerusalem."

FIVE

MONTY PARKER

Jerusalem, November 1908

From a mile or so away, Monty Parker could see the gray walls of the Holy City as they staggered up and down the top of the hill. From the distance, Jerusalem looked like a fortress, or at least a long-ago attempt at one. Seen in bits and pieces peeking over the wall, its limestone buildings interlocked like some uneven puzzle. An ethereal cupola stood over the right wall. Monty looked at the scene, awash in shadow.

In the shadows of the famous cypress trees, Monty spied the single minaret at the west gate. People moved about the few villas outside the gates with their baskets of washing. As Monty rode closer, he saw the famous Dome of the Rock rising from behind the wall, one of the holiest places in Jerusalem, built and controlled by the Arabs. Juvelius and Hoppenrath rode behind him, talking in Swedish.

When Monty passed through the gates into Jerusalem, his hat was over his eyes and he wore a scarf over his mouth, with his pipe sticking out. The interior of the city was filled with tiny staircases and narrow streets. Monty saw merchants and pilgrims, Jews and Christians. The Arabs ran to prayers in their flowing robes. Ottoman Turks in their trim suits walked by on streets that seemed to wind in on themselves in a never-ending, rolling labyrinth. It was a shared city, but the differences were plain to any eyes. The city was romantic and ancient, that much could be felt in the air, but it was also crowded, noisy, and exceedingly filthy. It smelled of warm bread, thick incense, wisteria, and rot.

Juvelius began talking again. Hoppenrath paused, then translated for Monty.

"Twice this city has been completely destroyed, literally razed to the ground. Yet there are many holy sites and artifacts here for all three religions. The Chapel of the Holy Ghost, Armenian and Georgian mosaics, the old tombs, the old hospice of the Teutonic Order. The great Kufic, Karmatian, and Arabic texts of the khalifs and sultans of Islam, who founded or repaired the beautiful buildings in the Haram. And two Holy Sepulchres, multiple Zions, possibly three Calvarys, and at least two Geth-semanes."

Monty looked to Juvelius, who was smil-ing, confident in Hoppenrath's translation. Perhaps this man was more human than he seemed. Juvelius continued, via Hoppen-rath.

"Of the holy places, almost the only thing we know for sure is the Temple. It is still in its old place. There is no doubt a huge hid-ing place beneath the ruins of the Holy City that could perhaps change our entire base of knowledge."

Monty saw an Arab appear in one of the minarets of a nearby mosque. He spoke out a long, tremulous roll of words, calling the faithful to prayer.

The next day, they rode donkeys out of the city from the Dung Gate to the Kidron Valley, just outside the city to the southeast. Monty saw the very Mount of Olives, filled with thousands of graves, frame their way to the countryside. The atmosphere was dusty and hot, but the sky was bright and there were deep green grasses poking through the sharp rocks. Juvelius pointed to the opposite ridge and an irregular clumping of huts and caves that hung to the side of the mountain.

"That's Silwan," said Hoppenrath. Juve-lius suddenly stopped and said something else. "This valley, the Kidron, is also called by the Arabs Wadi-en-Nar. It means 'Lake of Fire.' "

They rode a little farther down into the valley. Juvelius took out the cipher and began reading aloud. Hoppenrath translated:

In the entrance of the place of refuge and
    where the stairway of the aperture /
The stairway of the aperture / Well the
    cistern! / And then the hiding place
Praise the Lord!

Monty looked around. He saw some houses, and a short tower-like structure, but that was all.

Juvelius got off his donkey and started walking down the side of the slope, toward a small building. Monty and Hoppenrath followed. They walked about over the uneven ground, dust and pebbles and grass. They seemed almost in a daze. Juvelius wandered off toward the tower. When Monty looked up again, Juvelius was shaking, almost jumping. He was shouting.

By the time Monty and Hoppenrath reached him, Juvelius had a look of what could have been relief or fear. He was talking very rapidly. Before Hoppenrath could translate, Monty ran up and saw what he was pointing to. For some reason, he felt the whole scene looked familiar. He looked down.

He saw a set of stairs, falling into the darkness, just as the cipher predicted.

Monty had been impressed by the cipher when he saw it in London on pieces of marked-up paper, but there was an abstraction to it, an almost mathematical quality. To see its results now, here in the ground of the Holy Land, was an entirely different story. Juvelius, bursting with pride, read something else from the cipher. It was a line from Isaiah:

Hearken to me, ye that follow after righteousness, ye that seek the Lord: look unto the rock whence ye are hewn, and to the hole of the pit whence ye are digged.

That night, as they sat around a table in their hotel, Juvelius, through Hoppenrath, told Monty more about what the cipher revealed about the location of the Ark. The Philistines had captured the Ark from the Israelites for many years, but when David got it back, he kept it under a simple tent, called the tabernacle. The Lord spoke to him and said, "I will appoint a place for my people Israel and will plant them that they may dwell there and not be moved hence any more." David then began gathering the raw materials for a temple worthy of God, whom he loved, one that would stand forever, though he knew he would not build it himself because of his own sins, which were many. David told his son, Solomon:

> My son, I had it in my heart to build a house to the name of the LORD my God. But the word of the LORD came to me, saying, You have shed much blood and have waged great wars; you shall not build a house to my name, because you have shed so much blood before me upon the earth. Behold, a son shall be born to you; he shall be a man of peace. I will give him peace from all his enemies round about; for his name shall be Solomon, and I will give peace and quiet to Israel in his days. He shall build a house for my name. He shall be my son, and I will be his father, and I will establish his royal throne in Israel for ever.

When David died, Solomon brought all the things David had gathered and built the First Temple, a magnificent house of God made of white and gold and lined in cedar.

Not only did the Temple house the Ark in the Holy of Holies but it became the physical and symbolic center of Jewish life, high upon the Temple Mount.

But, said Juvelius, the cipher suggested another possibility. The Lord had also spoken to Solomon. "The Lord said that he would dwell in thick darkness," said Solomon, and "I have surely built thee a house to dwell in a settled place for thee to abide for ever." This all connected, Juvelius said, to the cipher's claim that the Ark was still in the fixed and secret place where David had first put it. It was somewhere in the dark.

Jerusalem would fall, many years later at the hands of Nebuchadnezzar, the king of Babylon who wore a long, square beard. In the name of Marduk, his demon god, Nebuchadnezzar spread the blood of his enemies across the table of the civilized world. It was during the second siege in 587 BC that he destroyed and looted the First Temple. The Ark went lost at exactly this moment, unmentioned in the lists of what Nebuchadnezzar and his forces took to Babylon.

The important thing, said Juvelius, is that the cipher revealed that the Ark was still there. That the "thick darkness" Solomon spoke of was the original tabernacle, cut deep into the mountain. The Ark was so holy that even the high priest went before it only once a year. Such a location made sense. Part of the covenant was to keep it fixed, like a nail. It was there, he said.

"Here," corrected Monty. "It is here."

Six

CYRIL FOLEY

London, June 1909

"Tell the story, Cyril, come on."

A few men — it was hard to tell how many in the jumble of shoulders and forearms — were huddled around the circular table. The center of the attention, finishing his drink with a flourish, was Cyril Foley. He had a high forehead, a dashing dark mustache, and a well-set jaw. He was not smiling.

"Lads . . . ," he said, looking around with a mean and serious look.

He took a long pause, before a brief, inevitable smile appeared.

"It was 1893, July sixth, and we were playing Sussex at Lords. . . ." The men cheered. Cyril continued, drawing his head closer to his audience. He enunciated all the right words and used his hands when needed. He had told this story before and knew the best way to tell it.

"A tremendous crowd was there because

it was the day that old King George V was married." The men nodded. "So with all those people about, many of them came up to see the cricket." He stopped for another swig.

"A Sussex bowler named Gutteridge bowled me a ball which narrowly missed my wicket; struck Butt, the wicketkeeper, on the pads; and rebounded into the wicket. Butt replaced one bail, and I the other. As I was preparing to receive the next ball, Henry, the umpire, said, 'You're out.' I was flabbergasted! 'What for?' I asked."

"For handling the bail, said the umpire."

"Well, I was stunned," said Cyril, opening his arms. "I walked about like a man in a dream. I reached the pavilion and ran into Buns Thornton, who said, 'What did they give you out for, Cyril?' "

"For handling the bail, I said."

"Go back," said Buns. "The umpire can't make the rules!"

"But I shrugged it off," said Cyril, with a grimace. "I went upstairs and took my pads off. Now back then, the dressing rooms were located in the back of the pavilion, so I never saw what occurred, but I believe the crowd invaded the ground, and there was a devil of a row. In about a quarter of an hour, W. L. Murdoch, the Sussex captain, came up to the dressing room and said to me, 'Cyril, I want you to go in again.' "

Cyril Foley, forty-one, an Eton man, second lieutenant veteran of the Jameson Raid, and son of the late Honorable Sir St. George Gerald Foley, raised his cup to his lips. "Of course," he said. "I was quite ready and managed to add some thirty-odd runs." The men at the table clapped as he finished his glass.

"In fact, I believe I am the only person to have ever been accorded two innings without the sanction of the umpire." The crowd laughed. "Oh yes, and I was wearing the opera gloves I wore the night before." He shrugged. "I didn't see a reason to change." They roared again.

"I later asked Gutteridge why he had appealed. I had not handled the bail. I'm sorry to say he was suspended for two years. No one knows why he did it."

As the table dispersed, Cyril Foley took their handshakes and admiration. He was a legend to these men: a soldier, cardplayer, shooter, bachelor, and most of all an accomplished batsman, having played in one hundred first-class matches in England and the West Indies. He was an adventurer-gentleman who was always good for a tremendous story. So when his good friend

Robin Duff walked in, with his close-cut dark hair and mustache that defied gravity, Cyril knew that some game was up.

"Good to see you, Duff!" said Cyril, clasping his hand.

"Same. Do you have a moment? I have a fantastic proposition for you."

By the time his friend had told him about Monty, Dr. Juvelius, the cipher, and the Ark of the Covenant, Cyril Foley had only one thing to say.

"Duff," he said, shaking his head with a half grin, "should I call the police?"

Seven
JOHAN MILLEN

London, July 1909
"The doubt of the Bible must be doubted!" Johan Millen was standing in the middle of the dark room. He had come to share his knowledge of the Ark, which was significant, before the expedition left. He felt it was very important they know certain things.

"Externability and authority must disappear!" Millen was a magnetic speaker; his accent, flattened out with *v*'s and *z*'s, often changed in pitch midsentence, sometimes ending on a higher octave. It sounded more like a chant than actual speech. His words had an authority, like song.

"The Ark was made to God's own specifications by Moses and two engineers in the desert after they left Egypt," he said to his rapt audience. "It was constructed out of the sacred shittimwood, then gilded. The box measured two and a half cubits in length, one and a half in breadth, and one and a half in height. In it were placed the Ten Commandments of the law, in some form or another.

"After the people reached the promised land, the Ark was stolen by the enemy, the Philistines. But everywhere they tried to place it, sickness, in the form of tumor and woe, followed its every move. The Philistines were so distraught that they returned the Ark to an outlying village of the Israelites. King David, who was then early in his reign, was so pleased at the Ark's return that he ordered it loaded onto a cart and driven to Jerusalem with a great escort of his people.

"As they passed over a farmer's threshing floor, one of the oxen carrying the cart stumbled on some of the loose kernels. A man named Uzzah feared that the Ark might fall, so he bravely jumped forward and used his hand to hold it steady."

Millen paused and looked down. He was saddened, but direct.

"Uzzah's deed incurred the wrath of the Lord, who smote him where he stood. When David came upon the scene, he was filled with horror. Taken with an unnatural fear, he ordered the Ark to stay at the farm and for everyone to return to the city.

"Later, in consulting the Scripture, David found that he had not followed the rules of the law, that said the Ark should be transported with two long wooden poles and could not be touched. David tried again — following the rules this time — and they moved the Ark back to Jerusalem, with David dancing, with all his might, in the dust at the front of the procession." Millen did a little dance here himself, to some laughter. He was a mercurial man, in both thought and deed. "They put the box in the tabernacle, where it was hidden by a veiled curtain."

"The power of the Ark is real," said Millen, pointing upward. But then he moved his finger to his temple. "But what was explained to superstition in the ancient past can now be explained by the scientist, not the fanatacist. Eventually, the ancient miracles, one after the other, dissolve into natural phenomena. In this case, Dr. Juvelius and I are in agreement that the dangerous power of the Ark was due to the substance we now know as radium. But!" — and here he raised his finger again — "We believe that the duration of its rest inside the box will have made it long inert.

"The Ark had peculiar effects on people," said Millen, "but its purpose was clear. It was a means of communication with God." Millen produced a small print of the Ark. He pointed to its golden lid, topped with two golden cherubim. "This is the mercy seat, the space for the presence of God," he said. "When the high priest came before the Ark, we think, according to the texts, that it was not with a blank mind, but with a question!"

Millen got very quiet, there in the firelight. "But not with speech. One cannot simply talk to God. Urim and Thummim are the means by which we think the Ark was communicated with. They are the wise stones, as they were called by the medieval alchemists."

His audience looked at him blankly, as if he were a ghost.

"Let me rephrase," said Millen. "The priest could not confer directly with the Lord. He was too powerful. And sacrilege! That is where Urim and Thummim are used. In Exodus 28:30," and here he took up his own black edition, "it says, 'And thou shalt put Urim and Thummim into the court of the world, that they may lie upon Aaron's heart when he enters the face of the Lord.' "

Millen rummaged through another book until he found a picture. It showed a golden rectangle covered with flat, colorful jewels. "Aaron, the high priest, wore a breastplate, called *hoshen*," Millen said. "It was gold

88

and covered with twelve gemstones, one for each tribe, lapis lazuli, amethyst, and moonstone among them. But it was not mere decoration or ceremony. This was part of divination." And here Millen stretched out his arms and closed his hands. "In each palm, the priest held the rocks of Urim and Thummim. He would then ask a question, and the stones would reveal the will of God.

"Some believe the priest would know which hand to overturn, others believed it was a kind of psychic sense. Some complex questions could have been answered by great rays of light shining out of certain jewels on the breastplate; each jewel was taken to represent different letters, and the sequence of lighting thus would spell out an answer. Urim means 'lights,' after all. Or, and I believe this version, it was more simple.

"One meant cursed, the other faultless. The stones were essentially used to answer the oldest question of all: Innocent or guilty? True or false? Life or death?"

EIGHT

CYRIL FOLEY

Mediterranean Sea, July 1909

Fine white sand stretched out under a sky the color of Wedgwood blue. Just beyond the shore, Cyril saw the slow, foaming waters of the ocean. The sea breeze sifted gently through the palm trees. The air was warm but not harsh; it was perfect. Cyril allowed himself a long, calming breath. Then, suddenly, his stomach rose, and a thick taste filled the back of his throat. He took another breath and held his hand out in front of him, against the blue sea, the sand, and the sky. He wavered for a moment, but then steadied. Cyril smiled again. He could feel it again, the magic of the place washing over him like a balm. Then he began to shake a little, first his finger, then his hand. The horizon tipped over.

Cyril saw darkness. His thin blanket was pulled all the way up to his face, which was covered in seawater. His limbs awakened to

90

a chilling cold. He looked up to see a gigantic mast and sail swaying in the night air above him. Cyril felt the hard deck beneath him and could hear the walls of waves splashing the boat, the wood creaking like bones. His stomach was in his mouth again. Cyril shut his eyes and tried to dream again of Jethou, one of the minor Channel Islands. He had made up his mind that he was going to buy it once they found the Ark.

A few days ago, they boarded the *India* at Victoria at half past eleven in the morning on Thursday, July 22, 1909. Their party was motley, consisting of Captain Monty Parker, Captain Robin Duff of the Guards, and Mr. Clarence Wilson. It had not taken much convincing for Cyril to join the group. They seemed like a good lot, and he trusted his man Duff completely. The war had sealed that.

Cyril also knew that he was one of the last to join. In fact, by the time he did, the Syndicate itself had changed. There was apparently a bit of bad blood between Vaughn and Monty Parker, the expedition leader. Vaughn had gone bankrupt because of some past deals and had been replaced (more or less) by Wilson, the long-haired aristocrat who was providing some of their expenses. He had been injured in the Boer War but seemed first-rate. Cyril, like Duff, was born into a noble family, but he was not a member of the Syndicate. He would be accorded his share of dividends once the Ark was found.

There were others. Otto Von Bourg was a clairvoyant. Some of the boys said that he had once, in London, used a crystal to solve the case of a missing gentleman. In a séance, Von Bourg communicated with the spirit of a man who had been murdered, then led police directly to his body. When he shook his hand, Cyril tried to clear his mind. Von Bourg was joined by a mysterious man named James Lee, another thought reader, who was said to be a friend of Juvelius.

They were also joined by Agop Macasdar, an Armenian who would serve as their much-needed interpreter. Monty had found him in Constantinople. After their trip to Jerusalem, Monty had gone there — several times, in fact — to negotiate the precious digging rights from the Turks. This had been a long and delicate negotiation given the unsettled politics of the area. The year before, the progressive Young Turks masterminded a march on Constantinople that persuaded Sultan Abdülhamīd II to return to a constitutional form of government.

Though the Young Turks were, at times, amenable to the expedition, numerous changes in their leadership posts made a signed agreement difficult. It was only when an accountant named Mehmet Cavid Bey was named finance minister and intervened on Monty's behalf that the accord was sealed. Cyril heard from the others that Monty had secured the digging rights for five hundred pounds sterling for three years. Two Turkish officials would join them in Jerusalem as observers. Cyril wondered what the split would be.

From England, they traveled in a steady, speedy line to Marseilles, where they stopped, changed course east, then headed straight to Port Said in northern Egypt. When they landed on July 27, two men waited for them on the dock. One of them was Mr. Walsh, one of the head engineers of the new pier at Dover and the London Underground. "Invaluable," thought Cyril, as he clasped Walsh's rough hand.

The second man was thin and wore a high collar, a vest, and trim boots. Cyril almost laughed; he knew exactly who this had to be.

"The great Juvelius," Cyril said sardonically. The man looked up and nodded; clearly his English was sparse, but he knew his name. Everyone disembarked from the *India* as hired men moved their luggage. Juvelius clutched his bag close. They were going to transfer to a small boat that Clarence Wilson had docked at Port Said, before heading on to Jaffa.

When they approached Wilson's vessel, the *Water Lily,* Cyril expected to see a fine and practical English supply boat. Instead, he saw a bright white racing yacht in impeccable condition. The boat was not very long (though certainly more than enough for their needs), but it had a bangingly tall mast. It pushed up into the sky like some great biblical tower. Cyril elbowed Wilson in jest, though he had to admit he was jealous. Within a day, they set sail for Jaffa.

Now, in the grip of a midnight storm, their smooth sailing trip seemed like a suicide mission.

"That ridiculous mast," muttered Cyril as he again looked up at it, swaying like it was drunken. Cyril tumbled to his feet, hunched over, and wrapped the blanket around him. All around him, his companions were lying on the deck in similar straits. They had decided to lie on deck so they wouldn't roll overboard, though that no longer felt like such a wise decision. It had now become some sort of lunatic contest as to who could last the longest before getting sick. Cyril laughed. The mind men had already gone belowdecks. Cyril shambled to his feet in his blanket and moved forward like some old Egyptian mummy. He looked over to Walsh, the engineer, and nodded. The spray from the waves blasted off the sides of the boat.

"Look out!" someone yelled.

A swell of cold Mediterranean water surged against the boat, causing it to dangerously tip. Cyril looked at the safety angle: they were several degrees over the limit. He held his breath.

The boat hung there a slow, captivating moment, tipped halfway over, then fell back onto its hull with a punch and splash that made everyone stumble. Cyril looked behind him, hoping that each new rhythm of the swell wouldn't bring an even bigger wave that was lying in wait for them, hoping to spill them out of the boat like so many little fish.

He saw Monty standing up against the waves, a shadow in his hat in the dark of the storm. Cyril wondered what his share in this was. He didn't know much about him. He knew he was in line to be Lord Morley, though it was unlikely because he was the second son. Cyril knew that Monty had been in the Second Boer War, after he and Duff. Cyril heard that Monty had been injured there, though he saw no visible limp or scar.

The storm never really ended that night, though after it reached its peak, it began to settle down. Their little competition a soggy disaster, Monty retired belowdecks around one in the morning, his easy demeanor showing that he had no need to prove anything. Robin Duff, who had never been seasick in his life, gave in at three a.m. Cyril, who had never withdrawn from a race or match, managed to stick it out, but only just. Lee and Von Bourg had spent the night below. Everyone heard their unfortunate retching.

When Cyril woke up, it was still dark, but it had stopped raining and there was enough early-morning light that he could finally see beyond the yacht. This time, it was Juvelius who was perched at the stern, looking forward. Cyril followed his gaze. As the sun started to push up, the dim outline of an ancient city rose on the horizon. In the haze, it looked like some magnificent version of a child's blocks, all piled up on top of itself. This is how the *Water Lily,* bruised and slow, reached the port city of Jaffa.

By the time the morning sun was comfortable, most everyone had risen, or at least most of them.

"How is Von Bourg?" asked one of the boys.

"He passed away just before sunup," answered the steward, without flinching.

There was a pause, then the men laughed.

Though they could see the city, they could not yet land until they were cleared to do so. They cast the small anchor over the *Water Lily*'s edge. It clinked, then splashed, then sank. As they floated in the open, Cyril got a better look at Jaffa. The city itself was long and stood on the edge of a ridge, old and crumbling. The city was said to have been named after Japheth, the son of Noah, who built it after the Flood. Cyril expected a short trip in Palestine; they would have the Ark in tow and the wind at their backs in a couple of days at most. But he found the sight of Jaffa, romantic and deep, to be exotic.

At nine o'clock in the morning, a small boat came up to them, carrying a pilot and passenger. The latter was the port medical officer, a dry, serious man. He wore a light uniform and had an air of control to him.

"You cannot land," he said, matter-of-factly, "until I have vetted the lot of you."

Jaffa apparently still had problems with the plague.

"Fantastic," said Cyril, probably too loudly.

The *Water Lily* was a small enough vessel, so it couldn't take too long, Cyril thought. Besides, the medical officer looked a little seasick himself.

Monty stuck his tongue out first, with the barest minimum of enthusiasm, and let the medic look into his eyes. Cyril was next, and then down the row. The medic got through the rest of them rather quickly, including Juvelius.

"Is that all of you?" asked the medic.

It was just then that a very bleary Lee and Von Bourg, both looking a quite gruesome shade of gray, climbed up the stairs to make their grand entrance. Cyril thought of making a statement about the miraculous resurrection of Mr. Von Bourg but thought better of it. The medic took one look at the two and shook his head. Cyril's spirits sank. They might be stuck out here for days, even weeks. Cyril thought of his island with the light breeze. He looked over to Jaffa.

He had an idea.

Cyril looked closely as the medic waited to examine the two psychics. The man wearily sat down on the edge of the rail and wiped his brow. He *was* sick, observed Cyril. Maybe the *Water Lily*'s propensity to make people ill because of its small dimensions could be used in their favor. He grabbed Macasdar, and they slipped over to the launch that the medic had tied to the side of the boat. The pilot looked up at them. Cyril smiled a hello.

"Tell him," he told Macasdar, "that his master wants him to return to harbor and remain there till signaled for from the yacht." Macasdar looked at Cyril.

"Trust me," said Cyril. "But don't tell him that." Macasdar relayed his words. The pilot looked over at the sick medic, nodded, and pushed the boat off.

When the medic realized what had happened, he had a fit. Cyril was right that he had hoped to stay on board the queasy *Water Lily* as short a time as possible.

"You can recall your launch by signal at any given moment," said Cyril. He looked over at Monty.

The medic was getting greener by the moment. He glared at them through a fully developed flopsweat.

"And I would point out," said Cyril, slyly, "that the signing of our landing permit would synchronize with the hoisting of the afore-mentioned signal."

The medic was nearly spasming, so he gave the signal and signed the papers. When his pilot returned with the boat, the medic didn't even speak to him. Cyril imagined that he was planning on saying quite a bit more on the way back.

"No shaking hands?" asked Cyril, as they sailed off.

They were not yet on Palestinian soil and already they were breaking the rules. Cyril felt as if this was going to be the beginning of a grand adventure indeed. Jesus had calmed a storm in this very sea with the power of God; this lot had used good old-fashioned blackmail.

They rolled up the anchor and set off for the port. As they got closer, Cyril grabbed Walsh and pointed to a massive crag of stone that was pushing out of the sea.

"See those rocks?" he said. "That is the place where Andromeda was rescued by Perseus from being sacrificed to the Kraken. The Kraken! And here" — he pointed to the city itself — "the Egyptians once took this city by hiding in sacks that were carried in by donkeys! Two hundred years before the Trojan Horse!" Walsh regarded Cyril with a cool eye that seemed to project equal parts incredulity and fear that this sort of exchange might become a regular occurrence.

"I went to Cambridge!" said Cyril.

When they landed, Cyril found Jaffa to be beyond compare. It was a very Eastern town, which was the best word he could come up with for it. He loved how absurdly narrow the angled streets were. Cyril was admiring a particular shop window full of rugs when he turned the corner to find an enormous camel standing directly in his face. Cyril ducked out of the way, only to see the camel open its long mouth and chase poor Clarence Wilson for two hundred yards. Cyril laughed. He thought it brilliant that these great beasts could knock you down, bite you, or lick you, depending on their mood, all while carrying some stupendous burden.

The party purchased donkeys and rode into Jerusalem on a long and tedious journey. When they arrived that same day, at six o'clock at night, Cyril was so tired that he noticed very little of the Holy City itself. The last thing he remembered before falling asleep was that their particularly dirty hotel was most likely the cleanest in Jerusalem.

■ ■ ■ ■

PART TWO:
UNDERGROUND

■ ■ ■ ■

NINE

BERTHA VESTER

Jerusalem, 1909

Mrs. Bertha Vester was in her kitchen, standing over the grated oven that was set into the counter, making upside-down mutton. She took the copper pan and tipped it to and fro over the flame. The chopped meat inside was roasting in the pooling yellow butter. Bubbles formed on the grease before disappearing with tiny pops.

"So, Mr. Tarsha! What are those Englishmen on the hill up to?" Bertha asked the exhausted bearded man at her kitchen table. He was eating bread and drinking water and looked washed-out from a long day in the sun. Next to him was a toddler, a girl with blond hair, playing with the remains of a crust.

"Mrs. Vester!" said the man. "I should be cooking for you!"

"No, no, you have been cooking all day. Sit."

The mutton was sizzling, its grassy smell filling the small kitchen. Bertha added a layer of sliced eggplant that proceeded to fry. With the American Colony's ranks growing, Bertha and her husband had rented a larger house and sublet the old one to Mr. Tarsha, who was cooking for the group that was conducting archaeological excavations on the side of Mount Ophel. Not much was known of them, so Bertha was naturally curious. She needed to know if there was any way the Colony could help them. Or if they posed a threat.

When the eggplant was nice and crispy, Bertha added the cooked rice. She then seasoned it with salt, pepper, a bit of cinnamon and allspice, and some saffron for color. Her fingers brushed together in a quick and practiced motion. The smell changed, instantly and almost imperceptibly, becoming something heavenly.

Bertha pushed her shawl back and turned toward the table. She was thirty, but still had her long hair pinned up like a girl's. She was wearing mostly white and crossed her arms to regard Mr. Tarsha.

"They're not building hospitals," she said.

"Oh no," said Mr. Tarsha.

Bertha had lived in Jerusalem nearly her whole life and had enough friends that she heard things almost as soon as they happened. The rumors around the Englishmen were many. They seemed to care little of the history of the place they were digging in. Apparently not one of their number was even an archaeologist. As Bertha placed the dish onto the table, steaming and framed with slices of lime and onion, she gave a look to Mr. Tarsha that she needed more information.

"They are digging. And with some care. But the parties! So many!" said Mr. Tarsha. He was staring at the upside-down mutton. "The Turkish pasha was at the last one! I had to cook it all! And speaking of food, guess what they use for target practice when they are bored? Oranges! Full, ripe oranges! They use their guns and" — he made a gesture with his two worn hands — "blow them to smithereens! I saw the children scrambling to gather the bits!" He gestured at the little girl, who gave him a wide-eyed look.

Bertha sat down, held their hands, and led them in Christian grace, which was the only cost of sharing her table. Once it was over, Bertha began doling out the food.

"They have hired a great many workers from Silwan," said Mr. Tarsha, "but overall, they are very nice men. Though," he said, with a humongous gulp, followed by a pause where he closed his own eyes. "Ah, excellent." He took another forkful. "Your brother will not like them!"

"No, he will not," said Bertha.

"One other curious thing I saw. They ride to the dig on donkey-back. Once, I saw that they all switched places! The English were running alongside the donkeys, whooping and yelling, while the boys rode on the donkeys!" He swallowed again. "Madness!"

"They are certainly the oddest archaeologists I have ever heard of," said Bertha. "Well, I am sure we shall meet them before long."

Sure enough, a week or so later, Bertha and her husband, Frederick, with his long horizon of a mustache that Bertha found to be very handsome, were at a reception — they went to so many — when the Englishmen walked in, confident and straight. They looked sharp, though perhaps a fraction out of place. Bertha slowly made her way over to their party, moving from one conversation to the next as if they were rungs on a ladder. Once she reached their party and was introduced, their leader gave a measured, if slight, bow.

"Captain Monty Parker," said the tall one with the hat.

"Mrs. Bertha Vester," she replied.

Monty narrowed an eye at her accent. "American?"

"Yes. My father and mother came here from Chicago when I was three."

"Ah," said Monty.

"So, I hear you are digging. Have you found anything yet? In the Pool of Siloam? Or in Hezekiah's Tunnel?"

Monty looked greatly reduced by Bertha's salvo, which gave her a small amount of glee that she was not altogether proud of. When she asked about the work of Charles Warren, it was clear to her that this man Parker had little to no knowledge on the subject. He was no archaeologist. What then were they doing? As was her nature, Bertha didn't question to be cruel. She wanted to help.

"You should talk to my brother," said Bertha.

The next day, when Bertha told her brother Jacob about the exchange, he was, as predicted, quite upset.

"They have the privilege of excavating there, and they go to parties? And ride donkeys?" He sulked. "I have to talk to them." Bertha understood. Her brother's favorite hobby was archaeology, and he took great pride in it, as many locals did.

Soon after, the mayor of Jerusalem, Faidie

Effendi al-Alami, hosted a picnic. Jacob went as a representative of the Colony and, as planned, saw the British men, this time congregating under a shady tree. They were watching the mayor's young son and daughter playing with some other children. He walked to them with haste.

"Hello," he said. "You met my sister the other day. I am Jacob."

"Captain Parker," said Monty.

"I wanted to tell you," Jacob said, with some difficulty. "You are digging on the most historical spot in Palestine."

Monty looked like he was bracing himself for another barrage. The others inched closer, but he held them back with a slight raise of his finger.

"And if you would carry on excavations there," flashed Jacob, as he pointed at Monty, which drew some eyes, "without leaving any record . . . well, it would be a great harm to the whole archaeological world!"

Finished, Jacob caught his breath. Monty seemed almost to smile but stayed serious.

"Those caves are holy," said Jacob. "Trust me." Jacob pushed his hand into his pocket and gave a piece of paper to Monty. "Promise me you will talk to this man. His name is Père Vincent. He belongs to the Dominican fathers and is the head of the École Biblique et Archéologique in Jerusalem. He is an archaeologist."

When Jacob returned home and told his sister what he had done, she was proud of him indeed.

TEN

FATHER VINCENT

Jerusalem, August 1909

"Father! They're back!"

Father Louis-Hugues Vincent gave a sudden twitch from his chair. He was not sleeping, but merely deeply involved in his book, though at this very moment he failed to recall its exact title.

"They're digging on the hill again! Come look!"

Father Vincent marked his page, set his book on the table, and gathered up his white habit around his thin frame. He stood up, grabbed his large, circular hat, and walked out onto the little white courtyard of St. Stephen's Basilica. His bald head was surrounded by a halo of black hair, the unmistakable mark of his Dominican order. Father Vincent pulled his glasses over his long nose and placed his hat on his head, adjusting its tilt to where he liked it. He pointed his bearded chin toward the boy and smiled. The hat made his face look like the sun.

"Come on!"

They made their steps outside the city gates and toward the Kidron Valley, southeast of Jerusalem. As they took the road down on the eastern slope of Mount Ophel, Father Vincent could see the men his young friend was referring to. They were swinging pickaxes and hauling out dirt. They had set up a wooden platform with a pulley and rope. They were digging again. Watching over the operations was the familiar silhouette of a man in a captain's hat with a pipe in his hand. Father Vincent had been watching them for days now. He knew exactly where they were.

"Let's get closer," Father Vincent said.

Mount Ophel was more of a slow swell than an actual mountain, rising out of the valley in the shadow of Mount Olive. Everything was slow and rolling there, bleached by the flat sun with thatches of bush and low trees. The land was alive with heat and insects, but Father Vincent was interested in its other attributes, the old and dusty things that people had left behind a long time ago.

"Are they from the Palestine Exploration Fund?" asked the boy.

"No." Father Vincent was studying them

through squinted eyes. It was a good guess, as the leaders were obviously English in dress, but they did not look very official.

"They are on their own, I think."

"Who are they?"

The question went unanswered as Father Vincent studied his subjects, these hazy people with their shovels and picks. They carried long ladders and planks. Whoever they were, they were well acquainted with the archaeological history of the spot to have started here. Either that or they were incredibly, preternaturally lucky. This was where Charles Warren, the Englishman, had uncovered an underground shaft into the mountain almost forty years ago. It seemed as if these new men were trying to open it up again. Perhaps, Father Vincent thought, it was time to answer the question of who "they" were.

As Father Vincent slid closer, he realized there was an official perimeter to the dig site. Signs in various languages warned that all visitors would be turned away. At this distance, he could see that he had mistook two of the figures from afar. The fezzes gave them away: Turks. They stood along the back, with their broad mustaches and uniforms. In fact, Father Vincent noticed a fair number of other foreign men, marked by dress or habit, gathered all around the mouth of the dig. The Turks were obviously there in an official capacity, but these others? Father Vincent was unsure.

Father Vincent took off his hat and wiped his head with a handkerchief. Since the men had arrived, people from nearby villages and even the city had tried to get a peek, though they were mostly unsuccessful, which only further added to the mystery. The whispers scampered through the crowd like little mice. Hushed voices said that the men from England were unholy treasure hunters. Pilferers.

Raiders.

Father Vincent knew this accusation well. It was, most unfortunately, not without its own eternal truth in Palestine. There had been grave robbers and thieves all throughout the region for centuries, stealing from churches and tombs. They came from all over, looking for gold and treasure. This happened even under the Turkish rule. Some were thieves in the night; others came during the daytime, with permits and uniforms. Father Vincent shook his head. All those discoveries scattered away. All that history lost. The true story of the region was lost on such men. The tragedy, Father

Vincent knew, was that it was then lost to all.

He watched the Arab workers, locals from the small village of Silwan, haul debris from the tunnel without complaint. Father Vincent circled around one of the signs and snuck a closer look at their leader. He was dressed in khaki and had a mustache and a pipe. His white hat was getting dusty, and he kept beating it clean with an annoyed look on his face. Father Vincent saw a spark there, among all the swagger. He could not say if it was faith. One thing was clear: the man in charge was no archaeologist. In fact, he did not see any of their ilk, with their telltale instruments of tape and paper.

"Interesting," said Father Vincent.

The next day, Father Vincent returned to the digging site with a letter of introduction on official letterhead from the École Biblique, the French archaeological school next to St. Stephen's, where he had worked since 1891. He showed it to someone who called over the man in the captain's hat. The leader of the expedition walked up, gave Father Vincent a quick but direct look, and took his papers. He took a moment to read them, with a few carefully punctuated "hmms" and "mms." Father Vincent shifted his feet on the dry rock as his qualifications were being read. At age thirty-six, he was no ordinary priest. Called the *petit saint* by his brothers, he studied archaeology and languages and was even a writer. Because of his frailty, he was sometimes excused from some of the more rigorous aspects of his order, but he embraced his calling with such passion, with such natural curiosity, that his brothers could not deter him even if they wanted to. The man simply loved the study of archaeology, especially here, where tunnels and catacombs were said to somehow reach all the way to the center of Mecca itself. Vast distances shrank to almost nothing in the face of the tunnels of Palestine. The Bible even told of a smoky passage that led straight to Gehenna itself.

The man in the hat finished and handed the letter back. The look on his face was almost stern. Father Vincent's heart seemed to disappear.

"I'm Captain Monty Parker," said the man, stretching out his hand. "Your reputation precedes you, Father. Welcome aboard." Father Vincent smiled, and shook Parker's hand as vigorously as he could.

As he did so, a thin man with a slight beard came up to show a map to Monty. This man had dark, hollow eyes.

"You'll have to excuse me," said Monty.

"My attention is needed elsewhere. I am leaving on some business for a few weeks. By the time I come back, we should have cleared the opening somewhat on the other side and we can go down together." He smiled. The thin man kept his eyes on the ground.

As Monty walked off, Father Vincent felt relieved. He had tried not to allow himself the want of jealousy, but he had been unsuccessful. As he walked away, Father Vincent felt the spark of a dance at his feet, like King David himself. More sacrilege, he knew, but he let it take him, if just for a moment. In the end, he was overjoyed to be going back to his favorite place in all of Jerusalem.

He was going underground again.

ELEVEN

CYRIL FOLEY

Jerusalem, August 1909

Cyril Foley wiped the back of his neck with a handkerchief. It had now been well over forty-eight hours — weeks, in fact — since they had arrived in Palestine. They had not found the Ark, and he was definitely not on an island, or any richer, not even by a half penny. If anything, he was only dirtier and greatly baked from the heat. For the last two weeks they had been working at clearing out the Gihon Spring, or the Fontaine de la Vierge, or the Ain al-Adra, depending on who was asking. There were so many languages here. Cyril put his handkerchief back and returned to observing his man Walsh, who was marking out a wooden post.

Walsh, it turned out, knew his stuff. One of the first things they did when they arrived was to sink a shaft into Warren's old site to make things easier to clear out. So accurate was Walsh in his overhead estimate that at sixty feet down they hit it right on the nose. The ground then gave way rather easily, ending in what looked to be a pile of small boulders. Cyril thought it a great performance. It had been the height of their excitement. Mostly, they just stood around and watched the local workers clear out the dirt.

"Where's Juvelius?" asked Walsh, in his flat manner.

"We sent him off by himself down the hill," said Cyril. "Him and his notes." Cyril motioned in the general direction, but Juvelius was already gone. Probably lost in his own head, thought Cyril. He found Juvelius to be somewhat of a boor, but not as much as Von Bourg was. At a recent conference, Von Bourg had suggested that the Ark was actually on Mount Ararat and that they should move the entire works, planks and all, based solely on his psychical impression. Von Bourg was banned from speaking on the subject again. Cyril didn't have anything against mystics, but he supposed this group had tipped their quota. Rumor had it that Juvelius was going to be joined soon by a friend from Finland. Cyril hoped he had no psychic powers.

The early days had been going well, practically speaking, though they were not without incident. Two days after sinking the shaft, on August 16th, the chief rabbi of Jerusalem died. Cyril walked up the hill and watched from afar as all the Jewish women collected on the Women's Wailing Ground. They arrived slowly, wearing long patterned shawls wrapped down over their heads. They clutched their prayer books across their chests.

"My word, they really did wail," Cyril told Walsh later. "It was really so impressive as to be unforgettable."

The current aim of the expedition was to clear out the fountain area. At the bottom of the stairs was a cave, with a long tunnel leading out from it. Another side led to a dead end, a sheer vertical tunnel that was unclimbable. This was Warren's Shaft (since he discovered it), but the locals called it by its much older name: the Dragon Shaft. One of the expedition's long-term goals, at least engineering-wise, was to connect the tunnels in the ground with the shaft on top. They had old maps to guide them, but those were sketches at best, two-dimensional representations of the hard dirt and rock that spread out below in three directions.

On August 20th, Monty and Duff had gone home to England for a month's holiday. Cyril and Walsh stayed behind to watch the seemingly endless parade of diggers bring dirt from the tunnels. Cleaning out the fountain was necessary work, but it quickly outpaced their patience. It was repetition of the infinite. Cyril chastised himself because he was actually — while looking for the Ark of the Covenant in Palestine — feeling the pangs of boredom.

The next Sunday, Cyril jumped off his perch, motioned Macasdar to come over, and approached one of the head Arab workers. After the incident on the yacht, Macasdar feared the worst.

"Please tell this good man that I have a wager for him," said Cyril. Macasdar sighed but then spoke some words in the husky, gurgling language. The worker tipped his head, then looked at Cyril.

"Tell him my fellows and I have just made a bet that he and his men can't clear one hundred and fifty buckets of earth in one hour," Cyril said. He knew that the buckets had to be filled and manhandled for one hundred yards in a tunnel four and a half feet high. Cyril knew it was a sure thing.

The man squinted at him and nodded.

"All right boys," said Cyril, walking back. "Start counting."

Fifty-one minutes later, the workers had won. Cyril was truly astonished, and promptly doubled that hour's wages. When the victorious group ended their shift, looking only slightly more spent and quite a bit richer, their replacements did not look pleased.

One night, at their rented house on the main floor, Cyril sat with Walsh, who was trying to read a book. The house was old and dark, almost like a castle, but Cyril liked it much more than the horrid hotel they had first stayed at. Cyril had demanded a change, for comfort if not their own reputations. Cyril looked around and, as always, started talking.

"No offense, Walsh, but this place could use some members of the fairer sex, though I daresay they would be horrified by our conditions here."

Walsh offered a glance, possibly. It was enough.

"So, I was at one of the castle balls," said Cyril, getting comfortable, "spending time with a Miss Gore-Booth, who was considered the outstanding star of that season. She has since become Countess Markievicz. Anyway, she had danced quite a bit, so that I was seated at one of the tables and a well-known gossip said to me, 'I saw you dancing a great deal last night with Miss Gore-Booth; how does she dance, and has she much to say for herself?' I said, 'She is a very nice girl,' but this would not satisfy the inquisitive old woman.

"She wouldn't stop pressing! 'Now, Captain, tell me, would you prefer Miss Gore-Booth as a dancing partner or as a talking partner?' Annoyed by this inquisitive persistence, I said, 'I should personally prefer her as a sleeping partner.' There was a dreadful silence, only broken by bubblings from the man next to me."

Cyril set back into his chair. "I was duly reported to and spoken to by Lord Houghton during our daily ride in the Phoenix before breakfast the next morning, but I fancy he was really more amused than angry."

Walsh continued to read. After a long sigh, and a rare quiet moment, Cyril shot up like a thunderbolt. He looked at Walsh with a fixed eye. It took a moment for Walsh to fall for it.

"Let's have it," said Walsh, dreading the answer.

"The Dragon Shaft!" shouted Cyril.

Walsh raised his eyebrows, then got back to his book.

"No," he said.

Not only did the Dragon Shaft appear to be unconquerable, but even the workers kept clear of it. That, they said, muttering and pointing to the tunnel, was where a monster lived. There were stories that back in the ancient days, the beast issued steam and all sorts of growls from its lair in the earth. But Cyril did not believe that the workmen were scared of the place because of some antediluvian reptile. Cyril believed that they had not attempted it yet because it looked exceedingly steep and dangerous.

"No," said Walsh again.

"Monty is gone. Juvelius is staying in the city, so he won't stop us," said Cyril, trying to persuade him. "Think of it, Walsh. A difficult athletic and engineering task, to be sure. But let's get down to it. What better place to hide the Ark?"

Walsh looked up, then closed his book.

They gathered up all the six-foot ladders they could, ten of them, and dragged them out to the site. They clattered the ladders down the stone stairs and into the underground. The way through the cave was winding and their ladders could barely navigate the curves, but they eventually pushed them all through the square tunnel toward their destination. The only light was their candles, and they wore waders through the small stream. The water was up this night, as they had not yet completely dammed it up yet. Except for the work and the echo of the water, it was dead quiet. They were underground, the workers were gone, and no one knew they were there.

Cyril thought of his island again, calm and bright.

As they pushed forward through the main tunnel, Cyril watched as Walsh looked at the walls with a mixture of professional respect and romantic love. Cyril could not believe that this tunnel was man-made. Clearing it out was the expedition's ultimate goal, as they believed it led to the Ark. All the tunnels were connected somehow, but this long burrow, Hezekiah's Tunnel, was the key.

"Can you imagine it?" asked Cyril. "Old King Hezekiah tells his commanders, 'You must divert the waters at Gihon through a tunnel, which I wish you to cut right through the hill, and bring it out under the wall of the city into the Pool of Siloam. You can begin it at both ends to save time, though I suppose you will be at least twenty feet out when you try to meet in the middle. Let me have your plans by sundown! And by the way, we're at war with the Assyrians." He looked at Walsh. "Now that is, I take it, what happened."

This had long been the legend of Hezekiah's Tunnel, that during the war with Assyria in the eighth century BC, the king had ordered a tunnel dug to safeguard their water supply from the enemy. But Cyril shook his head. "I would not say that the Jewish historians told deliberate untruths, but there is no doubt they were prone to exaggeration. The historians make one imagine that Hezekiah gave an order, and hey, presto! The thing was done. I guess it would have taken them five years at least. How long would it take you to cut this tunnel?"

"With modern implements?" Walsh looked around. "Eight or nine months."

"Time and space meant nothing to the Jewish historians," said Cyril.

They stopped and let go of the ladders. Cyril stretched into the small space he was given and raised his candle as high as he could. It flickered against the smooth walls. He swept its light slowly to the right and then the left. Nothing. He raised it higher.

There. The Dragon's Shaft yawned above them.

Cyril could see a ledge about ten feet up. It was wide enough for the ladders. He breathed a sigh of relief.

"Let's get the ladders together," he said.

For the next four hours, they managed to

join seven ladders together and with great difficulty hoisted their monstrous creation onto the ledge above them. They pushed it up slowly through the darkness, all the while waiting to hit an obstacle that never came. The ladder kept rising. It finally reached its full, almost impossible height somewhere in the void above them. Though they had entered the tunnels somewhat even with the ground, they were now under the mountain itself, meaning the space above them was now much greater. It was disconcerting, this feeling, that it was all bigger on the inside. They leaned the ladder against the stone.

Walsh raised his candle again to inspect their invention. The work was not up to his usual requirement, and Cyril feared the man might demand a complete redesign. They could both see that the ladder was swaying somewhere, up in the dark. Walsh narrowed his eyes.

"It'll do," he said.

Suddenly, Cyril was not very keen on ascending those thin dowels into the mystery of the void and possibly a dragon's stomach. Cyril looked at Walsh.

"Let's toss for it, old man."

Cyril dug into his pocket and produced a coin. He flipped it in the air, and in the pool of candlelight, it slivered in gold.

128

Walsh won and was the first to attempt the summit. Cyril didn't say it out loud, but he thought his friend was really the one who had lost. Walsh spit on his palms, took a breath, and started up, his candle in his mouth. Cyril stood underneath him as Walsh's boots dripped water onto his head.

Within moments, Walsh had disappeared into the gloom.

Cyril stood there, steadying the ladder, though he didn't know what precious good it would do. He felt the ladder groan with each steady footstep, like a creaky heartbeat, somewhere high above him. Cyril did not shout out to his friend; he didn't want to scare him. Cyril raised his wavering candle up as high as he could. He could not see Walsh's light anymore. There was nothing there above him, only emptiness. No, not that — it was darkness. A total darkness. It felt colder than it was. He tried to think of his island.

The ladder stopped moving. Cyril looked up. He braced himself for Walsh's large body crashing onto him after a long, murderous fall, but nothing happened.

Cyril knew the story about the dragon was utter nonsense, probably. But he also knew that the Bible had mentioned it more than once. Jeremiah said that when Jerusalem was finally conquered, that it would be overrun with dragons. The Virgin's Fountain itself had been called the Dragon's Well by Nehemiah. The old stories seemed to repeat themselves in one fashion or another.

The ladder creaked again, and suddenly, Cyril could feel the weight moving again, but this time in the opposite direction. His friend was coming down. After several minutes, Cyril saw a yellow glow moving down toward him.

"I've had rather an exciting time," Walsh said, as first his boots, then his legs, then his candle (and the rest of him) emerged from the shadow and he plunked down to the ground. He dusted off his shirt and took a drink of water. "There's a slope of rock at the top of the shaft, and I got on to it, but it was so slippery I slid back." He took another swig. "If I had not luckily struck the top of the ladder, you would have seen me much sooner." He paused, as if trying to convince himself of something. "There's an iron ring up there, set into the wall. They probably used it to pull something up."

"Something heavy."

Cyril looked up and swallowed. The whole trip up and down had taken about twenty minutes. And it was now his turn. Cyril put his boot on the first rung and began to ascend with his heart in his mouth as well as a melting candle.

When he got to the top, Cyril found that Walsh had spoken true. The tunnel moved abruptly away from him, at an angle of even less than forty-five degrees, with the top of the ladder extending above the slope, under a domed ceiling. Cyril moved his candle and saw huge boulders stopping up a half-filled passage to the right. They looked very precarious, and Cyril wondered if they might be part of some elaborate booby trap. He looked ahead to the long slope. By the dim light of the candle it looked a grim and ghostly spot. Cyril clutched the ladder as tightly as he could. He realized two things: one, he was not going to leave that ladder for anything, and two, he was probably the fourth human being who had looked on this place in eighteen hundred years, the first and second being Sir Charles Warren and Sergeant Birtles, who made the ascent in 1867. He had read Warren's work, of course, and it was vivid, but it was nothing like being *in* the place, standing on a ladder, deep underground, looking into a place that breathed pure mystery.

Cyril stopped there for a moment, in the near dark. He had moved his foot slightly off the rung to begin his descent when he heard something shift from up in the passage. He slowly moved his candle forward. Before he could move, he felt a motion, like wind but of much greater substance. A dreadful shape hit Cyril full on the shoulder, knocking the candle out of his hand. As he watched it fall straight down, Cyril was gripped by a sheer terror he had not felt since Africa. He took one short breath before he immediately fled down the ladder as if he were trying to break a record. When he struck the ledge at the bottom, not having even known it was there, he turned a complete somersault, and landed with a sickening splash into two feet of water.

"I was attacked," said Cyril, as Walsh helped him up. "By a bat!" He caught his breath. "It was attracted to the candle." He sputtered out some water. "And no second-class bat, either."

After seven hours on the job, Cyril and Walsh walked home. They left the ladder in the tunnel. Cyril was now convinced that he knew exactly what the Dragon Shaft really was. In Chronicles, during the siege of Jerusalem (then called Jebus), around 1000 BC, the city was held by the enemies of Israel. King David had the plan of sending someone to go through these tunnels and "get up the gutter" to make a surprise attack on the Jebusites from within their walls. David's nephew Joab volunteered, slipped in undetected, and led the way to a rout and the capture of the city. He was made commander in chief for his bravery. When Cyril was on top of that ladder, he knew he was looking at that very same gutter. Walsh was, as always, impressed with his friend's knowledge of the Bible, and they retired to a well-earned supper.

The next day, Clarence Wilson could not believe what his friends had done. Cyril and Walsh took him down to the ladder to show him. Wilson gave a look, then climbed up himself. On returning, he said nothing, but quietly picked up an eighty-foot rope that they had brought with them and ascended again. Cyril didn't rightly know how, but Wilson not only carried the dead weight of fifty feet of rope up, but he actually got onto the forty-five-degree slope and, with the rope, crawled up the "Bat Passage" (which Cyril had now named). Inspired, and perhaps less leery of bats now, Cyril set his teeth and went up next. When he reached the top of the ladder, he heard Wilson's voice out of the distance telling him to throw him a candle. Cyril knew that, even though he had once thrown a cricket ball 107 yards, he did not feel equal to throwing a candle with his left hand round a corner from the top of a ladder, balanced in a fifty-foot underground shaft. He politely declined.

"Are you ever coming up?" asked Wilson's voice, from the Bat Passage.

"Probably never," replied Cyril. "Is the rope tied to anything?"

"It is not," said Cyril. "I'll tie it around my body." The rope appeared and rapidly slid toward him like a snake.

"Don't shake the rope coming up," shouted Wilson. "There are a lot of boulders, and if you start them rolling, God help you!"

"Thank you!" said Cyril, who was already starting down the ladder. Wilson spoke up again.

"I've come up, and so can you," he said.

Cyril stopped. He looked over at the smooth slope, shining in the light. Cyril took his hand off the ladder and sidled onto the rock somehow. He grabbed the rope and worked his way up the steep passage. He scuttled over great rocks of a kind that the Jebusites used to roll down the shaft on their enemies. He saw the ring fixed in the wall, gleaming in the wet. When he reached Wilson, it was at a small cave that seemed to go up higher, though it was covered by stones that looked familiar. Cyril had seen them, from the other side, when they sank the shaft from the surface. If they knocked those stones out, they could join the tunnels together. There was no Ark in this cave; it was empty. But it was full of other things. There were fragments of pottery. People had been here. Cyril and Wilson made their way back down the slope, though it was much more difficult. The rope was greasy, and its natural hang was some six feet away from the ladder.

On September 24th, Monty and Robin Duff returned, bringing with them a new member, Cyril Ward, a black-haired gentleman and the uncle to Lord Dudley.

"Any news?" asked Monty, as he walked into the house and brushed off his hat.

"Cyril and Walsh went up the Dragon Shaft."

Monty paused.

"What?"

After lunch, the new arrivals rushed off to go up the ladder themselves. Cyril stayed at the house. When they returned, Duff came into Cyril's room with a stunned look on his face.

"Who took the rope up the shaft?" he asked, almost out of breath.

"Wilson," Cyril said. Duff walked straight

across the hall into Wilson's room and gave the man a hearty handshake. Cyril never saw his friend so moved.

Cyril heard later that when Duff had gone up, he saw the slope and deemed it impossible. Like Cyril, it was only pure shame that induced him to leave the ladder. But halfway up the slope, the rope got loose from a rock, and the slack let him down toward the abyss. Cyril asked Duff what passed through his mind during those brief but awful seconds before the rope got taut again.

"I thought of Juliet," said Duff.

Cyril smiled. "How loyal and wonderful we men are, are we not?"

The new man, Ward, had followed him next, but he got violently sick when he joined Duff at the top. Ward had been a middy in the HMS *Victoria* disaster and had sunk — twice — before finally being rescued. Cyril imagined that Ward would probably rather go through another shipwreck than ascend the Bat Passage again. He made a mental note to tell the poor man to avoid the *Water Lily* by all possible means.

TWELVE

FATHER VINCENT

Jerusalem, 1909

Father Vincent tested his sandaled foot on the first step of a staircase that seemed to fade into the ground. Monty Parker was a few steps in front of him. The edges of the steps were smooth and rolling, capable of holding four, maybe five, people across. Father Vincent picked up his habit and moved slowly down. It was easier to go down in a kind of sideways manner. He was very excited.

"I am very excited," he said.

"Did you know the Arabs call this Um ed-Derej, the Mother of Steps?"

"I did not," said Monty.

For nearly a month, Father Vincent had been waiting patiently around the dig, watching the daily routine of hauling. Father Vincent's initial hypothesis had been proved correct. These Englishmen knew what they were doing. After opening Warren's Shaft, they moved to another site down the hill that Father Vincent knew quite well, the very stairs they were descending. They labored day and night in four-hour shifts under the light of gas lamps to get rid of the debris that had choked the opening.

Within days, Father Vincent was being enthusiastically greeted with handshakes each time he visited. Mostly, the Englishmen would watch the workers and sometimes laugh at their own stories and jokes. Sometimes they would jump in and help pull out a particularly irregular boulder. The presence of the Ottoman delegates seemed only to ensure that the workers did not confiscate any treasures for themselves. Father Vincent sometimes saw one of the Englishmen talking to the Turks, but they never entered the tunnels themselves.

Sometimes, at night, the workmen used the magic of the magnesium wire that burned like a tiny, angry star. They chanted their strange, wonderful songs, meant to counteract the monotony of the mysterious passageways that seemed to stretch endlessly into the very heart of the mountain.

By September 26th, Monty had returned from England. He summoned Father Vincent to show him what they had uncovered at the bottom of the steps they were now descending. With Monty at the lead, lamp in hand, they made it to the bottom. Father Vincent looked up at the arch above him. His eyes widened as it passed over him, monumental and heavy. With its delicate curve, it was a most curious construction.

As Father Vincent passed under the arch, he found himself on a spacious landing under a vaulted ceiling. The walls were the familiar sandy yellow of Jerusalem limestone, curled and balled up in spots like it had been boiling, though it had, as Father Vincent knew, formed slowly over an endless span of years. He looked down. At the end of the natural platform, veering to the right, were more steps, steeper this time, and then darkness.

"We finally cleared it out," said Monty. "A start, at least."

Father Vincent followed silently. His eyes saw what perhaps others did not — that something was very strange about these steps. He had seen them before, but not like this. They had cleaned away the garbage of the ages. But Father Vincent also saw, or perhaps "felt" is the better word, what this place really was. He heard a small noise. A gurgling sound from the blackness below.

"The Virgin's Fountain," he said.

"Yes," Monty nodded.

"It was here," said Father Vincent, with a gesture, "after the birth of Jesus, that Mary herself washed her son's swaddling clothes!" Monty nodded and looked down. "It is known as the Gihon Spring, of course," said Father Vincent, "but everyone calls it the Virgin's Fountain."

He looked around for signs of water. The spring would bubble up from time to time, and the people from Silwan would come. There were other stories, too. Father Vincent stopped on the landing and began to recite Scripture as effortlessly as if he were talking about the weather.

The king also said unto them, take with you the servants of your lord, and cause Solomon my son to ride upon mine own mule, and bring him down to Gihon.

And Zadok the priest took a horn of oil out of the tabernacle, and anointed Solomon. And they blew the trumpet; and all the people said, God save King Solomon.

"First Kings," said Father Vincent, with a wink. Not only had the clothes of the baby Jesus been washed here, but nearly a millennium earlier, King Solomon himself, the son of David, was anointed in the same waters.

As Monty began to explain how they had rid the stairs of the debris, Father Vincent's eyes lit up again behind his lamp. He was seeing strange things that were far from easy to explain. The very entrance into the fountain was fraught with mystery.

"There were some bits of pots here," said Monty. "We have them outside for you to examine."

Father Vincent nodded. He had already seen the small bits of ceramic flake that remained in the corners of the landing. Father Vincent ambled down the next set of shorter stairs, leaving Monty on the landing, a little amused at the *petit saint.*

"Look out!" said Monty. Father Vincent looked down.

The second set of stairs, which were much steeper, ended with a gap of two feet or so. Father Vincent teetered for a moment, but then half stepped, half jumped over the gap. Monty followed, then pushed his light forward.

At the bottom of the stairs, there was a cave that was about the size of an ordinary dining room. Father Vincent looked at the broken rocks on the floor, which appeared ragged in the light. This is where the water sometimes flowed, swelling to fit the cave and cascading down the slopes into the

141

Kidron Valley. This was where the people of Mary's time would come get their water or wash their clothes. Father Vincent looked around. He took out his notebook and began sketching.

He marked the tunnel he could see on the western end and made notes for two more openings. One was quite low and seemed to be in the shape of a large rectangle. At the end of the cave was another tunnel, veering to the left. Father Vincent turned around: to the west was a small oval cavity that dipped below the surface of the floor.

"Shhh!" he put his finger to his mouth and dropped his head. "There! Can you hear it?"

His face was beaming with discovery. Father Vincent dropped to his knees and placed his head against the smooth floor, listening for something. At the bottom of this opening was where the spring emerged. He could hear it. He turned his head back. Now he was trying to see.

"This is surprising," said Father Vincent. "There is a slight slope here." His eye followed the floor down to the stairs he had just stepped over. There was a gap between the stairs and the floor. There was something behind them.

He stood up again, pushing off one knee.

Above him, the ceiling was elegant, forming a natural cupola. He saw little cavities everywhere. He knew they probably led to further tunnels and no doubt an entire hidden labyrinth. Father Vincent again felt the swell of the place. But he was a man of science as well as faith; they existed in the same soil that was dirtying his hands. As Father Vincent made his way through the water and mud, he became aware of something very profound.

"We are not alone," he said.

The presence he felt was not of a ghost or spirit or even God, not entirely, but someone else — the person who had designed the construction of these mysterious tunnels. Though the caves were natural, someone had molded and connected them to a higher purpose. Father Vincent was seeing the evidence of one very human, very gifted man. He had no real name or face, not that he knew, but Father Vincent was beginning to make his acquaintance. He called him the Master Architect.

Father Vincent turned to Monty, with an immense smile on his face.

"Thank you for showing me this," he said.

"We have much work to do."

THIRTEEN

DR. JUVELIUS

Jerusalem, 1909

Dr. Juvelius stared ahead, shifting uncomfortably in his seat. Directly across from him, a young lady was sucking sherbet out of her glass of burgundy with a bamboo horsetail straw. The woman, a brunette in stylish clothes, had a pretty face, he guessed, as it was mostly obscured by an enormous hat. She had asked their waiter to bring her the drink as a guard against climate fever.

"Are the summers in Jerusalem always so blazing hot?" she asked, in French, to really no one in particular. She took another slow draw and seemed to look at Juvelius, who shifted again.

Seated next to the woman was her husband, Captain Hoppenrath, who laughed loudly at the display. They were seated in the lounges outside the German hotel where Juvelius had been staying, far from the noise of the Englishmen. They met here most every day, to exchange information and talk, away from the cloudy dust of the dig. Hoppenrath was also staying in the city, at a different hotel, with his wife, though Juvelius could not directly remember her name. They were joined by Pertti Uotila, a childhood friend of Juvelius who had lately arrived in Jerusalem. Juvelius was overjoyed about this. Uotila had studied ethnology in Paris and Berlin and would be a great help to him. Uotila had known about the cipher for years and had always been a great supporter of his friend's work.

Juvelius took a long drink himself. He smacked a bug biting at his neck. The days had become long and hot: endless in their repetition. Juvelius would watch as the rope ladders clunked down, wooden planks were passed along, and lines of workers came in and out of the earth. He watched from afar, just in case there were falling rocks or radium traps. Juvelius kept his precious cipher on his person. He held it close enough that when he felt the papers bend, he relaxed his grip to keep them safe.

When workers needed instructions in the tunnels — right or left, north or south — Juvelius would join them. He would leaf through his papers in the candlelight, often in silence, as he read the cipher aloud, incanting it as if it were some sort of magic spell. Juvelius would then come out and find Hoppenrath to translate his instructions to Mr. Parker. Hoppenrath would nod, then turn to Monty and say words in English with a great flourish: "Six spear lengths forward!" "Disturb the water!" Juvelius could only recognize some of the words. Sometimes Hoppenrath's version seemed longer than his own — or far shorter — but he supposed that was the nuance (or lack of it) of English. Juvelius was very appreciative of Hoppenrath. He was a good friend. Hoppenrath was Swedish but, for one reason or another, had resigned from the military to serve instead for various other states, in Algiers, Tunis, and even Turkey. He spoke a great many languages. That was another reason why Juvelius liked him — he could speak to him — but it also highlighted why Juvelius was, most days, very much alone.

Hoppenrath was the opposite sort of man: he was big, kind, active, and ingenious. Never was the job going better than when Hoppenrath was in the tunnels. If a vertical shaft had to be emptied from the bottom up or if a bursting water vein threatened to drown everyone, Hoppenrath was the resourceful and quick-witted one who came to the rescue. He had unmatched physical power, which aroused awe in the Bedouins. He even knew their language.

One day at a café, on the way back from their first trip to Jerusalem with Mr. Parker, Juvelius and Hoppenrath were alone. Hoppenrath raised his glass — not his first — and said, "Be wary! In the eastern countries, you should never be with an Arab or Jewish woman! It can produce twenty centimeters of cold steel between the ribs!" Here the man downed his latest sip and paused.

"Fortunately, there are always plenty of Italian women!" He laughed and finished the glass. Juvelius looked on. He was disgusted by the man's cynicism, but then again maybe he had misunderstood him.

Juvelius took another drink. He was frustrated. They had been excavating for weeks, chipping away at the hidden tunnels under the mountain. Juvelius knew they had only barely penetrated the hidden surface of the network. The complex corridors were artificially filled, tightly closed with rocks and gravel. Even the new man, Father Vincent — whom Juvelius quite liked — seemed confused by the interior of the maze. Were they going hunting for the great treasures of Solomon only to find bits of broken pots? The cipher was clear, but the stopped-up tunnels had made it difficult to determine how long their work might take, an especially important question given the amount of time and money they were putting into the enterprise. Juvelius had lately felt the stares and heard the snippets of hastily ended conversations in his vicinity. Mr. Parker had even suggested that Juvelius pay a visit to a local rabbinical scholar for direction. Even Father Vincent had agreed this would be a good action. But Juvelius felt as if he was being challenged. The cipher was clear.

Juvelius took another drink. He had already circulated news that he would have to be leaving soon anyway.

The next day, Hoppenrath arrived at the hotel on a new horse, a beautiful half-Arabian that he had just purchased. The look on his face was glowing. The animal was a deep brown color and seemed of exceeding grace. But as it clopped forward, the beast's back legs stopped, then wavered a little, startling Hoppenrath, who quickly tried to explain it away as the presence of a most uneven, sharp ground. Juvelius realized that the horse must have been more affordable than he had previously thought.

Hoppenrath's wife was delighted with the shiny horse. She wore new riding boots and carried a riding crop in her hand. She gave her husband an earful that she wanted a woman's saddle. By the time Hoppenrath had slinked to the table and had his first drink, he had agreed to the saddle, along with some much-needed riding lessons.

Later that day, one of the Englishmen, one of Mr. Parker's men, appeared with a message for Juvelius from Monty. He needed help with part of the cipher and was riding his own new horse, a magnificent Damascus that must have commanded a lofty price. Hoppenrath made a sour face as his wife jumped to pet the beast's nose. After yet more pleading, Hoppenrath had agreed to let her take a riding lesson with him right then and there.

As Juvelius and Hoppenrath went over the clarification, the Englishman trotted his horse across the dusty commons with Mrs. Hoppenrath high in the saddle. "Very good, my dear!" said Hoppenrath from the table. Uotila excused himself for a moment.

"So, you're really intent on going then?" asked Hoppenrath, turning to Juvelius.

"Yes," said Juvelius, in his slight voice. "I must return to the school. But I will return once the tunnels are cleared, or at the end of the rainy season." Hoppenrath didn't agree, but he understood: Juvelius was recently been made director of the Vyborg

Workers College and had been on leave but could take no more time.

"Uotila will be able to use the cipher in my absence," added Juvelius. "He has my most complete trust."

"What about your next report?" asked Hoppenrath. "Why haven't you given it to me for translation?"

Juvelius straightened up. He had planned on writing a final report for Mr. Parker to help guide the cipher's use in his absence.

"I am still formulating it myself." Their usual mode was for Juvelius to write in Swedish, then hand it over to Hoppenrath to translate. He had not given him anything yet.

"You know they will only keep it secret," said Hoppenrath in a low voice. Out on the road, his wife screamed with delight as her instructor hoisted her off the horse by grabbing her waist.

"Will Mr. Uotila get to see it?" said Hoppenrath, pointing to the man, who was returning from the hotel's entrance.

"Now you're talking about things you don't know," said Juvelius.

Hoppenrath looked almost hurt. Juvelius knew that he had not liked that Uotila could speak to him just as easily. Juvelius felt some shame. Mrs. Hoppenrath giggled again. She

150

was almost falling off the horse. The Englishman had to use both of his hands to support her. Hoppenrath looked on as she laughed. He sighed, then got up to intervene as Uotila returned to the table.

Uotila leaned over to Juvelius and nodded toward Mrs. Hoppenrath.

"Nemesis Divina!" He laughed. "It's pretty clear who is teaching who."

The riding lessons stopped soon after.

That night, in his room in the German hotel, with Uotila next door, Juvelius continued working on his report. It was very difficult for him. He wanted to convey his thoughts about the expedition's next steps accurately to Captain Parker before he left for Finland. But since he wanted to touch on a number of sensitive issues, he did not want to show it to Hoppenrath, so he had been trying to write it in English. He was filled with the pangs of guilt at his actions. The man was his friend.

The next day, at their customary table, Mrs. Hoppenrath was distraught over the sudden cancellation of her riding lessons with her handsome English teacher. "He's simply too busy," said Captain Hoppenrath, in a syrupy tone. After a few minutes of the usual news of the tunnels, Mrs. Hoppenrath smiled at Uotila.

"Tell me, Mr. Uotila, do you ride?"

She was crafty, thought Juvelius. Hoppenrath looked Uotila over — trim, handsome, but slight, with a philosopher's pallor and a slightly expanding hairline — and agreed that Mr. Uotila might be a perfect instructor for a riding lesson the next day. Hoppenrath did not seem even remotely worried about him. Juvelius did not think that could be taken as a compliment.

Over the next two days, Uotila rode with Mrs. Hoppenrath. On the evening of the second day, Juvelius was again at work on his report when Uotila burst into his room. He knocked off his heavy gloves and seemed highly excited.

"You will not believe it!" said Uotila. "Guess what the hell he had?"

"What is wrong?" asked Juvelius. "Had what? Are you drunk?"

"I wish," Uotila said. "No, it is Hoppenrath!" He sat down and tried to catch his breath. He continued: "I was at their hotel, for a riding lesson. It was fine. But she invited me inside, and Hoppenrath was busy, and I saw . . . I saw . . ." He was breathing heavily.

"What?" Juvelius had an idea what he might say next.

Uotila looked at his friend with an exasperated look.

"He had a full survey of your work!" Juvelius was aghast; that was not what he had anticipated. Uotila pointed to Juvelius's papers on the desk. "He came in and confronted me. He asked questions that could not have been asked without the guidance of the cipher!"

Juvelius was surprised. He knew that Hoppenrath wished for more information on the cipher, but not like this.

"I acted completely ignorant," said Uotila. "He wanted more information. He was distressing me — he was really distressing. But I didn't say anything. Finally, he complained, '*Mon Dieu,* you do not understand me!' and declared it a misunderstanding."

"He rode with me, silent, all the way home. But as soon as he left, I was so excited I turned around and rode to the house, to tell the Englishman what happened."

"What?"

"I had to know. You don't understand. He admitted that Mrs. Hoppenrath had tried to get some of the secrets of the report from him during their riding lesson." Juvelius considered this carefully. The Englishman had full access to all of Juvelius's reports. Hoppenrath had seen a great deal of it, but he clearly wanted more interpretation that he did feel comfortable asking for directly.

"Did he betray us?"

"No, he's a good man."

Juvelius was relieved. He knew that one would have to have mediocre intelligence to think they could milk secrets from an English gentleman.

Uotila was silent for a moment and added: "This is not a story that you read in novels. The lady was clearly trading herself under . . . certain conditions." He stared at Juvelius, who knew what he meant. "These men and their wives — these adventurers!"

Juvelius sat on the bed. What was to be done? Juvelius thought about reporting it to Mr. Parker, but that could be catastrophic with the people involved. Mr. Parker was too much of a gentleman to have to decide between his man and them. Juvelius couldn't see a way forward. He had to gain Mr. Parker's trust.

The next day, Juvelius, along with Uotila, made their way to the house where the Englishmen were staying. On the first floor, the men had set up a series of tables to catalog their archaeological finds. Father Vincent was down at the very end of one, peering at some old piece of cookware.

Juvelius found Father Vincent to be an

extremely pleasant, well-educated man. The men gossiped that he had been born in a noble castle in southern France and had earned degrees in law and philosophy from the University of Lyon. His future had looked full of fortune when he suddenly turned to the ecclesiastical life and locked himself into a monk's oath. Juvelius found it impossible to dislike the man. His fine nobility, beautiful dark eyes, eagerness for intelligent discussion, and deep expertise in every area of life made him very amenable.

Father Vincent motioned Juvelius and Uotila over. He looked quite comical wearing his magnifying glass; his left eye looked enormous and liquid under the lights. Father Vincent showed him the particular chip of clay he was investigating. It was clear that he was very pleased. Father Vincent regarded his guests.

"You should go," said Father Vincent, translated through Uotila. He understood that Juvelius had reservations about seeing the rabbi that Mr. Parker had recommended.

"You could do great trying to find out rabbinic opinions on some of the things that are in the context of our research," said Father Vincent. "He speaks several European languages quite fluently."

"I'm not a diplomat," replied Juvelius. "Maybe you can't go yourself?"

Father Vincent gave a slightly malicious smile. "Ah, I'm afraid it would attract too much attention," he said, gesturing down to his consistently filthy robes.

As they rode home, Juvelius was still wrestling with the question of how to proceed.

"What are you going to do?" asked Uotila.

"If I go see the rabbi, it will satisfy Mr. Parker, and perhaps get him on our side. But I think it would be unwise to take any conversation with the rabbi. He could get a hint of what we are doing. Of our information." He paused. "But I need Mr. Parker to believe my report. We'll put it together, you and me," Juvelius said. "You could help me so we can keep it out of Hoppenrath's hands."

"Of course!" said Uotila. "That's why I am here."

"There's something else," Juvelius said. "We have somewhere to go first."

Fourteen
MONTY PARKER

Jerusalem, 1909

The hour was late when Monty finally got up to his room at the tall ramshackle house that they were renting from the mukhtar, the chieftain of Silwan. Monty walked up the creaky stairs. Its high ceilings were guarded by very stubborn spiders. The men had turned the first floor into what appeared to be a Jerusalem version of a jumble sale. There were bits and pieces of digging equipment scattered over handsome Persian rugs, pickaxes propped up against heavy cracked bowls spread out on the Turkish divans. Wall shelves and cupboards had been repurposed to temporary storage spaces. But all was not lost: there was a smoking table full of fine Havana cigars and Egyptian cigarettes in the corner. They were English, not barbarians.

Monty clicked his door shut and walked over to the closet. As he passed a mirror, he caught a glimpse of himself, or at least a version of it: different, but generally recognizable in the moment. He walked into the closet — it was still dark — and switched on the special bulb. He looked into the shallow tray on the small table before him. A shadow had begun to form, like smoke, on the surface of the paper. As the image began to fade in, the strange black cloud solidified into a sharper rectangle. Monty shook the tray a little, before grabbing it with the tongs. He then placed the print in the stop bath, where he could get a clearer look. He had not taken this many photographs since the war. Looking at the image, three and a half by three and a half, he remembered that a photograph always held three versions of the subject: the one on the paper, the one in his head, and the real one somewhere in the past. He patted his big camera on the way out.

Monty shut the door to his closet, walked across the Persian rug, and sat down at his chair before the fireplace. The night was cold, and the room was crackling with the warm light of the flames. Monty grabbed a mostly empty glass from the end table, sniffed it, and took a drink. He lay back into the chair and groaned. This dry place was not Saltram, but he decided it would do.

He took another swallow. He reached for his bag and took out a folder that was wound up with a string. A book spilled out, but he let it lay. As leader of the expedition, Monty was in charge not only of the day-to-day running of the excavation but also something far less exciting: the bloody paperwork. He had expense reports due and was late in sending an update to the Syndicate in London. He had to admire Foley. Ascending the Dragon Shaft was a bold maneuver, though he knew it was probably Walsh who had done it first. But the Ark was not there. Monty took another hard swallow.

There was mail to return. He looked over the newest packet of letters. Nothing from his younger brother Jack or his sister Mary back home. Nothing from the earl, either, he chuckled. Monty could only imagine what his older brother might think of where he was right now.

There was nothing from her, either. Obviously. Monty pinched the bridge of his nose with his fingers and shut his eyes. He wanted to write a letter, telling her everything of his adventures, but he knew he could not.

Monty sighed and set the letters aside. He saw the pages of the cipher, bound in thin red ribbon, peeking out from the bottom of the pile. When Juvelius had finally handed it over to Hoppenrath, Monty took the originals to John Venn & Sons, a notary on Cornhill, to have them translated. Monty could only imagine their reactions as they worked on the document, but the firm was quite reputable, and Monty knew he could rely on their discretion. Still, the frontispiece must have been an eye-opener:

TRANSCRIBED FROM THE SWEDISH A
SUPPOSED CIPHER WRITING IN EZEKIEL
SEEMS TO REFER TO THE HIDING PLACE OF
THE ARK OF THE COVENANT AND THE
ARCHIVES OF THE TEMPLE
Signed V. H. Juvelius

The translation was completed in pencil with a long, looping cursive over seventy-four pages imprinted with a light red and blue border. Monty looked through the messy interior. Words had been scratched out and replaced willy-nilly. Some portions were flipped on their side and extended into the margins.

This was the document, full of strange words and numbers, all spread apart on the page like some unfamiliar game of cards, that had launched the entire expedition. The cipher was difficult to read, most likely because of the multiple languages it had gone through, but also because Juvelius did not — except for one example — show his work step by step. At first, Monty found the words to be an impenetrable morass, like a riddle with no solution. Juvelius explained in the beginning pages that the cipher was "intentional symbolical writing," which meant that any interpretation must involve some guesswork. After all, the whole point of the cipher was to offer a trail of crumbs to something that its ancient writers still wished to conceal.

But over time, it had begun to make more sense. The cipher claimed that there was a hidden chamber, a "hiding place" or "asylum," where the Ark had remained untouched, somewhere behind a walled-up tunnel. Through analysis of the cipher solutions, Juvelius believed that there were three possible entrances to this secret place: the Dome of the Rock, the Virgin's Fountain, and a less-specific third entrance from the lower valley. There were no exact maps to get to the asylum, only clues locked into the ancient words.

Monty sat back in his chair and looked through the pages, trying to find something he knew he had seen before. Much of it was devoted to Ezekiel, the prophet who had clairvoyant dreams of Jerusalem while in captivity in Babylon. Monty pulled out the Bible he had brought with him, with the black leather cover that looked brand new, and turned to Ezekiel. It took him a while to find it. Monty read the verses where Ezekiel has a vision of the water of life as it wells up from the Temple of Jerusalem and flows out into the valley, healing the land in its wake. The prophecy is shown to him by a nameless man whose appearance is like shining brass:

> Afterward he brought me again unto the door of the house; and, behold, waters issued out from under the threshold of the house eastward.
>
> And when the man that had the line in his hand went forth eastward, he measured a thousand cubits, and he brought me through the waters; the waters were to the ankles. Again he measured a thousand, and brought me through the waters; the waters were to the knees. Again he measured a thousand, and brought me through; the waters were to the loins. Afterward he measured a thousand; and it was a river that I could not pass over: for

the waters were risen, waters to swim in,
a river that could not be passed over.

Juvelius had worked from the ancient Hebrew, but perhaps Monty could check the tone and message. He read the cipher's interpretation of the same verse:

The Flame Has Disappeared
Into the hiding places / lead / its hole /
    cunningly
Hewn. / The body of water / collects itself
    / together
Covers / the refuge of the cave / and roars
There is / The place of refuge / that
    which /
Does not flow over / Publish / Provided
    not (in fact)
Wrong counsel / empties out / and
    wickedly
Fractures / the vault's water / and leads
    away
The water's dam / and the vault's
    protection
And the Threshold! / Be silent!

As he read the words, Monty could see Father Vincent moving down the stairs and into the cave of the Virgin's Fountain, his eyes darting around like arrows. Monty could see him look at the strangely carved passage at the cave below. "Be silent!" said the cipher. Monty could see Father Vincent putting his head down to hear the sound of the spring, of the water. "The refuge of the cave," Monty read again, "cunningly hewn" and "roars." It fit almost perfectly.

Monty felt a chill on his spine. There was no doubt that the solution sounded very much like the cave of the Virgin's Fountain, not to mention the water in the main tunnel. Monty quickly flipped back to the first page of the cipher.

Juvelius had written it in 1907.

Two years ago.

Monty read on. "The stairs" and the "noise of the waters" were common themes in the entries. The cipher also kept referring to the "hollow stairs" — did that mean something was under the steps of the Virgin's Fountain? Monty thought of the main stairs back home at Saltram, which hugged the walls in two flights separated by a landing. The stairs in the great hall were supported by nothing; they seemed to be some strange magic trick, floating in the air. There were good, darkened places underneath to hide or hang a painting.

The cipher was less straightforward about what the stairs meant.

(The entrance of the filling water) subdue, behold, the steps of the hollow and 80 rooms between, 80, unstable, shakes the steps of the hollow staircase:
Separates itself. ("The dragon RAHAB.")
(The Pleiades' behold!) "The Nails" "the nails" close
(Behold) Mountain, "the morning star's the healing (Behold the opening)

The Pleaides? Was there a clue somewhere in the sky? It would not be the first time a star was used as a direction to a divine place. Juvelius further explained this connection in a footnote:

/ "STAR" = the symbol of the Ark, Messiah was also called "the son of the star," perhaps with alluding to the taking out of the Ark by the appearance of the Messiah.

Monty turned the pages forward. The other recurring subject was "the tunnel."

And the tunnel (?) / and the surroundings / tear asunder
The living body / Raise itself / that oh!
The shovels / the noise of the waters / the holy place

165

Hezekiah's Tunnel was the main route between the Virgin's Fountain to the Pool of Siloam that they were currently beginning to clear out. Warren had made it through decades ago, but Monty was beginning to wonder if it was possible. The cipher directed that by the "rivers of water / The tunnel was long ("The distant lying answer")." Juvelius wrote that his "opinion" was "that in the middle of the tunnel there must have been a perpendicular shaft full of water . . . but it has now been emptied." Monty immediately thought of the Dragon Shaft. In the light of their recent discoveries, the cipher seemed to have become clearer somehow. Juvelius explained in the text that he thought Ezekiel was envisioning a sluice, part of an ancient waterworks that could drain the tunnel itself. The cipher said that it "could be entered through a higher way, or a lower one" — just like the Dragon Shaft, which could be accessed through the surface or from the ladder below.

Monty looked into the fire. The wood popped and hissed. Monty sometimes thought of his older brother when he saw such a fire. In 1903, right before their father died, Edmund had been on the steamship *Ovalu*, off the coast of Australia, when the ship caught fire. The hold was filled with

166

copra kernels, so the flames spread fast. They headed for Lord Howe Island, some six hundred kilometers away. As they got close, the fire accelerated, and they got into the boats. As they rowed for the beach, the fiery ship behind them began to hiss terribly. It then exploded and sank to nothing. His brother was fine. The newspapers proclaimed him a hero.

Monty had wondered if the cipher might be a fake. But how could it be so tantalizingly close to being accurate? Juvelius might have used existing maps, Monty supposed, but Warren's work was incomplete in this area. A more daring question lay right behind it. How could the things described in the cipher — the stairs, the hidden shaft, the water, and the tunnel — be things that they were seeing with their own eyes and dirtying their hands over right now?

Juvelius explained that the verses he had found in the Scripture functioned as part of a larger message, "forming a complete whole by themselves and containing within themselves everything necessary to complement and illustrate each other — all the links are firmly welded together — no gaps exist." By looking at various books in the context of one theme — finding the Ark — Juvelius's cipher had ironed out its own kind of truth, and it was not just vague direction; it seemed to be a story. "The flame has disappeared" the cipher claimed. The Ark had been lost. But "the solution" was "confirmed and reliable" to recover it.

Monty was beginning to feel a sense of welling excitement. "In spite of the terrifying long way," Juvelius explained, "one should not allow oneself to be dismayed, because the ark is here." Once the secret chamber was found, the instructions were clear:

> And push against / the ornament of the
>   crown / and the dividing wall
> Swings round / opens on the hinges
> And something / beautiful / resplendent /
>   seek
> (and) measure / the entrance!
> IT!

Monty Parker was tired, sunburnt, and weary, but he could almost see it along the blurry edge of the fire. A long tunnel led to a hidden door that opened to a small room. There, in absolute and total darkness, he saw the shimmer of polished gold, somehow immune from the dirt and dust of the ages. He could see it gleam. Staves of wood were attached through rings of gold at its corners.

The lid looked to be solid gold and was covered by two cherubim whose wings were pushed forward like thrusting spears, meeting at their sharp, gleaming tips as all dissolved to fire.

Monty put his pipe to his mouth. He put the cipher down gently. These were great and serious things, he thought, as sleep came to his tired limbs.

Great and serious things.

FIFTEEN
DR. JUVELIUS

The Dead Sea Valley, 1909

"Wake up!" said Juvelius.

Uotila opened his eyes halfway, but once he felt the pain of the bright sun, he closed them again with a groan.

"Come on!" said Juvelius. "We are going on an excursion to Mount Nebo! I've hired a dragoman and everything!" Juvelius began packing for his friend.

"Where are we going?" Uotila mumbled.

"You'll see," said Juvelius. "Look . . . They are here!"

Uotila opened his eyes again and climbed to his feet. He looked out the window. There, on the ground, there were mules, a guide, and two Bedouins. Their cart was packed with a tent and supplies. Uotila closed his eyes, just for a moment more.

Several minutes later, they set off on the road east. The hills gave way to villages, which soon receded to flat ground and smaller groups of travelers. Within an hour or so, they seemed alone, on a landscape that was growing wilder and more desolate with each succeeding step. In the distance, they could see the reddish mountains they were riding toward.

They passed through a place where the remnants of a grass-covered stone foundation merged in and out of the landscape. There were some smaller houses and a larger, more modern three-story building in white.

"This is Jericho," said Juvelius. "The Ark was here, a very long time ago."

Juvelius knew that Uotila was familiar with the story, but like many stories it grew stronger in the retelling. Though they were going somewhere, they had nowhere to go, so Juvelius told the story of how Joshua, the son of Moses, took his people into the Promised Land. At the end of their long exodus, Joshua invited the Israelites to choose between serving the Lord who had delivered them from Egypt, the gods of their ancestors, or the new gods of the land they now occupied. The people chose to serve the Lord. Joshua was pleased.

God then told Joshua to conquer the Canaanites, who lived outside Jerusalem.

For six days the Israelites marched around

the walls of Jericho with the priests carrying the Ark of the Covenant. On the seventh day, they marched seven times around the walls, and then the priests blew their rams' horns, the Israelites raised a great shout, and the walls of the mighty city cracked into great fissures, then fell into stones.

As Juvelius spoke, Uotila looked back. The silence of the place, with its crumbled rocks and bright green grass, was altered only by the creak of their cart.

Juvelius continued: After Jericho fell, the Lord gave Joshua a grim command: "You shall not leave alive anything that breathes." The Israelites killed every man, woman, and child, as well as the oxen, sheep, and donkeys. Only Rahab, a Canaanite prostitute who sheltered Joshua's spies, was spared, along with her family. Joshua said that anyone who rebuilt the gates of Jericho would be cursed with the deaths of their firstborn and youngest child. It was the Lord's land to give or take.

As the day grew long and Juvelius and Uotila rode on, the ground grew very flat. They came upon a river, wide but not tumultuous.

"The Jordan," said Juvelius.

They dismounted and led their donkeys through the wide pane of water. Its depths felt infinitely refreshing, even as the sun was beginning to fall.

Juvelius kept telling the story, though now from an earlier point. After forty years in the wilderness, Moses had died, and Joshua bade them to cross the river. But it was the flood season and the waters raged. Joshua told the horde to stay back. And then the priests appeared, carrying the shining Ark, lifted up above them.

"And the waters shall stand upon a heap," said Juvelius, quoting the Scripture.

Though he was nearing the other bank, Juvelius stopped himself. He could almost picture it. The priests, robed in white, carried the Ark — the most precious thing the tribes had — silently toward the current. Juvelius looked back over the river, letting the scene unfold in his mind.

And the priests that bare the Ark of the Covenant of the Lord stood firm on dry ground in the midst of Jordan, and all the Israelites passed over on dry ground, until all the people were passed clean over Jordan.

Leaving their animals on the banks in the care of the men, Juvelius and Uotila swam in the Jordan, washing away an infinity of sand. They then set up camp on the eastern beach of the river. The Bedouins made their own up the bank. Juvelius picked thistles and placed them on the fire. He and Uotila, the two friends, then sat beside the flames, thinking of childhood, under the stars.

"I fear they do not get my meaning," said Juvelius.

"They will," said Uotila.

The next morning, they pulled up their sleepy mules and headed down the shoreline. They rode across the southeast, over the salt- and gypsum-covered earth, finally reaching a new gorge with a half-dry brook.

As they rode, a prickly sweat began creeping over them. They were in the valley of the Dead Sea. The atmosphere was hot and leaden; they were almost four hundred meters below sea level. Juvelius thought he could smell sulfur. They missed the Jordan terribly.

"Hold on," said Juvelius, looking at a map. They were near Har Megiddo and Petra, the city carved of stone. "Ah," said Juvelius. "We are close now."

A couple of hours later they were riding into a valley between three mountains. They were red with sunburn, tired, and wrung with thirst. The Bedouin scout, who was riding ahead, shouted:

"Ayun Mûsâ!"

They descended from their saddles. The Bedouin cried out again; he was pointing at something. Three light-footed gazelles caught the slope of the mountain, already out of sight. Opposite them, they saw the bright rise of Mount Nebo, where Moses had looked out from the summit to see the Promised Land, only to be told by God that he would never get there. Juvelius felt as if they were traveling backward through the old stories, seeing them unfold in reverse.

The Bedouin was pointing to what looked to be a large circular well framed with stones. It was a spring! Juvelius and Uotila drank from it and looked up at the mountain. The Bedouins took the mules off to get water. Juvelius and Uotila set up their tent in a rut and ate their modest half-day meal.

"Well, dear brother, now we can talk," Juvelius said. "This is Wadi Ayun Mûsâ, the Valley of Moses. And it is where he is buried."

"This," Juvelius said quietly, "is what we should really be looking for."

Juvelius continued the story. When Moses died, he was one hundred and twenty years old. The version of the story in the Book of Moses revealed more than the Old Testament. Moses spoke with God, who was his friend. "Treat me also with love," said Moses, "and deliver me not into the hands of the Angel of Death." A heavenly voice sounded and said, "Moses, be not afraid."

Three angels descended from heaven and arranged Moses's bed with a purple garment and a woolen pillow. God stationed Himself over Moses's head and told him to cross his arms and feet. "I Myself shall take thee to the highest heavens," He said. God then took Moses's soul by kissing him on the mouth.

God then hid his body, for Satan wanted it, as did the enemies of the Israelites. God did not want others to use his body as an idol or symbol. There was something else about Moses that certain learned people coveted, a powerful word that was written upon the shield he was buried with.

"It was called the unspoken name," said Juvelius. "The very name of God, told only to him." He stopped himself from talking further.

"The most important thing," said Juvelius, "is that if we found the tomb of Moses, it would prove that he was real! There would be no denying it!"

"But how?" asked Uotila.

"The secret of Moses's burial place was

known to a select few and was passed on from one generation to another. When the Bible was committed to paper, the secrets were codified and incorporated into the text. Again, only very few knew how to interpret the open text. We just need the right key."

As he always did, Juvelius pulled out his notes. Uotila had never seen these before.

"Let me guess," said Uotila. "You have the key."

Juvelius shuffled his papers. "I have three ciphers here, three of them in Hebrew that writers have been hiding in the text at different times. It is clear from the writings that the place is in the Moab area. Listen!" Juvelius began to read from the papers:

Introduce / A ridge near the sublime body. And wake up six measures the mask at the point of discharge. The foundation of the cracked rock clump tore off, crush! Look, the lofty place.

Deliver two Dimensions! Destroy at that point! And notice cave corridor! Go ahead ten!

Clear! Intellectual trouble: Fraudulent eight!

The entrance is noisy.

Juvelius looked up at the mountain ahead of them and continued speaking: "From that mountain wall immediately facing us, at that time from the bottom of the valley, a small watercourse came inside the mountain from the cave. There was another, probably bigger one that went to a cave corridor that also had water. Through these corridors, the body of Moses was buried in the mountainside. The cipher says that it was buried in a special 'dry' cave that was ten feet high."

"What are we waiting for?" asked Uotila.

"Ah," said Juvelius, "would that it were that easy. After the body was buried, the exterior was plugged with stones and gravel. At the end, a large block of stone was beaten and placed to completely close the outside opening from the valley side. Only if this block of stone is torn off and crushed will the waters stagnating behind it burst forth! Then the way will be open!"

Juvelius took out his binoculars, and for a good half hour under purpling skies, he and Uotila took turns scanning the mountainside for such a boulder in the wall.

SIXTEEN

FATHER VINCENT

Jerusalem, 1909

Father Vincent stood very still. His candle was working hard in the dark, as if it were trying to breathe. Father Vincent had gone ahead of some of the workers into a new tunnel — a "gallery" — below the Virgin's Fountain. But the air was so thin that the workers had gone back, leaving him alone. He closed his eyes and controlled his breathing down to shallow exchanges. He was not afraid. He knew that he was not alone. He was in the presence of the Architect again. Even there, in the dark, Father Vincent could sense the work of the past in every notch of the caves. He was not afraid, but he was hoping that the workers would come back soon.

For three days each week, Father Vincent had gone excitedly down the dusty road from Jerusalem to the excavation site on Mount Ophel, sometimes alone, sometimes accompanied by Father Raphaël Savignac, his good friend and photographer from the École Biblique. Captain Parker had only two rules: never interfere with the diggers and don't disclose or publish anything until he said so. Father Vincent agreed and filled the space between those edicts with the gospel of work. On his days with the excavators, Father Vincent spent nearly all his hours in the sunless gloom of the underground. On those days he was away, Father Vincent stayed in his room and transcribed notes, worked on drawings, and stared at measurements until they blurred. These were perhaps not the normal tasks of a Dominican priest, and Father Vincent didn't always wear his habit in the tunnels, but it was his relentless curiosity that marked him. Dominicans were not called the "hounds of God" for nothing.

Father Vincent knew that there was an entire network of tunnels that were connected to the Virgin's Fountain. There were so many nooks and turns that it was difficult to keep them straight. Father Vincent focused on the Warren's Shaft system, which moved upward, and the Siloam Tunnel, or Hezekiah's Tunnel, the long passage that led from the fountain to the Pool of Siloam. This was the tunnel that he was most looking forward to delving into once it had been cleared of debris.

In the past week, Father Vincent had been investigating the galleries that connected to the cave at the bottom of the stairs; in his notebook, Father Vincent numbered them with Roman numerals. Every time Father Vincent strolled in to do his work, usually in pools of water, the workers, now familiar to him, raised a chorus to greet him. He shouted his own greeting in response and patted some of them on the back. Holding his paper and measuring instruments high to save them from a prolonged immersion, Father Vincent moved between the men like an eager friend. He believed that shared labor in the trenches of an excavation grew great companions.

Father Vincent, swallowing at air and trying to occupy his thoughts by thinking about how he got there, was currently in an area designated gallery II, discovered along the second flight of steps into the cave, around the sixth going down. The passage was only half a meter across. After about ten meters in, the candle in his hand began to flicker. The lack of air became more prevalent the farther they got from the fountain. The Architect was working perfectly in accord with the natural rock to make his work nearly invisible. They had found bits and pieces of things along the way: ceramics, a broken flowerpot, and other small artifacts. They had also found a strange mark that looked like an arrowhead cut into the rock near gallery XV. Father Vincent sketched it into his notebook and later showed it to Captain Parker, who looked at it for a long time.

Gallery IV was also very mysterious. When it was first discovered by the workers, Father Vincent immediately moved up the line to investigate. He was in a canal that was filled with rubbish to about a third of its height. They quickly arranged some drainage tubes to try to keep the water level down so that they could examine further, but whenever the fountain rose — which was always accompanied by a loud rushing sound from behind the rock — the water splashed everywhere, making further inspection impossible. They eventually dug ahead to a strange round chamber but were so afraid that the water might cause the wall of rubbish to slide right onto them that they left it there, thinking that an attempt from the other end — if they even found it — might be more practical. But as the workers abandoned the task, Father Vincent valiantly stood fast.

"Wait," he said. He had not moved an inch.

His keen eye had spied something — a thin line carved into the wall. It was too straight to be natural. He dropped to a crouch and began following it, first with his eyes, then with his finger, his candle always one step ahead of it. When his finger stopped, so did his breath. There was no mistaking what he had found.

He was looking at the base of a tablet.

Father Vincent thought immediately of the inscription that the boy had found, so many years ago, in these same caves. That inscription had been monumental to the study of these places and another find of its significance had yet to be duplicated, if it ever could be. Father Vincent looked closer. There was a giant chunk of clay that covered the top of the tablet. Father Vincent studied it with his eyes. The slab, it seemed, also rested against part of what looked to be a large boulder. Father Vincent raised his hands and tested the boulder very lightly; it was already loose. Father Vincent, who was normally very careful, was seized by the possibility of what he was seeing and let his notebook fall into the mud. He then tore away the clay from underneath the boulder. He did not seem worried whether it would fall, though the other workers clearly disagreed as they rushed up to hold it above him. Father Vincent scrabbled off the clay with his hands and began looking for the thin, telltale angles of Hebrew.

But there was nothing. They cleaned up the rock, brought up a stronger light, and searched it from every angle.

Nothing.

Father Vincent pulled at his beard. It was clearly a tablet, but it had never been engraved. Why?

The tablet had only been lightly cut out, and had not been polished or even prepared with the usual care to allow an inscription. But this led to another question: in the center of a deep tunnel, in an inconvenient and dark passage, what was the good of writing anything where no one would ever see it? The Siloam inscription was near the entrance and easily seen, though it had escaped detection for centuries. But this? This was different. What did it mean to prepare to say something — and then say nothing at all?

In all the days they worked around the Fountain, Father Vincent would often pause in his measurements and catch himself looking down the main tunnel, the subject of the Siloam inscription. The strangely rectangular tunnel filled with rubble and chaff was a great mystery. Captain Warren's heroic traversal of it forty years ago was still a legendary feat, but it had left many questions. In his spare time, Father Vincent waded about in its opening, each time advancing a bit farther. There was something — he couldn't say exactly what — that drew him back to this tunnel, even as other work begged to be finished. Was it related to the blank tablet? He was worried that he had missed something.

As the tunnel's mysteries occupied his mind, the workers finally returned with oxygen capsules and portable electric lanterns that they passed up the line. They eventually pushed a protesting Father Vincent out and back into the open air. As he sat down, gulping in great breaths, Father Vincent caught Monty smiling at him.

"Are you well, Father?"

"Of course! I love tunnels," he said, drinking some water. He raised his hand to signal that he wanted to continue, but he had to wait for his swallow to catch up.

"Tunnels are not just tunnels," he said. "They are stories. Everyone has a grandfather who knows of some legendary tunnel that connected two places. . . . This person, who always seems to live to the absolute apex of human life, knows of the draw, the oriental romance, of a simple hole in the ground. Sometimes it is rather difficult to distinguish between the truth and the superimposed tissue, but in no cases of the kind would it be wise to deny the existence of any subterranean mysteries at all." He stopped and smiled.

A few days later, Father Vincent was sitting outside the dig again, mopping his gleaming head, when a worker came out cupping something small and delicate in his dirty hands. The man, who looked scared, told Macasdar that he had found it. Father Vincent strapped on his glasses and walked over. The two Turks also noticed the commotion. Father Vincent beat them to it, getting the first look at the small object that was lain out upon a kerchief on a rock.

It was a small statuette of a head, with a strange, upturned face that had a look of horror on it.

"A Hellenistic pagan idol," said Father Vincent. "Fascinating."

Everyone had their attention on the worker as he managed a sheepish look from within the circle of people closing around him. The man said that he found it in one of the baskets of dirt they had been passing back to the surface.

That it had been missed when the rubbish was being cleared at the head of the line made his story very suspicious, especially given the rapid circulation of the baskets. This piece was also quite striking, and unusual. The Turks moved closer, and the frightened man cringed. Stealing from an excavation was a great crime. The worker cried out something in Arabic. Macasdar stared at him.

"It might have fallen out of somebody's pocket," Macasdar related to the crowd, his eyes still fixed on the man.

As they argued, Father Vincent crouched in the dust, staring at the head.

Captain Parker was motioned to come over. As Macasdar explained, Captain Parker looked the worker over, in his dirty clothing and terrified gaze, and narrowed his eyes.

"Just don't do it again," he said.

The matter was left there. The discipline of the works was a two-way street. Monty went over to Father Vincent, who was still studying the find.

"It's from the time after Alexander the Great conquered Palestine, around 300 BC." He held the unsettling face up to the sun, where it glowed orange and red.

SEVENTEEN

DR. JUVELIUS

Jerusalem, 1909

Dr. Juvelius stood in the doorway of his hotel and looked up at the gray sky, frozen with marbled clouds. They had somehow reached October, and the heat's ferocity had finally lessened. Juvelius put his hands into his belt. He had pushed off his leaving for the Moses trip, but he had decided that in a week or so, he would finally be going home. Though they had not yet found the Ark, there was just too much digging left to do before they could go in and freely explore the tunnels. Juvelius had his obligations back home and could put them off no longer.

Juvelius was still working on his written report to Mr. Parker. He had been writing it himself, in English, with his friend Uotila's help over many long nights. Meanwhile, Mr. Parker had again suggested that Juvelius pay a visit to the famous rabbi in Jerusalem. Juvelius finally agreed, hoping it would put him in good standing with Mr. Parker once the report was finished. So here he was, holding a rolled-up piece of paper with the rabbi's address on it. The meeting had been arranged for today.

The hotel door behind him opened and out stepped Uotila, dressed in white robes and a scarf. He was going to accompany Juvelius to see the rabbi.

"Is our guide here yet?"

"Not yet."

Juvelius had put this visit off as long as possible. He knew that Mr. Parker was really sending him in hopes that the rabbi might fact-check the cipher. Juvelius knew such an action was completely unnecessary. But he could nod his head for an hour or two if it meant that Mr. Parker would take his final report more seriously.

A dark-haired Jewish boy of about thirteen walked up from the street and looked at them quizzically. Juvelius handed him the paper. The boy looked at it, nodded, and began walking. Juvelius and Uotila followed at a short distance.

Although reluctant to admit it, Juvelius knew that there could be some value in seeing the rabbi. There were some references in the Talmud he was not completely sure he understood. Juvelius was also most interested in what happened in that time — the lost time — during the persecution of the Jews in the first century AD under the Roman emperor Hadrian. Juvelius wondered what ancient knowledge had been lost during that time. And could be yet retrieved.

"What do you think?" Juvelius asked Uotila. "What things should I touch upon?" Juvelius knew there had to be some subject that would not give away their plans and yet perhaps provide some help or insight.

"Maybe a recipe?" joked Uotila. Juvelius scoffed. "What about the number two?" asked Uotila, referring to the endless Christian debate of the nature between the Father and the Son.

"Too much," said Juvelius.

"What about Moses? The unspoken name you mentioned?"

Juvelius went quiet for a moment as they walked in the finely ground dirt.

"Perhaps," he answered, "Though there is great danger about such a question."

"I've been meaning to ask. Why was the name 'unspoken'?" asked Uotila.

"Because it could not be uttered. Even its shape was original and could not be known. The mystics said that the name produced a divine creative power. One just needed to write the name on a papyrus leaf, putting its letters in different combinations for different purposes. Then you could create — make from scratch — whatever you wanted."

Uotila paused, then laughed. He was used to such things from his friend Juvelius.

"There was a woman in the texts," said Juvelius, "who created a calf for herself with the name, which she later ate!"

"I think I should do that for myself." Uotila laughed. "The hotel's lunch today was a bit too sour."

As they walked along, the scenery began to change. The rabbi lived in Jerusalem's poor block. Juvelius thought it the dirtiest and most rambling section he had yet seen. He could smell the horse stables, which were too close to the street. They walked down the public bazaar, through the crowd, and turned a broad corner filled with heaping piles of vegetables. Juvelius could hear the mewling of something being butchered in the back of one of the shops. Uotila gently held a handkerchief against his mouth.

Their guide led them down narrow, complex lanes. There were several skinny long-bearded men who sat in the dust and begged for alms. An older boy began to follow them, his hand outstretched, shouting *bakshiish! bakshiish!* before collapsing in the road.

They went from street to street, stepping over offal in the dirt and feeling the wind from every corner. They eventually came to a hidden cul-de-sac.

"Here," their guide said, pointing to a low house. He took his money and went off on his way.

The shallow board gate was set into a dilapidated wall. It looked almost like the tunnels back at the dig. Juvelius tried the strange gate and was surprised to find it unlocked. Uotila said he would wait outside. If anything went wrong, he would knock on the door and come to get him. Juvelius thought that was unnecessary.

"Don't be useless," Juvelius said. "The rabbi is a civilized man. I'm only going to talk about serious cultural history."

"You're going to talk about things you don't have the right to know," claimed Uotila. Juvelius grumbled as he walked through the door. His friend knew him too well.

"Don't be too long!" said Uotila.

After passing through the gate, Juvelius stepped quietly into an outdoor area separated into two courtyards. The palms above him cast curved, swaying shadows onto the floor. In the first yard, there were nine shallow stalls made of loose cobblestones covered with sticks, twigs, and clay. Juvelius guessed these were for the donkeys.

Juvelius stopped. Straight ahead of him was a young Jewish woman staring directly at him with large eyes. She held a nursing baby. Juvelius was unnerved but nodded and continued past. He didn't look back. At the end of the second courtyard was the house proper, a single-story building. The door opened, and a dark-haired, nicely dressed young man greeted Juvelius. Curls hung down each side of his face. Juvelius had decided to use German on this visit, but for the sake of certainty, he tried some Yiddish.

"Ahlan," said Juvelius. The smiling young man stretched out his hand. Juvelius realized what was being asked and fumbled for his card. He gave it to the man and asked — this time in German — if the rabbi would accept him. The young man nodded and retreated into the house.

Juvelius waited for a few moments, trying not to appear anxious. He looked back, but the woman was gone. Finally, the door opened, and the man motioned for Juvelius to enter. He walked through the door and through a small dark room into a larger one.

The floor was covered with sand. Instead of windows, there were two tall openings in the wall. Juvelius saw some benches and a side cupboard with some pale china on top. There were long benches against the wall; in the middle of the room was a large table with a few stools that were covered in red cloth. The rabbi, a disheveled man, sat on a stool at the table. His face and smile projected a great warmth. The rabbi pushed aside a black book and welcomed Juvelius, who bowed.

"What a great honor it is to meet with such a famous scholar and expert," blurted out Juvelius, in German.

Juvelius regarded the wise man before him. He knew that this rabbi was very famous — and yet, to live so modestly. He could not believe it. Juvelius had expected the man to be stooped with age and in possession of an unkempt, frizzy gray beard. But the rabbi looked to be only forty-five years old. He was lean and, though somewhat pale, seemed the picture of vigor. His beard was soft and full, and his brown eyes were kind. He wore a fine, long robe tinged with black fur.

Juvelius sat down and, faced with an audience, began to talk. He chose his words carefully at first but was so disarmed by the situation that he quickly reached a state where he was not quite sure what he was exactly saying. In mere moments, his careful plans to check his output for the sake of security had dissipated to mist in the rabbi's presence. Juvelius felt a need to impress the man, so when the rabbi asked what his own work entailed, Juvelius nervously told of his theory that the biblical calendar was wrong because historical dates had been changed during the Jewish slavery by the Romans. Juvelius hardly knew what he was saying. He stopped and had to take a breath.

The rabbi moved visibly in his seat. He then spoke in a soothing voice.

"Yes, the reign of Emperor Hadrian was a severe test for us . . . ," but he then suddenly cut off his speech and looked at Juvelius. "Why do you ask?"

"I . . . ," stammered Juvelius. "I'm interested in the unspoken name." He silently cursed himself. Uotila was always right.

"Yes," the rabbi said. He then got up from his seat. He paused for a moment, considering his words. "I must apologize for accepting you here. I am, as usual, here for some of my care. But maybe I can invite you as a guest."

The rabbi opened the simple door on the back wall that Juvelius had thought was a closet. The rabbi passed through the narrow frame, and Juvelius followed through a dark hallway to a large, handsomely decorated room. All around him were richly ornate wall hangings and furniture in the Eastern style. Juvelius realized that this was not the man's house but a place he would come for relaxation or remedy. Juvelius felt himself to be in an almost completely different plot of the tale. The rabbi showed Juvelius to a low sofa next to the wall. A Persian carpet shrouded the wall, then descended softly in folds over part of the sofa and all the way to the floor. The rabbi walked over to a smoking table, picked up some cigars and matches, and sat down on a small purple blanket on the opposite mattress.

The rabbi lit his cigar and leaned over to do the same for Juvelius. They puffed for a moment.

"Your reflections are quite interesting," mused the rabbi, looking into the mingling smoke. Juvelius wondered if this change to an interior room had just been to allow the rabbi to collect his thoughts about a topic that had clearly disarmed him.

Juvelius exhaled. "There is a very old bust of Moses that has the first line of the letters of the name drawn on it," he said. "Two or so are clear, but the rest are vague or incorrect. But at least it tells us that the unspoken name had six letters."

"Six letters," said the rabbi, sucking in on the cigar so that its tip burned orange. "That doesn't go far."

"Of course not," said Juvelius. "The Hebrew alphabet of twenty-two letters in six-letter combinations would yield an enormous number of possibilities! The most reliable way would be" — he drew on his own cigar, carefully pausing to consider that he was saying too much again, but he had to know — "the most reliable way would be to try to find out about the tomb of Moses. I have written some about it, actually."

The rabbi glanced at Juvelius's belt. Juvelius looked down, confused. He kept talking. "The scholars talk about the human death of Moses, so it is clear that the details of his grave were, in the past, known to certain chosen persons. It also shows that the tomb of Moses was, at least during that time people were writing about it — and probably still today — untouched. What is there could be found, if one could only find the key."

Juvelius looked up to see the rabbi's face turn to a very strange expression.

"Have you learned the key?" the rabbi said, gently.

"I'm just talking about — my reports," stammered Juvelius. He had gone too far.

The rabbi held his cigar and stood closer to Juvelius's ear. He lowered his voice almost to a whisper.

"Are you — no, you are not?"

"No," answered Juvelius, understanding his question. "I am indeed a Christian."

The rabbi drew back and stood in front of Juvelius, his eyes tightly closed. When they opened, Juvelius saw fire in them. He remembered what Uotila had said and realized that he had said far too much about unauthorized subjects. He could not help himself. He never could. But he had to know what the rabbi knew.

With an altogether changed voice, the rabbi said, "Ah, I have been a very rude host! I'm so absentminded! A thousand times sorry! Please wait a moment!" He stood up and slid behind the heavy curtain.

Juvelius looked around anxiously. The room was dark enough to feel like dusk. If he shouted, would Uotila hear him? He had to compose himself. It had not come to that yet. Juvelius heard a buzzing whine of a mosquito as it circled behind him, then surged past his ear with a wail.

Endless minutes passed until the rabbi returned. The rabbi lightly apologized, sat down, and started talking again. Juvelius sighed. Everything seemed to be fine. The rabbi talked about the great merits of the Talmud and its versatility. "It is a microcosm," the rabbi said, "that encompasses all of heaven and the world. The Talmud urges its readers to study and, above all, to explore." Juvelius felt relieved, but noticed that the rabbi's gaze flashed, once or twice, toward the door.

The door finally opened, and a woman entered the room, bearing a silver tray. She was young and dressed in a white muslin dress. A crimson silk belt twisted around her waist with a tufted head hanging down the curve of her left hip. At her feet she had turquoise adornments on her saffron-colored slippers. Juvelius found himself staring.

"Ah, some refreshment!" said the rabbi with a glad voice. The girl dropped her round tray upon the cedar table. The tray had mother-of-pearl inlay and held a water siphon, a bottle of whiskey, and a Greek Santorini wine. She placed a tall Venetian crystal glass and a shiny earthenware bowl onto a golden base on the table.

Juvelius was entranced by the girl, though he wondered if she was older than seventeen. Once she had placed the items, the girl retreated to leave, and Juvelius thought that she had silently caught his long glance. At the same time, Juvelius thought he saw — though he could not be sure — a small, almost imperceptible hand gesture exchanged between the rabbi and her.

Or, Juvelius thought, was she trying to signal him?

The rabbi got up politely and gestured to the tray.

"Come!"

Juvelius stared at the wine.

"No, thank you," he said. Juvelius stood up and excused himself for taking too much of the rabbi's time. He said he was honored to speak with him about his own silly whims. As he began to walk away, Juvelius looked back.

The rabbi said, in a kind voice, how equally pleasant it was to make Juvelius's acquaintance. He asked if he had been in Jerusalem for a long time? He would like to see his writings.

"I am leaving soon," said Juvelius. "I have, unfortunately, not any writings with me. I left them back in my country. I deposited them to three people in three banks. Just to be careful." His voice trailed off. The rabbi moved to usher his guest through the curtain-door, but Juvelius did not move.

"I get lost so easily in the streets here, so I would rather leave the same way I came." Juvelius bowed his head, then walked — more quickly than normal — through the hallway, the door, and the corridor — much faster now — until he was through the courtyards and outside the gate, where Uotila was waiting.

"It's good that you came back," his friend said. "If you were three more minutes late, I would have broken in." He was smiling, but his face turned serious when he saw Juvelius.

"What's wrong?"

"I thought it was . . . it was fine. There was a beautiful Jewish girl." Juvelius was breathing quickly. Uotila pushed his friend along and they left the cul-de-sac. Once they passed the corner market and onto familiar streets, Juvelius began to calm down and was able to speak more clearly.

"The rabbi offered me some refreshments, but I didn't take them," Juvelius said. He paused. Things were making sense only now, after the fact. "I really have reason to think he wanted to put me to sleep, to study my papers. I guess I would have found myself later in some alley. I told him that all my papers are in my country, to be used after my death."

"That was wise," said Uotila.

As they walked, at a slower pace, Juvelius felt relieved. He was glad he had not fallen for the trap and he was glad that no one knew his papers were back at the hotel. He was also glad that he was going to file his report to Mr. Parker soon. Juvelius exhaled again. He felt that he was in control of his destiny for the first time in a long while. Until Uotila nudged him in the arm.

"Don't look behind you. At that corner."

Juvelius stole an awkward glance and saw the young man in curls who had previously given him entrance from the courtyard.

He appeared to be following them.

EIGHTEEN

CYRIL FOLEY

Jerusalem, 1909

On this morning, like all the others, by the time Cyril had pulled on his boots and walked out to the dig, the sky was already on fire. Cyril stepped across the dirt, ready to walk into what had become an everyday pattern of shuffling, clinking, shouting, and occasionally singing. But as Cyril stepped up onto the hill, he heard none of those things.

Something was wrong.

Cyril saw Monty standing over the staircase, looking down. There was a small crew scattered here and there but nothing like what would usually be working at this hour.

Had they found it?

Cyril started to walk faster, then broke into a run, his hat in his hand. But when he reached Monty, the captain's face was grim.

"The workers," Monty said. "They're on strike."

Cyril stared down into the open cave, made larger by the absence of the men. Cyril was angry but, then again, supposed he couldn't rightly blame them. They were employing three gangs of sixty men around the clock each day of the week except Sunday. Cyril wondered if his little wager back in August had something to do with all this, but felt no pressing need to tell Monty.

Cyril knew the problem was greater than some silly bet. Each group of workers earned their pay as contract wages that changed according to the amount of earth they moved out of the tunnels. This led to different groups often receiving different amounts of pay. Indeed, Cyril's winning troop had since proved considerably more efficient and earned almost twice as much as the other two groups. Cyril did a quick look around the site. Sure enough, it was those other two groups who were gone.

Cyril had to admit it was kind of nice and quiet. And fewer men crowding the works might make it easier to find the Ark. He also refrained from saying that bit aloud to Monty. Cyril knew they could not dig without them, even for a day. Cyril sighed and pushed his hand through his hair. They had hired almost everyone in the village who wanted a job in the first place, and it was already Ramadan.

"We're in trouble," he said.

"Well," said Monty. "We have a contract." He squinted — as he always did — and bit down on his pipe. "We'll take them to court."

"Court? Why don't we just pay them? What if we lose?"

"Well," said Monty, obviously thinking on the fly, "we still haven't had our official visit with the mayor yet. Now might be a good time."

Several days later, they met with the mayor in his offices at town hall. Hussein Bey al-Husayni was newly installed as mayor but had been in the hospital since their arrival so they had put off what should have been an immediate visit. Now, Monty, Cyril, and Macasdar sat across from his desk and assured him that everything was in perfect agreement with the Turks for the digging rights. The mayor asked this question several times before he was satisfied. He was committed to birthing a new, more modern Jerusalem and did not need problems, especially from old tunnels. He blessed their endeavors as they drank the local tea, *glezel tay*, served hot in a clear glass. They drank it through a sugar cube held between their teeth.

Monty eyed his watch. The court hearing for the strikers was scheduled for that same afternoon. Monty made a tidy goodbye of things with the help of Macasdar's translation, with a brief aside about the sordid affair of the strike. The mayor regarded Monty with some pause.

"Let me accompany you," he offered. Monty bowed his head in thanks. Cyril thought it timing of a most spectacular nature.

That afternoon, Monty took his hat off as they entered the courthouse, an old building of white stone. There, seated up front, were twenty of the leading strikers under an escort of Turkish soldiers. The commandant who was going to judge the case sat in the front of center. The case had already been called, and though Cyril could not hear Macasdar's whispered translation to Monty, he could get a good enough sense of what was happening.

The spokesmen for the workers stood up and began gesturing and speaking at a rate that Cyril felt must be challenging the limits of human endurance. The worker — who Cyril knew to be a good enough fellow, though he could not recall his name — spoke with greater and greater volume, until he was nearly shouting. At the same time, he was making motions with his arms that Cyril knew quite well. He was acting out — with some flourish — the motion of swinging a pickax.

"Too much work," Cyril said, nodding to Monty, who seemed to completely disagree.

Cyril was getting worried. If they lost their workers, they would have to go home. Not only would they leave the Ark here, somewhere in the dirt, but they would have to face the Syndicate with nothing but a case of heatstroke.

Cyril returned his attention to the speaker, who was getting even louder. Cyril soon realized that it was not the man who was adding to the rising noise, but his compatriots in the front rows. The strikers had begun chiming in, yelling out various words of agreement, with plenty of wild gesticulations. It was then that Cyril realized that the men were now disagreeing with their leader as they corrected and then outright shouted over his points and facts.

"Apparently," said Macasdar, "working for Captain Parker is hell on earth." Monty gave a defeated, hangdog look.

The shouting was now comprised of dozens of angry individuals, who each proceeded to give their own personal view

of the situation. Cyril had never seen anything like it. The commandant rolled his
eyes at the curdling wave of noise caused by
twenty men screaming at the same time. It
did not appear to influence the case in their
favor.

After about a half an hour of hearing such
grievances, the commandant raised his own
voice: "Enough!" he said, or Cyril guessed
that's what the commandant said, as he
continued speaking, making a strong gesture. The stern guards started moving the
workmen as they turned in place, dumbfounded by what the commandant had said.
He was apparently no Solomon, thought
Cyril.

"That's unfortunate," said Macasdar.
"He's committed them all to jail."

As the room sat stunned, the workmen
most especially, Cyril turned again to
Monty. The captain looked even more
sheepish than usual, though there was a hint
of a spark as he pulled his hand down his
chin.

Monty straightened himself and took his
hat in his hand, like he was preparing to
leave. The mayor seemed intrigued.

"Is there anyone here to defend them?"
asked the commandant.

Monty stood up.

"I would be pleased, Your Honor," Monty said walking slowly toward the front. The guards turned to stop him, but the commandant raised his palm.

"And you are?"

"I am Captain Montague Parker, their employer."

The workmen grumbled and sneered.

"Right then," said Monty. "Now I do believe I should have a say in the matter as I am the one they have wronged and hurt."

The judge took a moment, then nodded.

"Thank you," said Monty. "It is my wish that these men . . ."

Cyril saw the smile escape, that hint of some caper in the corners of Monty's eyes that was going to change everything, for either better or worse.

". . . should be set free."

The workmen paused for the translation, then cheered.

Cyril Foley smiled.

It was a masterstroke. Monty knew — or at least had bet — that he would be put in the position of savior. But what a gamble.

The commandant sighed, then declared the men free. The workers roared and spilled out of the courthouse in great spirits, pushing Monty through like a rush of water.

"Well done, old man," said Cyril, squeezing him on the shoulder. The mayor too gave him a look of admiration.

The workmen, now in uproarious spirits, cheered and hollered. There was no need to make it official; they would all be hired back. As they left, the commandant suggested that perhaps it would be a good thing for him to come down to the works and make a speech to the strikers. Not to be outdone, the mayor said he would do the same. Monty smiled and agreed, though Cyril knew he had no choice.

When they stepped out into the sun, Cyril saw their donkeys all in a row. Some Turkish troops were also there. Macasdar talked with the donkey boys; apparently there had been a misunderstanding. They thought Monty had ordered them to be brought to the courthouse.

"Let's ride them back," someone said.

Monty shrugged, and everyone got on their steeds. Cyril looked at Robin Duff, who at six feet tall towered above even the largest animal. Duff's donkey was pure white by nature, but for some unexplainable reason, someone had painted its tail and mane the brightest possible yellow. Once everyone mounted, they posed for a photograph. Cyril wondered if this was the only photograph of the entire expedition that would ever be taken. They had even managed to squeeze in the Turks, the Arabs, and the donkeys. As Cyril looked up and down the row, he was struck by what a group it was. He wondered what everyone would think of them, these brave English heroes, if they knew what they were really looking for. He wondered what the photograph would look like when they were posed around the Ark. He didn't know if it was their legal victory or just the camaraderie of the moment, but he felt hopeful for the future, if not a little wary.

Their procession through the city was a strange display of donkeys and horses. They were led by a troop of Turkish lancers with a flag, whose job it was to clear the streets. After them rode the mayor and commandant, at Monty's generous insistence. Next came their Turkish observers, various personages and hangers-on, and Duff, Monty, Cyril, Wilson, and Macasdar. A mass of Turkish gendarmerie brought up the rear.

The shortest way out of the city was through the old Jewish quarter. Very gradually, the streets became bumpier as the cobblestones got older by the step, narrowing as the high walls rose. They were surrounded by secret quarter arches and endless stacks of stone. It was a most romantic place, thought Cyril. One of a kind. He saw curious eyes begin to appear from open-air windows. He couldn't help thinking again: if others knew the purpose of the excavation, how they would feel.

As the street narrowed to a wandering contour, the donkeys fell into a natural single line. As they clopped over the ground, Cyril was able to get an up-close view of the quarter that he had not yet seen. The sides of this thin street were lined with shops and carts. Cyril thought that the shopkeepers, who were framed in their doorways, were less than thrilled at the sad parade. One old man, with his hair curling out in wisps along his beard, saw Duff's yellow-tailed donkey and screamed a terrifically long litany in Yiddish.

As they approached the halfway point in the quarter, Cyril watched as Kissam Iass, Duff's donkey boy, took his stick and casually gave two very forceful *thwacks* to the mayor's Arabian horse ahead of him. Duff watched in disbelief; he couldn't tell if the boy had not meant to use such force or if it was some nefarious plot — or perhaps he felt that the slow procession needed some speeding up.

There was a second of nothing. Duff sighed that they had avoided catastrophe, before the mayor's horse whinnied and sped off, swerving to and fro, slipping on the cobblestone as the mayor tipped right and left, trying to keep his balance. The mayor's horse then nearly broke into a gallop and went dashing down the street at a speed Cyril barely thought possible, his excellency hanging on for dear life.

Cyril watched as Monty jumped off his own donkey and sprinted after the mayor. Meanwhile, Duff was trying desperately to calm his own animal, who was similarly kicking and sliding. But the moment proved to be too much for the poor beast, and Duff was sent flying into the air and into the nearest shop. Cyril hoped it was a carpet shop, or a boot shop, but it happened to be a *rahat lakoum* and peanut shop. There was a huge crash as Duff collided into the front table where all sorts of things had been displayed. Cyril slid off his donkey and ran over to help. There, spread out under a pile of candy and innumerable peanuts, was Duff, overcome with a dazed look of almost overwhelming peace. He was seated in one of probably twenty-five boxes of overturned Turkish delight.

When the party finally emerged from St. Stephen's Gate and got down to the works, they had to cut Duff out from his saddle.

Turkish delight was like glue, thought Cyril: you either stop with it, or it comes away with you. Duff was brushing peanuts from his person for days.

The mayor (in perfect shape, if a little tousled) and the commandant gave perfectly rousing speeches, thought Cyril, to thoroughly tired workmen about very boring political affairs. It had been a long day. Cyril became worried when he saw that some of the strikers were gathered near the front of the crowd, speaking among themselves again. Cyril hoped that all this politicking had not made them reconsider their position against heat and time. He was not sure even Monty had the magnetism to bring them back twice. It was a good thing the speech seemed to be wrapping up. When it did, there was clapping as the mayor spread his hands and smiled. He really wanted peace.

But, sure enough, one of the workmen barked out some sudden exclamation that startled everyone. The worker turned and looked directly at the Englishmen. Macasdar, who had been, to the great regret of Cyril, translating the mayor the entire time, stopped. Cyril feared the worst.

"The men," said Macasdar, slowly, "are so grateful to us that they want to show us a new tunnel."

Cyril looked at Monty, dumbfounded. Had they been holding out on them?

"Go," said Monty. "I have to stay with the mayor."

The workmen grabbed their tools and started marching farther down into the Kidron Valley. Cyril grabbed Wilson by the arm, and they both followed the men. After a short walk, they found them stopped still under an arch in the side of a small hill.

Cyril had not seen this before. Had the cipher missed it? It was, like everything in Palestine, of an indeterminate age that veered somewhere between ancient and just old.

Then it hit him. Or rather, the smell did. Cyril knew exactly what this tunnel was. He started to laugh.

"What?" said Wilson, oblivious to what was happening. He had a terrible sense of smell since the war. "We have to explore it!" he said.

"I'm not going in," said Cyril, shaking his head, "it's the Jerusalem main drain!" Wilson harrumphed and went in anyway. He got thirty yards before he turned around. When he emerged, he was holding his nose, and his face looked purple. He did not say anything, only nodded his head in agreement. The workmen were laughing, and so was Cyril. As a token of gratitude, it was a failure, but Cyril thought it the finest smell of its kind in Jerusalem, all being said, and that being so, probably the finest in the world.

NINETEEN
DR. JUVELIUS

Jerusalem, October 1909

Juvelius and Uotila picked up their pace, even as passersby gave them disapproving glances. When they turned the corner at Jaffankatu, they hid behind a building and searched the streets for the man who was following them.

Juvelius watched nervously as the man crept into view and looked about. He was definitely the man who had let him into the rabbi's house. Juvelius and Uotila doubled around the other side of the block and took a parallel street to the hotel. Once they got in, they hurried to the window of the lounge and looked out.

"Look! He's speaking to the doorman!" said Juvelius. Uotila saw that the man was in conversation with the doorman, who seemed to be answering his questions. They finally ended their meeting and parted with a firm handshake.

"Can you believe this? In England this kind of spying would be impossible!" said Juvelius.

They immediately went to the hotel owner and complained bitterly. The owner looked the exasperated Juvelius up and down. He assured them he would speak to the doorman. When he came back, the owner said that the doorman had told the man that Juvelius and Uotila were with those — and he paused, knowing how it would sound — "English treasure diggers."

"Beautiful!" shouted Juvelius. The manager apologized and told them not to worry. But it was too late for that.

The next day, Juvelius met with Mr. Parker and told him about his interview with the rabbi. Mr. Parker was pleased that he had gone. But the more Juvelius went on with his story, the more he bit down on his pipe.

"He tried to angle information from me," said Juvelius.

"That doesn't matter," said Mr. Parker. "You were well to get out of there." He pointed to some newspapers on the table. "The press has already figured out that we are here, but not why."

"You did good work," he said, pausing, "Dr. Juvelius."

That night, Juvelius left his room to meet Uotila for supper. As he left his room, he noticed a man enter the room opposite his and shut the door, at almost exactly the same time that Juvelius opened his. Downstairs, Uotila was already waiting. Juvelius sat down quickly.

"Did you see?" he whispered.

"What now?"

"The room opposite to ours has been occupied!"

"So? It is a hotel, after all."

"Yes, but this hotel is always empty, which is why he caught my eye. And why across from us?"

"Was he Jewish?"

"I think so."

"He is probably just a tourist," said Uotila.

"Fine," said Juvelius, pushing the glass to his mouth. "You keep the first watch!"

When they left for the excavation site early the next morning, Juvelius noted that the door across from them was shut. They stayed at the tunnels all day, where the heat had unfortunately returned in an awful bloom. After a long day, they finally returned at dinnertime. When Juvelius got back, he immediately began changing his clothes, which were dusty and filthy.

Juvelius reached for his box of collars and immediately noticed something strange: they were not in order but had been separated into a feathery mess. He looked at the other boxes and found them in similar states of disorder. Frantically, Juvelius checked through his chests, his suitcases, and his desk. All was small, undeniable mayhem. Some of the books on the shelf had even switched places.

Juvelius went next door — quietly — to Uotila's room. His friend had just entered, so his door was open. Juvelius walked in and hurriedly explained what had happened.

"Did you leave your door open?" asked Uotila.

"Of course not! Have you checked your bags and boxes?" Within minutes, they found the same thing had happened to Uotila. All of his things had been emptied and then fully packed, hurriedly and unmistakably.

"Look," said Juvelius. He pointed to his friend's still-locked suitcase. It had been sliced open.

They called the manager again. He assured them that no man had traveled through this part of the hotel.

"But there is a tourist opposite us,"

remarked Juvelius.

"He left early in the morning," said the manager. "He got an apartment elsewhere." They followed the manager down to the desk and looked in the passenger book. The man across the hall had written that his name was Blumenthal, and that he was from Smyrna in Greece. And that he was an "agent."

Juvelius glared at Uotila.

They returned to Juvelius's room. After locking the door, Juvelius began to pace.

"This is the first consequence of my visit to the rabbi," said Juvelius. "I already thought I had misled him, but he had his own calculations."

"Have you lost any important papers?" asked Uotila. He was also clearly rattled.

"I don't think so. All my papers are sealed in the hotel safe . . . but wait . . ."

Juvelius searched a little with his eyes, then grabbed his Baedeker Palestine guide from the window shelf. He had placed some of his new ciphers from their trip to the Valley of Moses within its pages. He flipped through the book and stopped, then sighed. They were still there.

"What luck," said Juvelius. "These translations are not so much dangerous, but still. The Hebrew text could be used to open others." He sat on the bed in a heap. "If the Hebrew cipher were in rabbinical hands, it would have been an unfortunate accident. But this!" — he pointed to the guide — "was displayed too openly! He missed it! If he had just nicely put it in his pocket, the rabbi could have figured out the key! Now? He got nothing." He kissed the dog-eared guidebook.

They went back to the house of the Englishmen that night and told Mr. Parker. He listened to the entire tale, then stood.

"We'll be fine. But from now on, keep everything in the safe."

Juvelius couldn't believe that he wasn't taking the matter more seriously.

"If you'll excuse me, gentlemen," said Monty, "we've been invited to visit with the governor of Jerusalem this evening, and I must get ready."

Juvelius must have seemed excited, because the next look that Monty gave him conveyed the message that it was just the English who were being requested.

The next morning, Juvelius came downstairs to the hotel lobby. He was surprised to see Mr. Parker waiting for him. He had a serious look on his face.

"You were right," he said, as Juvelius sat down. He spoke slowly to make sure that

Juvelius understood his English. "Last night when we went to the . . . you know . . . the servants were out to, apparently they stopped in the city park to hear some Turkish music. They . . . ah, apparently after getting into the whiskey." Monty put his fingers at his temples and closed his eyes. "Anyway," he said, raising his head again, "our house was searched, just like yours."

"Were documents taken?" Juvelius was horrified.

"Nothing was taken. No documents. I had followed your advice and hid them, at least." Juvelius nodded his head. Monty said the next part very slowly.

"I understand that the rabbi is probably the one behind this. I think I can admit that I made the mistake of asking you to go to interview him."

Juvelius was surprised, but also pleased. He was also seized by the thought that this was the moment for him to directly communicate what he had been trying to write down.

"I have one more thing on my heart to you," said Juvelius, searching for the right words, and trying to duplicate the ones he had been working on in his report. "I do not find Hoppenrath to be completely trustworthy either. Mr. Uotila and Mr. Wilson agree." Juvelius told him in broken English about the horses, his wife, and the cipher. "That's what would now I am worried about a written communication and work plan for his translation," he said.

As Monty quietly regarded him, Juvelius knew that a shadow could easily fall on him at this moment. He knew that Mr. Parker greatly liked Hoppenrath. Everyone did. Juvelius thought about his words and spoke again.

"English gentleman," he said, "who personalizes honesty, you cannot even comprehend dishonesty in another.

"Hoppenrath is not true," said Juvelius. "He may be a spy."

Monty moved closer to him. He spoke very slowly and watched Juvelius's eyes to see that he was understood. "I think I have noticed that the spacing between you and Hoppenrath has not always been the best. And Mr. Wilson's relationship with him, well, it's a bit private." He paused, full of meaning. "Maybe we'll call it a family affair."

As Monty stood up and left, he said something in Latin. Juvelius was confused and angry. Were his words misunderstood? Did he understand his? It began to cloud his mind beyond all repair. He didn't know if it was the heat, the circumstances, or Jerusalem itself, but his feelings had a single, arrowlike trajectory. Juvelius wanted revenge on the rabbi, in ways he had never dreamed he would contemplate.

How could he think such things, he thought to himself. Mr. Parker was gone. Juvelius felt overwhelmed. These projects — perhaps unrealistic — were endangered by forces beyond their control. The heat of the East had surely, he thought, put him off balance. Juvelius felt tattered and torn by his surroundings and the otherworldly subjects within it.

In that lobby, with the people coming and going as blurs and shapes around him, a semi-imaginative atmosphere seemed to envelop him. As everything slid by him in waves, he saw someone walk up to him: a dark-eyed girl in a red silk belt, a graceful creature who caught his eye. She completely captured his thoughts, such that the only question in his mind, one that seemed more important than any questions about his more immediate problems was: Were her eyes brown or black?

TWENTY

DR. JUVELIUS

Jerusalem, 1909

Dr. Juvelius sat at his desk, trying to write. He had no fear about what he wanted to say. He felt better; he knew that Hoppenrath would not make a naked grab for his report, but he still had to finish it. But this had become an impossible task, an immovable boulder. Juvelius sat there at his desk for half days, writing and wiping out, without getting anything decent down.

"Good man, take the quin and lay down!" Uotila said with concern. He handed Juvelius a glass of aperitif.

"I have taken three full already!" said Juvelius. "My ears hum."

Juvelius threw a pen at Uotila and went for a walk.

He immediately felt more refreshed. It had just rained, and the air was pure for the first time in months. The dust of ages had finally been flattened to the ground. For a few moments, at least.

Juvelius stepped into his thoughts, with no drink needed. He saw himself in the alleys that led to the rabbi's residence. He continued firmly forward to the last alley and the second door of the low house in the cul-de-sac. He wanted to talk to the Jewish girl again. She had been foremost in his thoughts lately. He made up his mind; he wanted to thank her. He was now certain that she had secretly tried to warn him of the rabbi's intentions.

Juvelius walked for a long time among the bazaars and the Haram, the Dome of the Rock, the main streets and passageways. As he walked by a stand of steaming food, he saw Hoppenrath out of the corner of his eye. He was entering the Jewish quarter. Juvelius wondered if he was also looking for the rabbi's address. Perhaps he had gotten it from Father Vincent. Juvelius followed him. After a few turns, Juvelius was stunned when he saw — with his own eyes — Hoppenrath bow his head inside the rabbi's low doorway.

Juvelius did not understand. He had assumed that Hoppenrath was operating for his own concerns. Juvelius thought it not worth waiting and being discovered, so he returned to town, near the main bazaar again. Juvelius opened his lungs with a great breath; it was relaxing here. As he took in the sights and sounds of the place, he saw, off a side corridor, a flash of white.

It was her! The Jewish girl! She was dressed in a muslin suit, in the pattern of fine European fashion. Juvelius took in a sharp breath. He went right up to her.

"I am sorry," he said to her, "but I consider it my right to thank you!"

"Ah!" she said, remembering him. "I was so scared then."

Juvelius was relieved at her demeanor. "Isn't the rabbi your father?"

"He's my uncle. I was born in Frankfurt. I saw that he put something in the bottles, and I was so scared. He doesn't drink himself — no wine at all!"

"Let's walk," said Juvelius.

"Since the air was so fresh, I wanted to get out to see what color your eyes were. Brown or black?" He could not believe he was saying such things. She was a sophisticated woman, thought Juvelius, though still closer to the age and experience of a child. Her arms slid down and she smiled at him.

"Well, what color are they now?" she said.

"Black! Night black, sparkling and charming!" replied Juvelius.

Her natural feminine appetite had won

him over. It was a moment, there on the street, that he could see so clearly. She shifted her shoulders and spoke.

"I will not have long to discuss with you, though. I am engaged . . ."

"Engaged? And so young!"

"Yes," she responded. "With my cousin! We have been engaged since my childhood. I am now with my mother here for the first time. A month from now, when he turns twenty, we go get married.

"My uncle says," she continued, "that it is written that whoever is unmarried, after twenty years, sins every day and every moment before the Lord."

It was only when she was talking that Juvelius felt he could see how charming she really was. She had an essentially pure heart, he thought.

"And you will be happy?" he finally asked.

"I always used to think my husband Micha was my future."

"And you will gladly leave big, beautiful Frankfurt?"

"Wherever he goes, I go where he is. There I am me, too. It's our people's way."

"And your mother stays in Frankfurt?"

She nodded. There was a shy look on her face, and her voice shook a little as she said, "It has been said to mothers, 'Your sons

229

and daughters will be married to foreign countries, and without feeling sorry for you, you must leave them, knowing that they are chaste and happy.' But now I don't get married in foreign countries, but in Jerusalem!"

Juvelius was silent. He thought she was a saint.

"Now I have to leave," she said suddenly.

"But before that, please, I would know your name!" said Juvelius.

"Rachel Baumgarten." She uttered her name with great confidence.

"Rachel Baumgarten, goodbye — forever!" Juvelius bowed and kissed her hand.

As she left him, Juvelius felt that he had truly seen this girl, who had shown him an incomparable moral brightness. Her triumphant celebration of family ties and respect for ancestral customs was most worthy. That is why, he thought, the unbroken vitality of her entire landless refugee nation had endured.

When Juvelius returned to the hotel lobby, he had a fully developed fever.

Uotila chatted with him and soon realized his condition. He took Juvelius up to the room and wrapped him in strong felt coverings and gave him medicine for climate fever. Juvelius began to quiver.

In the morning, Juvelius felt quite brisk.

The accumulated vile materials were out of his system. His overnight sweating had a purifying effect on his constitution, much like a thunderstorm in nature.

"Well, how are you?" Uotila asked as he entered the room.

"Much better. I have to get to work here," he said as he eyed the desk.

"You slept for two days," said Uotila. "You kept going on about poisons and Jewish girls."

Juvelius seemed puzzled or perhaps ashamed. "I have to get to work."

"You know," said Uotila, "you tossed all night. It was only in the morning that you got to sleep with your eyes closed."

"I don't remember," said Juvelius. "Though," his mind wandered, "shortly before I woke up, I stole an ancient Hebrew home god from our own museum and hid it in a black-eyed Rachel's saddlebag."

Uotila stared at him, stupefied.

"Go write," he said.

Sometime later, there was a knock at Juvelius's door. It was Hoppenrath, with a warm smile on his face. He was looking for the new report to be translated. Juvelius let him in and gave him a long look through red eyes.

"I haven't started yet," he said.

Hoppenrath was genial and talked about some of his recent local adventures with his wife, including trips to the Suez Canal, the astonishing Petra, and even the summit of Mount Sinai. Juvelius nodded, somewhat in and out, of the moment.

"By the way," said Hoppenrath, "What was the name you once mentioned that was drawn on the bust of Moses? Can you write it down for me?" He took a piece of paper from the table and slid it toward Juvelius.

Juvelius regarded him. "Moses's bust is apocryphal, and I have never spoken to you about it. But perhaps the rabbi did when you met with him?"

There was a moment, or perhaps only the sliver of one, when Hoppenrath may have seemed surprised, but it passed so quickly as to be all but invisible.

"Now I remember!" Hoppenrath said. "Father Vincent mentioned it! Yes, I will be happy to tell him that he correctly interpreted what we found in that name on the pottery we found. Here you are!"

Hoppenrath took out a paper ticket from his wallet. "Four days ago, I brought a copy of the signature from the pottery for the rabbi to authenticate. See?"

Juvelius thought that Hoppenrath was as slippery as an eel. He was too cunning. He had taken everything into account.

After he left, Uotila was excited. "How did you know he visited the rabbi?"

"I followed his footsteps in the Jewish quarter," said Juvelius. "But notice how wise he is: I went to the rabbi three days ago. He claims to have visited the rabbi the day before me."

"But he went there yesterday? After all the burglaries!"

"Oriental diplomacy is different than Western," said Juvelius. "It's a good idea to go into the enemy's camp without them knowing it."

"What about Moses's bust? How did he know that?"

"Hoppenrath is a deceiver. He knows that the bust is important. The rabbi knows that. That's why he seeks the name. The rabbi is like a roaring lion searching for a lost key. Hoppenrath went to the rabbi yesterday to find out about our communication."

Juvelius and Uotila got to work on the document — together this time. Juvelius finished it in Swedish and passed it to Uotila to translate to English. They did not drink. By the next day, it was done, with just a little bit of translation left. Hoppenrath had been by twice to ask for the report, but Juvelius lied each time without remorse.

When he left the second time, Juvelius knew that Hoppenrath knew the truth — that Juvelius had included his thoughts on the tomb of Moses in the new report.

Juvelius also knew that Hoppenrath was going to try to steal the document.

"In a couple of hours, the translation will be ready," said Uotila. "It's already dark. I can take the papers for you to Captain Parker tonight. Hoppenrath won't be expecting that. I'll wear a dark suit. Nobody will see me."

"Neither of us goes tonight," said Juvelius, quite seriously. "The consequence could be a dagger in your back. The manuscript can wait for tomorrow."

They finished the papers and signed them. It was then that Juvelius knew it would be impossible to stop his faithful friend. Dressed in black, Uotila took the papers and exited from the back door of the hotel. He walked across the courtyard and out into the street before he disappeared. Juvelius felt a temporary pang of regret. Uotila was nothing if not versatile. He would be fine.

Fifteen minutes later, Uotila appeared in the back courtyard, limping. When he knocked at the room door, he was hoarse and breathless. He held up his left hand; one of his fingers dangled there, lifeless and destroyed.

After he collapsed onto a chair, Uotila took a drink and related his story. Two thugs had started to follow him. He was soon running for his life through the dark streets. Uotila wished he had his revolver, but it had been seized at customs. At one turn, he hid on the ground behind a corner, but fell into some building stones. It was then that they attacked him. He held up his hand again. He crawled back and finally got to the hotel. He was whining as he spoke; he was still in tremendous pain. Juvelius was hurting for his friend but also feared the worst. It was then that Uotila, with his other hand, pulled out the report, intact, from the back of his shirt.

A doctor was summoned to the room. The damaged finger was set. Uotila had also sprained his leg. He was given ice and bandages. "In three weeks," the doctor said, "he can get back on track."

"Can't he come back with me to Finland?" begged Juvelius "We would travel as comfortably as possible, the shortest way."

The doctor shook his head: "He would then have a limp for the rest of his life."

Juvelius looked at his friend. As he rested, Uotila finally fell into a fitful slumber. Juvelius returned to his desk.

In the morning, Juvelius was greeted in the lobby by Mr. Parker and some of his men, who were there for the report. Overnight, Juvelius had added a new epilogue about the incident. Mr. Parker assured Juvelius that they would implement the highest possible security measures to safeguard the document, even involving the English consulate. Juvelius asked him, in halting English, if there was any reason to suspect that Hoppenrath informed the rabbi about the existence of the report.

Mr. Parker listened thoughtfully. "The rabbi's involvement is obvious," he said, "though we cannot legally prove it. As far as Mr. Hoppenrath, I'm afraid your zeal has misled you. He showed me the interpretation he received the other day from the rabbi in the contents of the pottery writing. He mentioned it, laughing actually, that you had made some reference to him trying to steal a report."

Juvelius tried to breathe.

"I think that Hoppenrath is completely clean on this," said Mr. Parker.

Juvelius decided to spend the rest of the day in his hotel room tending to the sick Uotila. He was going to board the train tomorrow to go home. He sent his goodbyes to the English, and after a pause, to

Hoppenrath as well. Juvelius was then surprised when Hoppenrath appeared in the early evening at his door. He was dressed in a new riding suit.

Hoppenrath had come to accept Juvelius's earlier explanation that he had needed Uotila's help to finish his writing in time and that there were no hard feelings. But he had more to say.

"My work has been of greater benefit to the expedition than anyone," said Hoppenrath, close to his face and with spittle on his mustache. "The rest? I arranged the purchase of the land! Excavating is always when difficulties have been overcome, usually from my skill. I insist on being involved in all financial aspects of the company interests!"

"I think Mr. Parker has valued your work," said Juvelius. "But I can't do anything about those matters. You should ask him to bring your case to London to the board of the Syndicate."

"Now you don't know what you're talking about!" snarled Hoppenrath. "For me, all doors are open! What would stop me from going for a week, for example, to the Rothschilds? Do you think they would not be interested?" Juvelius knew that the French banker, the Baron Edmond de Rothschild, was not only greatly interested in Jewish interests in Palestine but had the nearly infinite resources with which to accomplish his goals. Were he to find out about their digging, the results could be catastrophic.

Juvelius said calmly, "That kind of speech has an ill name in every language. I still suggest that you turn to Mr. Parker, but I would not advise you to use the same language with him, at least in the presence of foreign men."

Hoppenrath left in a rage, grabbing his whip from his riding boot as he stormed out.

Uotila, who had been lying silently on the bed the whole time, finally spoke up.

"At last," he said in a thoughtful manner, perhaps a little dreamily because of the medicine, "I understand Hoppenrath's calculations, which I had always missed. I understand that he had intended from the beginning to betray us, but I did not know that his purpose was to do so for another party. I always thought it was about him. That's why he needed to collect all the information about us. And he used his wife, too!

"Hoppenrath went to the rabbi — who was truly interested in what we're doing — and promised to get him a copy of the report, provided he received a letter of introduction to Rothschild. If anyone could shut us down and find the Ark, it would surely be him. So even though Hoppenrath could not produce the report, he still got the rabbi to talk, at least a little. But I think he has that letter now, even if he bought it in pieces from explanations. Otherwise, he wouldn't have been so cocky and rude."

Uotila sighed and closed his eyes again. Juvelius regarded him silently. His friend was still in pain, and new bruises had been appearing by the hour. But there was no anger or thoughts of revenge from Uotila, only the awakening of understanding.

"You're right," Juvelius admitted. "We have been from day one the victim of unhelpful mistakes. But just my explanations won't be enough. Our enemies will still need the actual cipher. Without that, it will probably be difficult for them to do us harm.

"Maybe I should have gone to the Jews first," said Juvelius. "Remember what I said to you two years ago: if the Ark is a purely scientific question, the Jews would be the best to excavate it. But . . . in the hands of the Jews, the whole scientific material that might be obtained in the crevices of the mountain would remain their own private secret, unlike what Western research does in sharing such information.

"What is the significance of such a thing that could so cleanse our Western culture's misconceptions if it were hid? It would of course be useless. But I am not second-guessing myself. Neither of us have undertaken this to get rich."

Early the next morning, Juvelius left the bed of his sad friend, from whom he had enjoyed an unexpected amount of help these past months, and traveled by train to Jaffa and then farther on to home.

TWENTY-ONE
CHARLES WARREN

Jerusalem, February 1868
Forty-One Years Earlier

Charles Warren was climbing down an eighty-foot-long shaft on a twisting rope ladder that looked as if it was going to snap to twigs in seconds. He was sweating profusely but didn't dare try to grab his handkerchief, so he kept going. He reached one of the wooden beams and stopped against it for a moment. He did not look down.

He and Sergeant Birtles had bombed these shafts — at impossible depths — only twenty feet from the Haram wall. After his last trip, when they had walked through the tunnel at the Virgin's Fountain, Warren had somehow secured a permit to dig anywhere he wished, provided he avoided the specific religious sites, of course. So instead of digging at the Dome of the Rock, which was absolutely forbidden by the Arabs, Warren had decided to dig alongside it. Many

241

people were not happy.

When such persons came to complain, Warren would wave his official order around and bluff his way out of arguments, but he knew his days were numbered, which is why they were being so — reckless wasn't quite the word, perhaps forward-thinking — with their digging. Their shafts were so deep that none of the locals would even work for them anymore. Warren saw their point: there had been a few exceedingly close calls with cave-ins, but they were still alive; they were still at it. Birtles was pacing up top, on the lookout for prying eyes.

Warren plunked himself down on the ground and coughed up a mouthful of dust. He blew his nose and looked around. He was in the dry gallery at the southeast corner of the Haram that pushed up to about six feet away from the angle of the Temple wall. His goal, though he did not say it, was to find a way to . . . examine . . . the underneath of the Dome of the Rock from the side. He crouched and made his way up the passage.

When he reached the wall, he found stones exactly like those at the Wailing Wall, which was surprising at that level below the surface. As he brushed and swept away some of the dirt, Warren saw something else he was not expecting.

Words. Or letters? No. Something else. The figures looked Phoenician, though he did not know how to read it, the first language of words.

Painted in red on one of the big stones in front of him were three characters. They looked like the letters O, Y, and Q though he knew that wasn't possible. Not this deep in the ground. Warren could only guess what they were. Were they a sign? A warning? It was well known that Phoenician masons had designed and built Solomon's Temple. Were these marks meant to show where to place the stones? He did not know. Warren took a photograph, but when he had it developed, all he could see was the flame of his candle, which had wandered into the field of view.

Warren consulted an expert in the city named Dr. Julius Henry Petermann, a German. He agreed that they were Phoenician in origin, but did not know what they meant, only that they were a "seal" of some kind. Of what, he did not know. Another expert, Mr. Deutsch, agreed that they were masons' marks to help in the construction of the structure.

The writing greatly puzzled Warren, who did not like being puzzled. They had previously found some Phoenician writing at the south wall, near the underground opening by which the ducts made their exit from the Temple, carrying the refuse from the altar to the valley below. There, Warren had found pottery remains. Some had the sign of the king on them — El Melek — in the Phoenician or Hebrew character.

Twenty-Two

MONTY PARKER

Jerusalem, 1909

Monty walked up the stairs of the Virgin's Fountain and felt the wind whip across his shirt. The afternoon skies were dark, almost green, and the air was heavy. He stopped and looked out over the ridge. Any day now — or really any moment — the rain would come. But not just any afternoon shower, this would be the storm that would begin, end, and then be followed by three days of soft rain. This would repeat, with some clear weeks here and there, until February, when the rainy season would really be uncorked and Palestine would be cool and wet for months. Only in May would the sheets of water taper off, then end, giving room to the sun to parch the ground in July and August, before starting all over again. Every guide and expert had told them this. The Jews even had a name for the first drops: *yoreh.*

Rain was important, especially since they were excavating a tunnel once used to transport water. In the underground mud, rain was not something they could work around. Monty walked over to a tent they had set up outside. They all agreed that they would have to leave once the rains began in earnest. They would close the works and return for England. They would return as soon as they could, after the wet Jerusalem winter.

For only three months' work, they had accomplished quite a bit: not only clearing the stairs and exploring the Dragon Shaft but also starting work on Hezekiah's Tunnel. They had found many new passages and some artifacts, including Jewish flat lamps and sling balls made of metal. They had not found any trace of radium. To their disappointment, they had found nothing in the main tunnel yet. Any hope of a secret channel up to the Temple or a walled-up hiding place had been dashed by every foot of debris removed.

They had not found the Ark yet. Monty was not looking forward to going back to Saltram empty-handed.

Monty had his papers with him, in his folder. He spilled them onto the table, which was already covered with maps and some books. As always, there was the cipher again, almost taunting him. Monty pinched his nose and closed his eyes. Lately, the cipher had become somewhat infuriating. So many of the places they were digging appeared in its pages — the Fountain, the Pool of Siloam, Hezekiah's Tunnel, and Warren's Shaft — but they were almost static; they were destinations without direction. The cipher was so vague that they had to rely on Juvelius's interpretations, which were often just as murky. Juvelius said that abstraction was unavoidable; not only had the text been corrupted over thousands of years, but it was actively trying to throw them off the trail. This was not making things easier, especially with thunder at their doorstep.

Monty opened the pages and read into the layers of the cipher again. The words themselves plunged all the way down from English, to Swedish, to Hebrew, all the way to the apocryphal books etched out on ancient papyrus. And all the old voices and whispers before that. Juvelius claimed to be able to see the differences in these variations and account for them all, balancing them like a parcel of long metal rods clanging against each other as they moved. Monty was not sure how such a thing was possible. Juvelius was going far below the crust of things. Either he would find, as Juvelius claimed, the purest form of the Scripture in the form of the Ark itself, or it would be, in the cipher's own words, what was prophesized in Ezekiel:

And the entrance crooked fasten up /
Its hole (throat?) fortified with curse / the
heap of stones.

Juvelius had been adamant since the beginning that there were dangerous traps awaiting those who sought the Ark. The cipher warned "the infamous deed! Oh! / The lightning of wrath (for) the shamelessness to commit violation / And sudden misfortune strikes the destroyer!" But aside from some precarious rocks here and there, they had not had even a single accident.

The more they explored the main tunnel, and the less they found, Monty began thinking of the mysterious third way to the Ark that Juvelius had mentioned when they first came to Jerusalem. In the cipher, this was represented next to a crude drawing, presumably drawn by Juvelius, of a hand pointed east. Some of his sketches, especially the more geometric ones, seemed important. The passage that followed was one of special mystery:

How? The law / and a special? / Woe, /
    earthly asylums
Close to Molok / hundred steps? / to the
    cave / behold
The shame of the law / and "something"
    in connections!
(for) mark / the water / there in front of
As / the dam / see / the innermost (of
    the) / swells
Sinks / moves violently its water /-(so)
    "shivering?" / seek
The opening
Reach (?) / The staircase in the hole / —
    Not / Babel
(dishonour them) / nevertheless! / (No!)

It was followed by some of Juvelius's own
annotations:

A "special" = Molok!
The shame of the law = Molok
Something = the ark

This passage was also peculiar, claimed Juvelius, because it was protected by a "safety
lock":

Here Ezekiel has decided to give extremely dangerous information. It is in
question the entrance from the valley-side
an entrance which stood open for anyone.

249

> Ezekiel protects it [by] commencing his cipher series not from the letter 7 but allows this letter to contribute the seventh letter in the cipher series 1,2,3,4,5, with the seventh initial letter has been ticked off and taken into account as 7 in the series the safety lock.
>
> Behold the confusion!

Monty at least understood those last three words, if not what came before. The cipher had become almost nonsensical. Who was Molok? Monty knew he had heard that name before. He assumed he might be some sort of pagan idol, like Baal or the golden calf. The cipher had more to say on the subject:

> Molok. Compare in connection with this that in several traditions of the middle ages, the hiding place of the ark is taken in connection with Molok. Molok enters also of course in the mystery of the freemasons at the symbolical searching for the Ark and the law (Melander) Jerusalem's hidden temple treasures.

Monty wondered at these words and what they had to do with the mysterious third way.

He needed some air.

Monty stepped out of the tent and looked around. There were workers about, some of the men, the usual mess. Hoppenrath was in the city; even Uotila was somewhere else. Monty saw Juvelius walking up the same stairs he had just left. Monty motioned him over. Juvelius looked around. Not even Macasdar was around. Monty waved to him again.

Juvelius entered the tent, where it was just Monty and he under its very uncertain roof, which had waves rippling across it because of the wind. They had tried communicating many times to varied outcomes, many of them close to imaginary. But it was not impossible. Juvelius knew English and could read, even write. There were barriers and layers, but Monty would have to try to understand the man directly.

"What's this?" said Monty pointing to the word on the cipher. Juvelius looked down, then looked back up quickly.

"Molech" was how he pronounced it. "M'lek." He spoke something in Swedish, then stopped.

"King," said Juvelius. "*M'lek.* King."

Juvelius saw Monty's Bible on the table and picked it up. He opened and looked at it, with a moment of puzzlement, almost as if his eyes were adjusting to the light. He went through the pages quickly, went back, then forward, then stopped. He pointed to a verse; it was Leviticus 18:21:

And thou shalt not let any of thy seed pass through the fire to Molech, neither shalt thou profane the name of thy God: I am the LORD.

Was Monty wrong? Had Molok been some sort of local warlord? It was one of those words that you recognized and realized it was always there, sitting quietly under the skin of things.

Juvelius went to his bag and took out a book, bound in cracked brown leather. The scholar was never without his books. He went through the pages, much more confidently this time, before laying it open on the table.

There was an illustration, or perhaps a woodcut of a great creature — not a king at all, or at least not a human one. It was colossal in height, with the head of a bull, horns, and soft animal eyes. It stood from the waist up on a hilly countryside, holding out two great outstretched hands. There were open rectangles in its chest. Billows of smoke raised from below.

"Molok," said Juvelius. "Idol."

It was like Baal then, Monty nodded. It was one of the many pagan idols that the Israelites stamped out.

"No," said Juvelius. He knew that Monty was missing his point. He began pointing to the people beneath the beast, who were worshipping it.

"Canaanites. Also, King."

They were the nation of tribal people that had lived in Palestine before the Israelites conquered them. Monty knew that the Bible described them as large, wicked, and strong. They were descended of the House of Noah; specifically, his grandson Canaan, who was a son of Ham. Monty deduced that this Molok was a god they worshipped and sacrificed their oxen to for good harvests, fertility, and protection.

"Where?" asked Monty. Juvelius moved the book to the side and pulled the map into view. He pointed to a small valley right next to them. Hinnom.

The book with the picture had slid closer to Monty. He studied it more closely.

"What are the boxes for?" asked Monty, pointing to the openings in the idol's chest. He asked because they looked to be exactly the size of the Ark. Is this why Molok was mentioned in the cipher? He asked Juvelius again.

"No, no, no," said Juvelius, turning pale. He grabbed Monty's Bible again and found another passage, this time in 2 Kings:

And he defiled Topheth, which is in the valley of the children of Hinnom, that no man might make his son or his daughter to pass through the fire to Molech.

Juvelius pointed to the boxes again, and the twists of smoke rising around them.

"For children," he said. "For children."

■ ■ ■ ■

PART THREE:
THE KING
IN COPPER

■ ■ ■ ■

TWENTY-THREE
NATALIE MAURICE

Jerusalem, March 9, 1910

"Put your slippers on, everyone!"

The Reverend Charles H. Bohner directed his tour group over to the dragoman, who was handing out pairs of flimsy slippers. The American group, around a dozen in total, stood outside in Solomon's Court, in the shadow of the golden arch. The sky was overcast, but the air was warm and close.

"Agnes, your slippers! Come on!"

Natalie Maurice took two pairs from the dragoman. She sat her friend Agnes down on the step and removed her shoes, before easing the slippers onto her feet. It was difficult work because Agnes was so excited.

"We can't miss this!" she said.

Natalie adjusted the fit, then looked up and smiled at her friend. Natalie had light brown hair and gray eyes — and was equally as excited.

"Oh, they're very comfortable," said

Agnes. Natalie laughed.

"Where are you from?" Natalie had asked Agnes when she saw her sitting by herself on the ship. Agnes had blond hair and a round, pleasant face.

"Indiana," said Agnes. Since then, they had become inseparable, industrious sightseers on their once-in-a-lifetime trip. Though Agnes was twice her age, Natalie enjoyed spending time with her and indeed could barely keep up. They had seen incredible sites such as Jericho and the Jordan, and had ridden on horseback through rain and snow.

As Natalie helped her up, Agnes looked over to the rest of the group. Natalie had an idea what she was thinking of. It had been a hard week for all of them. The day before yesterday, an older lady who was part of their number had passed from heart disease. Agnes, and indeed all of them, had taken it hard. She hoped that this particular stop would help buoy their spirits.

"OK, all set. Let's go!" Natalie took Agnes's hand and led her to the group as they filed inside.

They were going into the Dome of the Rock.

When Natalie walked into the enormous, octagonal chamber, it was the curling smoke of the floral incense and the almost impossible height of the place that drew her senses upward. There, suspended above her like a second sky, was the glimmering mosaic of the great dome itself. Tiny, polished cubes of red and ochre, and orange and black, fit together into an overwhelming geometric pattern that seemed too awesome to comprehend in one glance. There must have been a million pieces above them, comprising one perfect dimension.

The honey-colored light from the high lunette window brought Natalie's eyes back to earth, down past more mosaics, and a golden ring of characters she couldn't read, all the way down to the square-cut floor, the burgundy rugs, and rising in front of them, a guardrail. The size of every part seemed related to every other part in some definite proportion, building together to a silent and harmonious chord.

"It's beautiful," said Agnes.

"Come on," said Natalie, pulling her to the front of the group. There were attendants in holy clothing moving slowly through the gallery. As one such man passed by, Natalie made one last push, passing the reverend and his wife. There, she saw it for the first time: the Foundation Stone itself.

The rock was gigantic, far bigger than

Natalie had guessed. It was also quite tall, at least six feet high; she could barely see over its ridge. The color of the rock was elusive; it was clearly made of a light-colored limestone, but in the light from the high windows it became warmer, almost otherworldly. As they stepped closer, she saw a crimson silk suspended over the rock by twelve thin columns. She pulled Agnes, who was oohing and aahing, along the gilded railing.

As they began to circle around it, Natalie saw that the rock's surface was in some places chiseled into rectangular holes, and in others left natural.

"Look!" she whispered. Natalie pointed to a small imprint on the stone. "That's it! When Mohammed began his ascent to heaven, the rock began to fly up with him, until the angel Gabriel held it down." Natalie excitedly pointed to a shallow impression. "That is his handprint!" she said.

"And" she said, trying to remain at least somewhat quiet. "The stone is actually still floating, suspended four feet in the air!"

Agnes looked utterly amazed.

"It's all covered up below." said Natalie.

"How do you know all of this?" asked Agnes.

"Oh, you know. I'm a librarian." Agnes

gave her friend a great smile. It had been their running joke.

As they made their way around the massive stone, Natalie remembered all that she had read, that the Foundation Stone was believed to be the actual place where Abraham sought to sacrifice his son Isaac, only to have his dagger stayed by the Lord's mercy. The first Temple of Solomon had been here. After it was razed by Nebuchadnezzar, it was Herod the Great who rebuilt it into a much larger construction. Natalie couldn't think of Herod without thinking of the story in Matthew of the massacre of the innocents, where Herod ordered all children two years of age and under to be killed, all in an effort to destroy the new-born Jesus, whom he saw as a great threat. Herod's temple was eventually destroyed by the Romans. The Arabs later built the Dome of the Rock directly over it, on the Foundation Stone, making it a holy place for the world's three largest religions.

Natalie and Agnes made their way toward a small structure in the left-hand corner of the room. Nathalie took a breath. She had read about this place for what seemed like such a long time, in her library. She knew where they were going next.

The Well of Souls.

This was the ancient cave that lay hidden under the Foundation Stone. David and Solomon were said to have prayed in this holy place. According to the Talmud, you could still hear the roaring waters of the Flood beneath it. Others said that it was the sound of departed souls, rushing through eternity as winding ghosts, restlessly waiting for Judgment Day.

The reverend got everyone into a line, then looked back at them. "We will go in with the guide at five o'clock," he said. "Just a few more minutes." Because they had tarried at the Foundation Stone, Agnes and Natalie were near the end of the line.

Natalie looked at Agnes. She noticed that her friend had closed her eyes. As Agnes's lips began to move, a shot of terror went through Natalie. She nudged her friend hard in the forearm.

"Ow!"

Natalie looked around to see if any of the Arab attendants had seen. She returned her attention to Agnes and vigorously shook her head no, putting a finger to her lips. Agnes took on a look of fear as she realized her error. The one rule for Christians in the Dome of the Rock had to be observed at all costs. No matter what, Christians were not allowed to do one thing above all others.

They were not allowed to pray.

Instead, Natalie took Agnes's hands in hers and they looked at each other, in a moment of silence.

The reverend checked his watch and nodded. They began walking down a narrow circular stair, passing a somewhat obtrusive outcropping of rock. As they made the turn, they saw a set of flat, broad steps leading into a cave with a low ceiling. Natalie peeked her head down with an excited smile, straining her ears to hear the Waters of Judgment. The dragoman was behind Natalie and Agnes; most of their group had already reached the bottom. The cave was brighter than Natalie had guessed. She could see what looked like a softly lit shrine. Natalie saw a man, an Arab, deep in prayer in the corner of the cave. She cautioned herself to be quiet.

Someone in front of her jumped, and a loud sound boomed though the staircase. Natalie stopped. Her leg, at the thigh, felt warm, as if she had spilled her tea. But she had no tea. Did she? She looked down to see blood on her dress. She had a feeling — pain?

The dragoman began to move past them. Natalie heard another sound — did someone drop something? — and a zing like a bee. A red line appeared — left to right — across the dragoman's face. Agnes screamed.

More shots called out and everyone scattered. Agnes saw the praying man emerge from the bottom of the stairs. He had a gun and was shooting at them. Natalie turned to her friend.

A shot thundered out, Agnes's left eye exploded, and blood sprayed out the opposite side of her nose.

Everyone began to scatter as the sound of more shots filled the small space. A rush of Turkish soldiers drummed down the stairs past them and through them. Agnes was bloody and screaming and Natalie realized she was, too.

The next day, the newspapers reported that Turkish soldiers were able to apprehend the assailant. They roughly dragged him out up the stone steps. His demeanor was very collected. He promptly acknowledged his crime and declared himself beloved of Allah. Authorities determined that he was a native of Afghanistan and had lately returned from a holy pilgrimage to Mecca. The shooter said that he was praying in the cave when a crowd came pushing their way into the room. He was not accustomed to being so disturbed in God's house, he said. The Turkish police, the *kavass,* believed that since the man had been in the city for several days, there was probably some greater plot that might never be known. Another report claimed that the man was praying when he saw that there were Christians in the Temple. He had never seen the infidel in a mosque before, so he fired his gun. Another newspaper stated that the tourists were mocking the man's praying, setting off his murderous anger. There was no trial by jury in Palestine, so the man's fate would be determined by a judge. The authorities said that he would be tortured to induce him to expose his confederates, if he had any.

The mayor expressed a deep detestation of the crime by the miserable fanatic who so ruthlessly shot the two American ladies. He declared his determination to do his utmost to have the severest penalty of the law dealt out to him.

Miss Natalie Maurice, reported the papers, had a flesh wound that was not serious. She would rejoin the tourists in a week or ten days. Miss Agnes Parker-Moore, an heiress, was less fortunate. She had to be taken to the German Hospital. Her left eye was destroyed. There was hope that she might be able to go home in a few weeks' time.

The Dome of the Rock was closed to visitors. The long inscriptions on the inner side of the octagonal arcade — that Natalie did not know the meaning of — stood over the guards below.

Do not exaggerate in your religion.

The Messiah, Jesus son of Mary, was only a Messenger of God.

There is no god, but God alone, without partner.

Saltram House, William Henry Bartlett, c.1832

Montague Parker,
age fifteen

Monty in Jerusalem, c.1909

Ava Astor, c.1910, Frances Benjamin
Johnston Collection, Library of Congress

Valter Juvelius, Jerusalem, 1909

Father Vincent, Jerusalem,
c.1911, photo courtesy of École
Biblique, Jerusalem

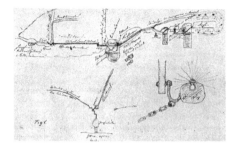

Detail from the Juvelius cipher, c.1909

The Virgin's Fountain, c.1915, G. Eric and Edith Matson
Photograph Collection, Library of Congress

Cyril Foley, c.1890

The Ark of the Covenant by James Tissot, c.1896–1902

Mounted, *from left to right:* Robin Duff, Habib Bey, Monty Parker,
Cyril Foley, Macasdar, Cyril Ward, the Hodja (a holy man), Clarence Wilson

The Illustrated Police News,
October 20, 1888

Bertha Spafford Vester and son John, 1915,
G. Eric and Edith Matson Photograph
Collection, Library of Congress

TOP LEFT: Jacob Spafford,
c.1910, G. Eric and Edith
Matson Photograph
Collection, Library of
Congress

TOP RIGHT: Molok, from
Athanasii Kircheri, *Oedipus
aegyptiacus*, 1652

BOTTOM LEFT: Hezekiah's
Tunnel, where the
workmen met, c.1911,
G. Eric and Edith Matson
Photograph Collection,
Library of Congress

Gehenna and Aceldama, G. Eric and Edith Matson Photograph
Collection, Library of Congress

Temple area, Mosque of Omar [i.e., Dome of
the Rock], c.1910, G. Eric and Edith Matson
Photograph Collection, Library of Congress

Temple area, Mosque of Omar [i.e., Dome
of the Rock], from above, c.1910, G. Eric
and Edith Matson Photograph Collection,
Library of Congress

The Well of Souls, from
*Picturesque Palestine, Sinai
and Egypt*, 1883

Twenty-Four

CHARLES WARREN

Jerusalem, Summer 1869
Forty Years Earlier

Charles Warren sneezed so hard he put his candle out. He was quite sick. After spending the night in a wet tent, he had been overtaken with a dreadful bout of rheumatism and neuralgia affecting his left side. He took it as just another sign that it was time to leave Jerusalem. He had made plenty of discoveries for the PEF, who would be pleased. But there was one last spot he needed to see. And he was looking right at it, though he was not sure what it was exactly.

Jerusalem had experienced some political upheaval of late, so Warren had finally been kicked out of his tunnels. He had taken the opportunity to meet with the governor-general of Syria. Warren was surprised that the governor was a brother Mason, and they had many subjects of common interest, including his digging near the quarries of King Solomon, near the Temple. The governor greatly approved of and encouraged Warren's work in this area.

The pasha was eventually removed from his Jerusalem post and replaced by someone who did not seem to have as fixed an eye on Warren's digging. Warren and Sergeant Birtles took advantage of the cover and began excavating on the side of the Kidron Valley, under the Moslem cemetery outside the wall of the Haram. Warren looked out over the crumbled graveyard. The only people there were the blind men, who were paid by sad widows to come every day and mourn for them.

Warren knew this was a dangerous undertaking, for many reasons: not only because bodily harm was possible in such a fragile place but also because if they disturbed or exposed even one grave, or scraped a single shroud, the resentment of the people would know no bounds. They would be run out of town, if not worse. Warren made sure to use special gallery frames to support the tunnels below. As he and Birtles dug underneath the cemetery, they always kept one eye on the ceiling of earth above them, looking for linen or toes.

Near the wall, in the underground, Warren

found a strange slit in the rock about eighteen inches wide and four inches high. He dropped a stone into it — it looked exactly like a London mail slot — and heard the pebble rattle away for several feet down into somewhere unknown. He called Birtles, and they chiseled for a few hours underneath the slit, finally breaking through into a passage.

Warren tried to concentrate. He was still shivering. As he moved his candle, he realized what the slot was for. The opening was not for mail (or pebbles), but had been a means of letting light in.

"Ingenious," he said.

He looked in and saw a forty-five-degree slope downward. Holding his walking stick for balance, Warren slid down about twelve feet to a flat surface. He winced in pain. As he stood up, a shadow of his head was cast onto the rock before him. It was an eerie feeling.

"A roof," said Warren, aloud. "I'm standing on a roof."

He broke through into another passage. The passage or gallery ran east and west and was two feet wide. It seemed to be almost eight feet tall at one point, but much of the old floor had been removed. Warren looked back west: there were three large circular holes carved into the rock. He knew that way would go all the way to the Birket Israel, the huge cistern outside the wall of the city. To the east — here he turned his head back — was the Temple. There was an opening there, almost four feet high. He was deep underground, but he knew exactly where he was on the map.

Warren then spied something. On the stone wall was a mark, not that unlike the red Phoenician letters. But this was different. It was the unmistakable shape of a Christian cross of the Byzantine period. He ran his finger over it, and then started searching around furiously.

He had missed something. He knew it.

There, to the north of the tunnel, Warren saw a dark shadow that he had previously taken at face value. As he crept closer, he saw that it was a hidden opening, about two feet wide. He came closer and saw, to his amazement, a staircase leading upward. He took a moment to orient himself; he was standing near the Haram.

He was looking upon things not on any map.

Warren grabbed his walking stick and plunged it into the darkness above the stairs. As predicted, it was filled with the usual mixture of stones and dirt. Warren kept fiercely stabbing the stick again and again, but the material began to come down with such great force that it not only further blocked the entry but threatened to bury him alive.

Warren inched back and leaned on his staff. There was no way up. He felt both angry and even further intrigued. He allowed himself the thought that, wherever the secret stair led, articles — such as the Ark — could have been concealed there at the time of the Temple's destruction.

Warren knew that between the cemetery, the nonexistent entryways, the deep slope, and the blocked stairs, they could not bring people down to clear the stairs. And they couldn't sink another shaft. This way, at least, was closed to him.

Warren made a note of it in his book, tarried a moment, then left the strange labyrinth and the mark of the cross behind.

Twenty-Five

FATHER VINCENT

Jerusalem, Spring 1910

It had been one of the longest winters of Father Vincent's life, not because of the weather, but because of the waiting. When Monty and his men — most the same, but some new, and some gone, never to be seen again — finally returned in spring 1910, there was no one happier to see them than Father Vincent. This time, the Englishmen brought new machinery with them, of a kind Father Vincent had not yet seen. The recent shootings still hung in the air, leaving everything in the region on a teetering edge. Even the stormy weather had still not entirely dissipated.

Over the past several months, Father Vincent had been studiously planning for his reentry into the tunnels. He knew that they were only a few weeks short of finally being able to fully explore the major conduit of the labyrinth: Hezekiah's Tunnel itself.

The gangs started right away, divided into two teams: one entered at the Virgin's Fountain, and the other at the Pool of Siloam. They worked for eight hours without pause, hauling out buckets of stuff. When Father Vincent went down among them, he was filled with happiness. The close air and bustle of the hearty workers produced an environment that was only barely tolerable for human beings. Father Vincent reveled in it.

As they removed debris to carve a way in, they were also digging down to the tunnel's true depth. Finally, one of the teams reached the original floor, having pared it down to the rock itself. In doing so, the height of the tunnel was raised up nearly an entire meter. This helped things along tremendously, and within a fortnight the two teams were able to work within earshot of one another, somewhere near the middle of the tunnel. The poetic nature of this was not lost on Father Vincent. The Bible said that Hezekiah had also ordered two teams to dig from each side to meet somewhere in between. In many ways, they had reenacted the very actions of the ancients they were trying to understand.

When they finally cleared it all the way through, the artifacts and scraps that had littered the galleries were still nowhere to be seen.

The secret tunnel of Hezekiah was empty, scraped down to its cold floor. And they had found nothing. Father Vincent was astonished. He stared down the passageway that looked like a black rectangular door.

When he returned outside, Captain Parker was slouched against a chair. They had accomplished a significant archaeological feat: they had diverted the spring and completely cleaned out the legendary tunnel. Warren had not even come close to doing this. Yet the Englishmen looked like they would just as soon go home. But not Father Vincent. He knew there were still secrets there. This was the tunnel where the Siloam inscription had been found. It needed the attention it deserved.

Father Vincent attempted to smooth out his dirty habit, took off his hat, and approached the men.

"Captain Parker, if I may?"

"Father," he nodded, his pipe held fast.

"Since the tunnel is finally open, might I be allowed to make a detailed plan of it?"

Captain Parker regarded *le petit saint* against the bright sun. Father Vincent knew that the English were disappointed. But this — the chance to measure out the tunnel free of water, brigand, or beast — had probably never happened since it was first carved.

Captain Parker offered to keep the tunnel open and not let the water through until Father Vincent was done with his inspection. Father Vincent shook Captain Parker's hand vigorously and almost sprinted off, once again struck by the obliging natures of the explorers.

The next day, armed with his tools, Father Vincent walked down the familiar steps. From September 26 to October 8, he had free rein of a tunnel that, save for a lonely puddle here and there, was completely cleared out. It was surely strange, thought Father Vincent. He hauled in instruments of all sorts: graduated rulers, water levels, graphometers, and even a portable darkroom. Father Savignac took detailed photographs of the tunnel, but mostly Father Vincent was on his own. Mostly, he was free.

They may have found little in the way of more pots and lamps, but there were still other mysteries. There were markings, he supposed you could call them. Father Vincent had found more of the hollow triangles that first appeared in one of the galleries. They were so asymmetrical, so capricious, that their meaning continued to elude him. Father Vincent could not reduce them, even summarily, to either old or modern numerical systems. Why hollow triangles, instead of the simple arrowhead? The difficult labor of chiseling a symbol into stone did not usually indulge extra work. He studied them for hours. He couldn't understand why there were also squares, some three and a half to four centimeters long. And these marks — whatever they were — could not be for measurement. They were the most inconvenient shapes possible with which to measure things when a simple line would have been so much easier. It felt like the Architect — the past — was taunting him. It felt personal.

Father Vincent decided to tackle the overall question instead. He turned and walked down the length of the tunnel, took his measurements, and then walked back and did it again. He repeated this process several times. There was a curve to the tunnel that he could almost pace off blindfolded. He walked to the middle again, where the passage swerved to the side.

He stopped. He was puzzled. Something was happening.

Father Vincent looked down at his map. The tunnel moved east to west like a snake and then shifted north to south. The northern curve had ostensibly been made to avoid a well under the town, allowing for people to draw their water in security or for the possibility of striking another spring someday. That made sense. But it was impossible to find any sign of an opening to a well in the whole length of the aqueduct. Father Vincent tested his sandal against the ground.

There was another dimension to this puzzle. The tunnel was also moving up and down.

Father Vincent then realized what he had missed. Though there were the normal variations one might expect on the floor of the tunnel, it was the unequal heights at both ends that were exceedingly strange. One would expect that a tunnel commenced with such spacious grandeur would gradually get smaller as it penetrated farther into the heart of the rock, but here it was quite the contrary. It was clear that the roof gradually sunk lower and lower toward the entrance. Had the floor sunk over time? Closer examination of the floor revealed violent gashes, especially at the openings of some of the galleries. Was this the work of the Architect? Why?

Father Vincent walked near the place of the meeting, the fateful turn where they knew the two gangs met — from opposite directions — in Hezekiah's time. He pressed his ear to the wall. He knew that others had heard the sound of running water here, even though there was clearly no fissure. He could hear it. It was similar to the sound heard in the cave when the Virgin's Well was active and loud: almost like boiling water for tea in a pot instead of a kettle, sounding far out of proportion to the actual amount of water moving behind it.

The key question was if gang A started at the fountain, how did they meet up with gang B from the Pool of Siloam if they had to avoid the water and were digging at different levels? Father Vincent liked explanations. But he was not finding any easy ones. He stood there, in the black tunnel, and thought about what he knew and what he didn't and what might explain that space of in between.

The solution jumped at him. It was the water. The Israelites did not have the technology to divert it as they did, so when it rose, their work became faster, sloppier, and the tunnel floor got higher. Only when the water naturally retreated could they fix these areas by lowering the floor. Father Vincent could almost see it in his mind, these Israelites, in leather and cloth, picking the tunnel out against the clock of an invasion by the Assyrians. The northern gang seemed to work faster in the water, slinging their picks with abandon, while the southern gang was more methodical. How wonderful was the past, thought Father Vincent. They probably knew perfectly well that the floor was too high, but they kept on because they knew it would be easier to correct later.

Father Vincent, with his eyes open, pictured their meeting. At the end, they were probably only about ten feet apart. They were shouting to each other. The clubs and axes opened a small opening, which was attacked with greater zeal. When the wall between them finally came down, a break between here and there, success and failure, truth and disguise, they must have cheered as they tore it down with abandon, not mattering the floor beneath them. The water was coming, as was the enemy.

Father Vincent realized that once the tunnels were finally joined, the gangs had to turn their attention to the ground and level it so that the water, when it came, would flow in a direct route. But that was a few days' work at most. The incredible scope of what these men had accomplished filled Father Vincent with awe. They had adapted to a changing geography and turned a plan into reality by their wits and will because the stakes were life itself. Father Vincent thought of the Master Architect and realized that his genius — his miracle — was that he was capable of being imperfect. He was just a man.

"They had driven a tunnel under a hill and saved a kingdom," Father Vincent said to himself. "No wonder they marked it with an inscription."

Father Vincent thought of the Siloam inscription, found by a young boy. The inscription he had read so many times that he knew it by heart:

Behold the excavation! Now this is the history of the tunnel. While the excavators were lifting up the pick, each toward the other; and while there were yet three cubits to be broken through . . . the voice of the one called to his neighbor, for there was an excess in the rock on the right. They rose up . . . they struck on the west of the excavation, the excavators struck, each to meet the other, pick to pick. And there flowed the waters from their outlet to the pool for a distance of a thousand cubits; and of a cubit was the height of the rock over the head of the excavation here.

The inscription was not about God, but the good works of men. The practical, scientific, imperfect works of men.

Walking back, Father Vincent paused and looked back at the stairs again. There was that gap, just under the last step. After breaking through a portion of it, Father Vincent saw a new conduit that penetrated under the stairway and led into a small cavern. He shimmied through and looked up to see a rocky step. Father Vincent sifted his hands through the ground. The floor was dust and sand. There were potsherds, but not a fragment was intact, not one showed a trace of pattern, though they all looked ancient.

Near the back of the dark cave, Father Vincent's fingers struck something. He carefully rescued the rough fragments of a fairly thick earthenware piece. It looked to have been a vessel of some sort, most likely a bowl or cup. He examined it there, on the ground, in the dark: it was reddish, perhaps even yellow, and not elegant in its working. The inside was glazed, though crudely. The piece had been baked very unevenly and was not the work of a skilled potter, which he could tell by feeling its sides. Father Vincent was confident in dating the piece, conservatively, to the ninth century BC, in the pre-Canaanite period.

On the north side of the basin, Father Vincent found an Israelite lamp in excellent condition, and certainly as old as the eleventh century BC. So many different peoples had used these tunnels — for water, for battle, and for worship, in many faiths.

As he tarried in the cave, Father Vincent could hear the rush of water building. Soon, they would release their dam and it would all work again, as it did all those years ago. The water from this spring would end up in the Pool of Siloam. He thought, as he often had in these tunnels, of John 9.

And as Jesus passed by, he saw a man which was blind from his birth. And his disciples asked him, saying, Master, who did sin, this man, or his parents, that he was born blind? Jesus answered, Neither hath this man sinned, nor his parents: but that the works of God should be made manifest in him. I must work the works of him that sent me, while it is day: the night cometh, when no man can work. As long as I am in the world, I am the light of the world. When he had thus spoken, he spat on the ground, and made clay of the spittle, and he anointed the eyes of the blind man with the clay. And said unto him,

Go, wash in the pool of Siloam. He went his way therefore, and washed, and came seeing.

Father Vincent sighed and smiled. He thought of what was going to happen very soon.

"Water," said Father Vincent. "The gift of life. Now we are ready to give it."

A few days later, Father Vincent surrendered the tunnel back to Captain Parker. He had books of drawings, notes, and photographs — enough to perhaps write a book someday. But he knew he might never return to these tunnels, at least as they were now. He was very grateful.

"Did you find anything?" asked Monty.

"You will receive my report, Captain. Beyond that, there is one thing I wanted to show you." He pulled out one of his latest attempts at a map, done in graphite and red, accompanied by a flowing script.

"Look here," he pointed to an overhead rendition of the Tunnel with its telltale curve. "We know it was meant to connect the Virgin's Fountain and the Pool of Siloam, which is from here to here, as you know." Here he drew a straight line between the two destinations, which the curvy tunnel did not follow. "I had thought that the

283

northern part of the tunnel bent due to the presence of a well, or another spring, or just the natural cut of the living rock. But I was wrong."

"You were wrong?"

"It happens. Yes. I believe that this curve was intentional. That the diggers deliberately avoided this area. I believe there was something there that they weren't allowed to touch." Here he circled the bulge missed by the Tunnel.

"What do you think is there?" asked Monty, his eyes flashing.

"A tomb," said Father Vincent.

TWENTY-SIX

BERTHA VESTER

Jerusalem, 1910

That night, Bertha went up to the rooftop. It was always a bit of a scramble, but it was worth the effort. Their location on the city wall afforded a magnificent vantage point: the Dome, now dark, and the stars above her seemed to glint with the same cord of light. The view was nearly unearthly. Bertha took a deep breath and did what she frequently did on these nighttime trips; she thought of her father. She felt close to him here.

Horatio Vester had been gone for many years, but he was still a powerful motivation for the Colony's efforts in Jerusalem. Bertha knew that he would be proud of all they had accomplished. The American Colony now ran a gift shop and a hotel, raised pigs, and had started a studio of photography. They taught handicrafts, made dresses and tailored suits, and funneled their profits into their philanthropy.

Because of the Colony's new reach, they had attracted many visitors. A few years ago, a man with a dark beard and a stoop to his neck asked to see the view from the roof. He was H. Rider Haggard, the author of *King Solomon's Mines* and the other adventures of Allan Quatermain. Bertha watched quietly as he gazed on the golden Dome. There were plenty of other renowned visitors, but Bertha, like her father before her, was drawn to the misfit characters, the outsiders, who had come seeking answers.

With the archaeological dig still in full swing on Mount Ophel, she had been thinking lately of one such man, Mr. Moses. He was a trader in rare antiquities and operated a small store in Jerusalem. He would look for ancient manuscripts in secret storefronts hidden behind rolled-down canvas doors. He would creep among the dusty hills looking for relics and inscriptions. He returned from one such trip with some ancient Canaanite idols he found in a cave somewhere in Moab. They were praised as an extraordinary find. Before they were announced to the archaeological world, Jacob's school was given the rare honor of displaying them. Jacob, who had been so excited at the prospect of seeing these important artifacts, took one look and quickly averted his eyes. The pagan idols were depicted in very specific anatomical positions.

Bertha laughed. Her brother Jacob was now a beloved teacher in the school and still looked at his shoes when she told the story. Mr. Moses was later discovered to have produced a scroll of great importance that the experts decried as fake. That part of the story ended quite awfully.

Bertha looked out at the stars, trying not to think of it. Whenever she saw a shooting star, she thought of Miss Poole, another of her father's favorites. She was quite a character, a charming, if eccentric, little Englishwoman who read astrology charts for tourists in Jerusalem. She would often engage in long, intelligent conversations with Bertha's father. Miss Poole would sometimes come to the Colony and stay for three days to make a particular point (and to enjoy the food). But she was welcome. They all were. One night, a huge meteor hurtled from the sky and landed right in front of Miss Poole's door. She called for Horatio and the men of the Colony came and moved the steaming rock, the very firmament of heaven, so that she might rejoin the world in her hoopskirt and curls.

Bertha felt close to her father when she thought of these stories. Mostly because of his credo, that their mission was to help others, not convert them. Her father's story was well-known to the public, but sometimes Bertha went through it in her mind, like a prayer. Horatio Spafford was a real estate lawyer, but the Great Chicago Fire took away his business. He and his wife, Anna, and their four darling girls finally found their way back and scheduled a trip to Europe to celebrate. A pressing business matter caused Horatio to stay home, giving them a promise to join them in England. His wife and daughters set off without him.

On November 22, 1873, at two o'clock in the morning and halfway across the Atlantic, their boat, the *Ville du Havre,* collided with another steamer, the *Loch Earn,* and sank, taking 226 souls with her. Her father waited for any news of survivors in a daze. He finally received a telegram from Anna in England. It carried only two words: "Saved alone."

Once they were back in Chicago, her parents plunged into religious charities to keep themselves from going mad with grief. They welcomed a new son, Horatio, but he tragically died of scarlet fever. Her father could not understand: what had he or his young wife done that they should be so afflicted by such pain? Horatio felt that people's eyes were looking at him in peculiar ways, wondering what abominable thing he had done. The Puritan strain of their Protestant congregation was strong in the Old Testament. Many of them believed that sickness or sorrow were the direct result of sin. One was the just retribution of the other.

Her father searched for answers in the Bible, but he still could not reconcile this harsh tenet of retribution with his concept of Christian teachings. He told Bertha that he remembered Christ's answer to the disciples when they asked whose sin it was, the parents' or the man's, that caused him to be born blind; Jesus answered that it was neither, but that the works of God should be made manifest in him.

Bertha's father was convinced that God was kind and that he would see his children again in heaven. This promise calmed his heart. He sailed on a boat to the exact place where his daughters had fallen into the sea. He wrote to his sister, Rachel, of his experience there:

On Thursday last we passed over the spot where the boat went down, in mid-ocean, the water three miles deep. But I do not think of our dear ones there. They are safe, folded, the dear lambs, and there, before very long, shall we be too.

He wrote a hymn to commemorate the moment, "It Is Well with My Soul." When he returned to America, Horatio voiced his views openly, and was removed from the church. Distraught with the constant ridicule and judgments, he took his family to Palestine to better live a life devoted to God. When they arrived, their new daughter Bertha was only three years old.

Bertha, now grown, smiled at the story, though it still brought her sadness. She looked out onto the city, the dark sky, and the tiny pinpricks of light behind it all.

Twenty-Seven
CHARLES WARREN

Jerusalem, November 1870
Forty Years Earlier

Charles Warren was riding back to Jerusalem from Jaffa when he was met by a wrapped-up Bedouin on his horse in the middle of the dirt road. Warren slowed his pace. Thieves were not uncommon here. The man was stopped directly in his path, as if waiting for him. As Warren rode closer, the man pulled down the covering on his face and greeted him.

"Effendi," he said.

Warren breathed a sigh of relief. After preliminaries were exchanged, Warren found out that the man had indeed been waiting specifically for him. Warren had been in Jerusalem for so long, digging in the ground, that he had garnered something of a reputation. Strangers were always coming to him with leads on artifacts and caves. This time was no different.

"There is a stone, across the Jordan," said the man. "A black stone."

Only this time, Warren knew exactly what the Bedouin meant. The Moabite Stone had been discovered nearly by accident in August 1868 by an Anglican pastor named F. A. Klein in a very desolate part of the Dibon. Standing nearly a meter tall, the stone was covered with thirty-three lines of writing, in Phoenician, and was almost completely intact. It was, for Warren and those like him, a find of incalculable worth. When Warren first learned of it a year ago, he was told that the Prussians were trying to negotiate its sale, possibly through a local antiquities dealer named Moses Shapira. Knowing that the addition of another party would almost certainly end in disaster, Warren decided not to interfere. A year later, he was told that the French were involved via a colleague and competitor, the young and talented Charles Clermont-Ganneau. Warren notified the British Museum and offered to act as their agent in any possible negotiations but received no reply.

"What happened?" asked Warren.

"The stone," the Bedouin said. "It is broken."

Warren's face and spirits fell. He grieved,

mourned even, for just a moment, before his instincts took over. He had to act fast.

"Have they taken a squeeze?" He was referring to the process whereby special paper was moistened and placed over an inscription to create a negative image that could then be read and transcribed.

"The French tried," said the Bedouin, "but they failed."

There was still a chance, then. Warren produced some squeeze paper from his bag and gave it to the man, telling him to apply it to any of the broken pieces of stone, or the whole if by some chance it remained intact. As the Bedouin rode off, Warren allowed himself a little bit of hope that this ancient wonder was not lost to the world forever.

A few days later, the man returned to see Warren at his house in Jerusalem. He produced a tattered squeeze. Warren quickly set it on the table and hunched over it, reading. But something was wrong; it was not Phoenician, but Nabataean. Warren straightened up and looked at the man. The Bedouin put his head in his hands. He knew his ruse had not worked.

"The stone is gone, effendi. Broken! They have buried the pieces to help the crops. I thought this other might be a substitute."

He looked physically hurt.

"Wait!" The man rummaged on his person. He stretched out his arm and turned up his hand. There, on his palm, was a small chunk of black basalt rock. He turned it over to reveal a single inscribed character. It was Phoenician; it was a piece of the stone.

The Bedouin explained to Warren that the tribe who had the stone had been put under immense pressure by the local and even higher governments to sell it to the Germans or French. This had so exasperated them that they put a fire under the stone. Then, they threw cold water on it, and it cracked into pieces. They took the bits and put them in different places in the fields and granaries to act as blessings. "They say that without the stone," said the Bedouin, "a blight will fall upon their crops."

Warren absorbed this new information. It was indeed a tragedy but there were still avenues left to them. He sent the man back after further remains of the real stone. Warren thought for a moment, and then decided to pay a visit to Clermont-Ganneau, who was also in Jerusalem.

He told him everything. His colleague took the news in silence. Even though they were competitors in the hunt, they shared the underlying ethos of the archaeologist that preservation was more important than anything.

After listening to Warren's words, Clermont-Ganneau had a bit of a smirk on his lips.

"The squeeze your friend said had failed? The one done by the French?" He directed Warren to a table filled with squeeze sheets of various sizes — all of the Moabite Stone!

"Not so bad, I think," he said.

Warren was very pleased. The squeeze was imperfect, and in fragments, but it existed. Clermont-Ganneau explained that he had, just a few weeks ago, sent an Arab to try to make a squeeze of the stone with the tribe's permission. But permission did not come easily. Apparently, when the Beni-Hami-Deh tribe finally gave their approval, a fight broke out while the paper was still wet. Clermont-Ganneau's man feared for his life, so he ripped off the paper when it was still wet, tearing it to pieces. He jumped onto his horse and sped off, clutching the remains of the squeeze, which he held on to even as one of the tribesmen struck him with a spear in the leg.

"It is not perfect," Clermont-Ganneau said, touching the papers. "There is much missing." It was then that Warren showed him his rock. It fit into one of the spaces.

They agreed to work together.

Warren's Bedouin friend returned sometime later with two squeezes of two of the larger fragments. Warren was impressed; they were of an excellent quality. The man then dumped out a small bag with a total of twelve small pieces of rock, each with at least one letter on them. Warren was ecstatic and praised his friend.

Warren went to Clermont-Ganneau and gave him what he had in hopes of filling in the gaps of the imperfect French squeeze. Clermont-Ganneau made copies of the rocks and offered to give Warren a translation of them. Warren said there were still more to find.

As they sat in the office and examined the new pieces, Warren noticed something curious. Clermont-Ganneau's own Bedouin appeared to have come that same morning with squeezes of some of the fragments Warren had just received. What's more, they appeared to be taken with Warren's own squeeze paper.

Warren talked to his Bedouin later about it. The man told him that the tribe was negotiating with everyone who was coming in looking for pieces of the stone. Clermont-Ganneau's man had money, and there was a lot of dealing happening on all sides.

Warren informed Clermont-Ganneau of this business, and they agreed to pool their resources. Warren wished he had money to buy some of the larger pieces, but he had still not yet heard from the British Museum.

As the two men worked at assembling the ancient puzzle, an article appeared in the London *Times* announcing the discovery of the Moabite Stone. The letter, from the head of the Palestine Exploration Fund, gave credit to Warren for finding the stone and even intimated that his actions resulted in its breakage. The article portrayed him as undercutting the Germans and the French in a mad competition to seize the stone for himself. When Warren read it, he was furious. None of it was true.

Warren slumped in the chair in Clermont-Ganneau's office.

"I never did that," he said. "Whether the stone got to Berlin, London, or Paris was a small matter compared with the rescuing of the inscription from oblivion. If any jealousy had existed between us, we might neither of us have done anything!"

Warren was not interested in false attribution or claims, nor did he want to make enemies of his fellow archaeologists. The truth was vital to their collective work. He drew up his resignation from the PEF but then wrote to the newspapers, and an apology was given. Clermont-Ganneau and he eventually resumed their work and soon published. Clermont-Ganneau did the very delicate translation.

The story of the Moabite Stone was narrated by King Mesha of Moab, who gave praise to Chemosh, his god. The stone listed King Mesha's many powerful accomplishments from dedicating sanctuaries and building strong fortifications to waging ongoing war against the Israelites, who had oppressed Moab. Chemosh told the king to take Nebo from Israel, so he attacked at night and killed all seven thousand of their men. King Mesha then took the Israelite women and devoted them to Chemosh. He took the vessels of YHWH and offered them before his dark god. Chemosh then told him to go down, make war, and take it all. Clermont-Ganneau's translation of King Mesha's response was direct and powerful. "And I assaulted it," the king said, "and I took it, for Chemosh."

Warren knew that the stone held implicit value not because of its composition or age, but because its inscription did not merely confirm but added to the world's knowledge of the Bible. Specifically, Mesha's story took a viewpoint opposite that of 2 Kings. In the biblical version, Israel wins the final battle with King Mesha and destroys Moab. King Mesha is so desperate at the end of this battle that he takes his first-born son and drags him to the top of the wall. The passage 2 Kings 3:27 recounts how it all ended: "Then he took his eldest son that should have reigned in his stead, and offered him for a burnt offering to Chemosh upon the wall."

The recovery of the Moabite Stone was an international news story. Warren himself wrote about it with exuberant reverence:

> Hardly any discovery has ever been made which has excited so widely extended an interest as the Moabite Stone. Other graffiti, such as those of Assyria, are found year by year, which bear more or less directly upon Jewish history, and are published in journals without producing an interest at all proportionate to their real value. The great and immediate excitement produced by this record of King Mesha is due chiefly, of course, to the utterly unexpected nature of the discovery and the publicity given [it].

But its meaning, because of its archaic nature, had to be mediated through experts.

Though Warren and Clermont-Ganneau had done the first real work on the stone, they had a competitor, the German professor Konstantine Schlottman, who had recovered a single fragment of it. He offered his own analysis in the press of who Chemosh was:

> The name Chemosh has reference to his taming, compelling power. Any one might suppose . . . that he was only nominally different from Jehovah: Chemosh is angry with his people; he delivers them into the hands of their enemies; he again looks mercifully on them. He drives Mesha's enemies from before his face and he speaks in the same manner as Jehovah. But the wrath of Chemosh was like his mercy, blind and fitful; not like the wrath of Jehovah, a symbol of that true Divine energy by which an eternal moral order is preserved.

The black Moabite Stone, glued together from broken fragments, with the spaces between filled in, ended up in the Louvre, displayed next to the pastiche squeeze that helped the world understand it.

Sometime later, when Warren finally returned to London, less dusty but with a lingering rheumatism, he went to the South Kensington Museum to take a glance at some of the artifacts he had sent the museum from Palestine. Warren was shocked by what he found. The items were all crowded together on old shelves, without a ticket or docket to identify them. It looked like the dusty corner of someone's garden shed. As Warren stood there, an older lady walked in. She looked around and seemed like she wanted to ask a question. Warren stood at attention, ready for her inquiry when she walked right past him to the policeman in the corner.

"Is the Moabite Stone here?" she asked, sweetly.

"Oh, yes, mum, I will show it to you," said the policeman. He proceeded to point out a morsel of a Hamath hieroglyph to her eager eyes.

"Oh!" she said, excited.

Warren did not make a fuss, only in his own mind. He felt, quite rightly, that the entire collection ought to be properly laid out. The pieces of pottery should have their own labels, at the very least. On one particular specimen, he found, to his dismay, "Carved wood from the Temple of Jerusalem," when the truth was that it was from a house at Jericho, from around the fourth or fifth century BC. And he would know; he had found it.

As he walked out in the mist of the afternoon, Warren thought, this should not be. But how could it be helped? He knew that the people did not spontaneously fill the coffers of the fund, and so the results from the excavations had to be carried about from place to place to make money. It was nobody's fault, he thought. Someday, perhaps, a greater museum might be established. Yes, he thought, feeling better about the state of things, at least in the future. Jerusalem must yet be laid bare and examined further anyway, he thought, so perhaps not for ten, or maybe twenty years.

Monty stopped reading and put the book down. His eyes were tired. Warren was difficult to make sense of, even on a good day. Monty was thinking about those stairs in the cipher. But not really the stairs.

He was thinking about where they might lead.

Twenty-Eight

CYRIL FOLEY

Pool of Siloam, October 1910

Cyril Foley ran his fingers through his already tousled hair in a doomed attempt at grooming.

"What do you say, Walsh?" he said, showing his best side.

Walsh seemed at a loss, but then began trying to rouse the dust from his own hair.

"There he is," said Cyril. "The mayor of Silwan."

The mayor arrived, whom they all knew, clearly commanding a field of respect on this important day. He had come to celebrate the grand occasion of the reopening of the Virgin's Fountain. Now that the tunnel was clear, they had fixed and altered the cistern with some cement and — thanks to Walsh's ingenuity — were going to turn the water on so that the spring could function again. This project had not been on their official list of Syndicate objectives, but Cyril was quite glad they had done it anyway. Today was going to be a fine day.

His eyes scanned the ridge. They had been told to be on the lookout for strange men in the area. There were rumors that the wealthy French banker Baron Edmond de Rothschild may have taken an interest in their digging. Cyril knew that most paranoid notions about money or treasure seemed to always concern a Rothschild.

"Did I ever tell you I know Lord Rothschild?" Cyril said. He was referring to Leopold de Rothschild, head of the British branch of the famous family and cousin to the French baron.

"I hunted with the Whaddon Chase after Cambridge, and the Lord and Lady Rothschild lived close by. They often participated. They were most kind and hospitable." He looked up the hill and squinted.

"One night," continued Cyril, "I was at a party at the castle with a friend when the debutantes entered from the left, their eyes watching the floor. The ladies were, of course, introduced by their full names. First was a Miss Arabella McGinty followed by Miss Arethusa McGinty. Now, twins are not that uncommon, but it was the girl after that — who looked very much like the previous two — who was making things interesting. 'There can't be three of them, can there?' my friend asked. 'Impossible,' I replied.

"Of course, it was then that Miss Araminta McGinty was announced, and we could barely control our laughter. When Miss Annabella McGinty was introduced next, we completely broke down."

Cyril had returned to Palestine in time to finish the cleaning out of the tunnel and to get ready for this grand event. Unfortunately, because of obligations at home, he could stay only a month. But perhaps that was just fine. They had not found the Ark. He would miss his little island, the one in his head, but he imagined it would have its own problems, in the end. Terrible bugs or something.

The mayor of Silwan and his villagers were assembled at the Pool of Siloam. At a given signal, the wall at Gihon that was holding back the water was going to be blown up, and the water was going to rush into the pool. That was the plan.

"You better be right on this," said Cyril to Walsh. "Or they might remember that hospital we were supposed to build."

The signal for the dynamite was going to be the firing of a shotgun by one of their men, Thompson.

BOOM!

Out of the corner of his eye, Cyril saw Monty jump at the blast, much like he himself just had. The shotgun echoed through the old valley. He could feel his hands shaking.

Silence.

Cyril took a breath. At any minute, they would hear the dynamite blow, and the water would come gushing into the pool from the tunnel, making them immortal heroes in Silwan for giving the locals a newly restored place to wash their clothes.

Any minute now.

The mayor was smiling and had apparently no clue what was going on. They all started to edge, step by step, toward the pool, but there was still no water. Monty gave a nod and one of the men took off to see what was happening. Monty then smiled at the mayor and moved in to shake his hand. It would be any minute now.

Five minutes passed, then ten. At fifteen or so, Cyril began to laugh somewhat uncontrollably. This did not go over well. He looked over at Thompson, who was somehow still holding the shotgun in some feeble gesture of hope.

"Did I ever tell you my shotgun story?" asked Cyril. Walsh may have groaned. Not another one.

"I was in Africa. In Kimberley, which we called the Diamond City because it, well, had so many diamonds. So, on one dark and rainy night, there was a robbery at the post office. Someone had broken a small window and stolen two or three mailbags. The problem was that the bags were filled with a monthly shipment of registered letters — that were all stuffed with diamonds.

"A friend of mine, J. B. Currie, had a poor boy staying with him who soon became a suspect as he suddenly began paying off debts and making plans to return to England. In fact, he was on the boat ready to sail, when J.B. and the detectives boarded and searched his luggage. But no diamonds. My friend and the law felt mighty small as this was just some kid. They left the boat and as it began to drift out, the boy just couldn't help himself and said, over the rail, 'You forgot to check my gun!'

"J.B. put his arm out over the water, caught the boat, and stopped it long enough for the detectives to board. The kid had an old double-barreled shotgun — and both barrels were chockablock with tiny sparkling diamonds.

"True story," said Cyril. "The boy got five years' hard, but J.B. took it worse because he found out he had stolen for his old mom. It was rank stupidity, madness, bravado — call it what you like. But can you beat it?"

Cyril laughed a bit, as he always did after his little stories. He looked up to see Walsh looking right at him.

"Was that before the raid?" Walsh asked.

"Yes, yes." Cyril seemed disarmed.

"What was that like?" his friend asked, quietly.

"I haven't told you about it? Not too much to tell. I went to Africa on a shooting expedition and ended up a mounted policeman. Sounds like me, right? It had gotten a little bit better there when suddenly they found gold in the Transvaal. The British wanted it, so Cecil Rhodes, the governor — and also the largest man I have ever met; he drank stout and champagne from a silver tankard, like a bloody Viking — hatched a plan. He thought he could provoke an insurrection among the unhappy Utlanders so that they might need some English assistance, giving us a path to the gold. Dr. Jameson set up a plan — a raid — to get in and cause just enough trouble to light the fire.

"Naturally, I signed up. In fact, I was only the sixteenth living person to hear of it. I have to say, it takes a lot to take your breath away when you are in good health and only twenty-five years of age, but that cockamamie plan did it. They said we would be disavowed by England if we were caught, but that was enough for me. 'Put my name down right now,' I said.

"We marched toward Johannesburg. Halfway down, Dr. Jameson was summoned back. He even received a telegram, but famously ripped it up. It was recovered after it all ended, from soggy pieces in the road, but it was hard to say what it really meant. Either way, we were in it. On New Year's Eve, the Boers opened fire on us. My wristwatch stopped.

"We lay in at Krugersdorp, a ridge about twenty miles from Johannesburg, and waited, knowing that they were close. One of my recollections of that terrifying night was its intense darkness. It was literally impossible to see your hand in front of your face. At about midnight, someone lit a match in the hospital wagon. That was the signal. They opened fire. I was more frightened than I have ever been in my life. For some reason, I spent the entire night looking for my horse because I thought he might be frightened. I didn't find him until the next morning.

"I ended up the target of three Boers. But

it was then I saw one of our boys jump on a Maxim gun and let off half a belt at a thousand yards. It shredded the Boers, and they lay there, on the ground, with their horses.

"They were shelling us, and we were overrun. A few of our number and I ran to a white farmhouse at Vlakfontein, behind which we took cover. There was a black mammy there, who was feeding her baby some mealie-pap, the yellow corn porridge that everyone ate there. Not having had anything to eat for thirty-six hours, we shared the disgusting mess with the child, who screamed her disapproval. Her mother just stared at us, shaking. That is the only time I have ever taken food from a child.

"She wore a white apron. My friend Harry White took it. I asked him what we should do, and he said, 'Oh, put the damn thing up, I suppose. I'm going to blow my brains out.' He then rose and disappeared into an orchard behind the farmhouse. In spite of being very fond of him, I was much too tired and hungry to care.

"We raised the flag and surrendered. They still kept shooting. But I was genuinely glad when old Harry came out of the orchard five minutes later, munching an apple.

"After that, it was quite strange. Shooting

continued even as our leaders negotiated our safety. Melton Prior, the famous war correspondent, ran by and saw a man covered with a blanket who was kicking like a shot hare. It was Charlie Coventry, the son of Lord Coventry, and if anyone ever looked *in articulo mortis,* it was he. Prior reported him dead and ran off, even though he was not. When his family got the telegram that Charlie was alive — which they received at his own memorial service — they danced on the green, top hats, frock coats, and all.

"We went to jail, then court, and eventually got traded home to face punishment. We rode back to England on the troopship *Victoria.* A major there was put in charge of us; he gave us ten indestructible orders. The biggest one was that on no account were we to speak to any of the officers' wives who were there on the ship. 'They have been warned not to speak to any of you!' he said. That was a mistake. If you order a woman not to speak to a man, the result is almost inevitable." Here Cyril finally laughed. "Within forty-eight hours, every one of us had an officer's wife under our wing. The major was furious, but we had sized him up immediately. He had not realized that we were criminals of a certain social status. We violated all ten regulations the very first day.

"When we arrived on British soil, we were taken to court. And we were a sight, having not changed clothes in weeks. I myself wore a khaki tunic (that was filthy), a Stetson hat, and bell-shaped corduroy trousers that were not mine. When we got to the courthouse, we were mobbed by people. We thought at first it might be a rescue. They thought we were heroes. But we were quite a sight. We were raiders, and we looked the part.

"We ended up out on bail, though our leaders had to serve some time. We eventually found out that the African government was seeking a great amount of damages because of the raid: 677,938 pounds, 3 shillings, and 3 pence, to be exact. Personally, I thought that the strangely precise 3 shillings, 3 pence was directed straight at my stolen trousers.

"Speaking of, at my first visit to White's Club after the raid, I was asked by the proprietor if I would give him my Kruger trousers. I sent them round by my servant. Some two days later, I happened to go to the club and saw them exhibited in a case over the fireplace in the lounge. It really was the limit. They remained up just as long as it took me to remove them, which was not a lengthy period."

Cyril looked out over the pool. Nothing

had changed, but a few minutes had passed, with the help of a story. "They didn't listen to me after that. The officers, I mean. I told them that war with the Boers would need a lot of men." He continued looking off. "They didn't agree." He nodded toward Monty. "And men like him paid the price."

"What happened to Monty?" asked Walsh.

"Does it matter?"

Another, farther *BOOM!* sounded, and they could see smoke over the hillside. Cheers broke out among the crowd.

It seems that the wall took longer to blow up than they had reckoned on. In fact, before the long-awaited blast, the good mayor thought he would walk into the tunnel in the pool, which at the Siloam end is tall, and have a look round. He had been accustomed to seeing a trickle of dirty water come through only rarely and never anticipated anything else.

When the dam finally blew, the wave of water was, thought Cyril, more of a miniature Niagara than a rivulet, traveling at twenty miles per hour and over four feet in depth. Cyril watched, gape-eyed, as the mayor was slammed by a palisade of water and swept past the terrified villagers. He was recovered downstream and hobbled back, but unfortunately never retrieved his hat, which was a pity. This unfortunate incident rather spoilt the show, thought Cyril, but the villagers, who washed their clothes in the Pool of Siloam, were genuinely grateful to the party for supplying them with clear spring water undefiled by the silt of three thousand years.

As the pool filled and people laughed and splashed, Cyril Foley looked over at Monty, who was smiling. The water that now flowed through those ancient caverns, which they had spent over a year excavating, had been given back to the valley.

Cyril would leave within days, so there was only one thing left to do. One last adventure to have. He raised his hands to his friends and workmen alike.

"How about a match, lads?"

As they prepared the field, Cyril looked over to his man, Walsh.

"Next time I'll tell you about the time I fought Dracula.

"I'm not kidding!" he said, on his heels, his voice trailing off as he ran toward the game. It was then that Cyril Foley, smiling from ear to ear, played in one of the more disorganized but satisfying cricket matches of his life. At one point, he hit a six into the Pool of Siloam itself, which caused him to whoop with joy.

"That is a thing," he shouted, "which has never been done before!"

"Not even by the Hittites!"

Twenty-Nine

MONTY PARKER

Jerusalem, Christmas 1910

Monty Parker stood at his balcony window and watched an almost unthinkable phenomenon: for the first time in decades, snow was falling over Jerusalem. It had done so for seven straight days, in fact, heavy and white. The snow had piled itself into curves along the streets of the old city. Boys near the school had built sleds out of crates and wooden planks. There was not a pair of feet in Jerusalem that were not wet with cold.

Monty turned and walked back into his room, shutting the glass doors with their leaden panes closed. He took his hat off and placed it on the chair. The fire was roaring and just holding its own against the winter outside the door. He heard clanking and bustling downstairs. Because it was Christmas (and with the unspeakable snow), Monty and his men had opened a makeshift soup kitchen downstairs. Amid the potsherds and relics were now tureens and ladles, set at attention to feed the people of Silwan. They had even managed a spindly tree.

Monty clamped his pipe in his mouth and paced. The expedition was in trouble. Real trouble, for the first time since they had first arrived. Their hope of slipping in unnoticed under the pretense of constructing a hospital or school — what were they thinking?

They had been found out.

Members of the Syndicate back home had warned Monty that short articles had begun to appear in the newspapers. A few came, as Monty suspected they would, when they first left for Jerusalem, but they had little to no information, though some of them referred to their expedition as "mysterious." More concerning were these new reports. They were short and not overblown in terms of headline, but there was something much more alarming about them: they were true. Monty looked through the clipped articles the Syndicate had sent him. One was titled "Strange Treasure Hunt" and had details of their work in the Dragon Shaft and in Hezekiah's Tunnel. The article even mentioned their Turkish observers — by name! Luckily, these articles did not mention the Ark, opting for "King Solomon's treasure" and "the crown of David," instead.

The other item of concern from London was, of all things, a book of fiction. The author William Le Queux had come out with a new potboiler titled *Treasures of Israel*. The Syndicate had sent Monty a few of the summaries from various newspapers. One reviewer wrote that the book was about "the whole science of textual criticism of the Bible, for there is a cipher readable only by the most learned professors of ancient Hebrew," as he and his companions sought "nothing less than the Ark of the Covenant." Monty hurriedly grabbed another review. In the book, the Ark was apparently "hidden in a secret chamber concealed by water tunnels somewhere in the vicinity of Jerusalem."

"The story," the reviewer wrote, "is one of frankly melodramatic mystery and treasure hunting, with lovers, and a villain of the deepest dye. If marked by imperfection when regarded as history or revelation, it is delightfully convincing in its own way."

Monty clenched his hand into a fist.

Treasures of Israel stood, according to the reviewer, "among his best work."

This man, this Le Queux, had obviously talked to someone in the Syndicate. But there was nothing to be done now. There was an even greater threat. Someone else had also found out about their expedition. Someone far more dangerous than any author.

The Baron Edmond de Rothschild was president of the French branch of the most powerful banking family in the world. He was rich beyond measure and collected rare artifacts. He was perhaps the one opponent they could not outfox or bribe. He had already bought up some of the land around the works so that they could no longer venture far past the fountain. In some places, he had even put fences up. What had taken them months of negotiation to accomplish seemed to take the baron mere days. And as far as they knew, he had not even set foot in Palestine, relying on personal agents and provocateurs. He had also officially approached the government and made a proposal for digging rights. The Syndicate had until next year to finish — finish! — so that there would be no overlapping contract concerns. This was personal to Rothschild — he was a Jew and a Zionist. There were rumors too of a Frenchman haunting the Jewish quarter and at some of the hotels, looking for information for the baron. Monty knew it was probably Raymond Weill, the French archaeologist. And who knew how long the Turkish government would last? Who knew how long any of it would?

Monty turned and walked again, his pipe glowing.

That, and they had found nothing in the tunnels. Pots, bits of pots, dust from pots, and finally some water. Father Vincent was ecstatic about all of it, but he didn't know what they were really looking for.

In a desperate gambit, they agreed to stay on through the rainy season. They knew it would be an impossible slog. And that was before the snow came. Monty looked out at the city again. It was calming and quiet. But it was all a disguise.

Monty took a drink. The cipher had failed them, of course. Catastrophically so.

He was on his own.

Monty picked up the latest batch of letters, still sitting in the envelope he had raggedly torn open with his thumb. Juvelius, though no longer with them in Palestine, continued to send him letters. They mostly took the form of new ciphers that Juvelius had uncovered since returning home. They were typewritten in a bleary blue ink and covered in typographic errors, marked-out sections, corrections, and squiggling notes. Juvelius had written these, then sent them to Millen, who translated them into English before forwarding them to Monty. It was unclear who wrote what without some amount of wishful deduction. That is what the whole thing had become: a wish.

Monty looked through the most recent set. Juvelius had given up his biblical analysis in favor of a stream of raw cipher messages, alongside some minor notes and drawings. Some of the same places were mentioned — "the hollow staircase," "the asylum" — but unlike the first ciphers, these (now mostly from Chronicles) seemed to give more actual direction:

(Six spearlengths, entrance the Ark's, the abode's, the black tunnel's, entrance of the mother's arms: break through!)
And seek! And the water 2 spearlengths addition. And behold like water!
(invoke "the cross"!)
Seek the entrance, seek! (Jerusalem!)

Monty was at least getting more adept at reading it all, though a fat lot of good it seemed to do him. "Mother's arms" was the Virgin's Fountain; "the black tunnel's" had to be Hezekiah's — but they had cleared both out. There had found some dummy tunnels, but there were no secret passageways, no lost mysterious chambers. And no Ark. Had they missed something? Or, the old thought raised its head again, was it all nonsense to begin with? Monty read on. The words seemed stranger, less coherent, even.

Seek indefatigably!
(Just the valley glen dale!) The hooks of the forhangings? Are enclosed by MOLOK SILOA, in the opening the swelling spring's. 4/

4/ SHILOA (The pond of SHILOA.) The swelling spirit (the spring of the Virgin.) and the cave of MOLOK are given as the entrances. As the last-mentioned was "the entrance" to the "infernal regions", it appears, that the channels of blood from the temple have debouched into the lowest labyrinth of cave.
/*"hump", blood-path's water = gibbous tunnel (?) Compare II. Chron. 33,6.
!! " 28, 3
/** "The valley" = "The valley of JOSA-FAT. (?)
/*** MOLOK = The ancient temple of MOLOK in the valley of "HINNON". (JEREM. 32,35) seems to have been the cave of "HAKELDAMA", where the en-

trance to "GEHENNA" (the infernal regions) also was found.

Monty was glad that Juvelius was no longer in Jerusalem. This new cipher only confirmed that to him. But something was intriguing here. The cipher said that the "cave of MOLOK" was one of "the entrances" with "channels of blood." Could it be the canal that was used to carry the blood of the sacrifice away from the Temple? Even more intriguing was that it finally had a location, in "the valley of HINNON" in the cave of "Hakeldama," where the entrance to Gehenna "was found." After his last conversation with Juvelius, Monty wanted nothing to do with Molok, but the blood canal, the supposed passageway from the Temple that carried away the blood of the animals sacrificed to the Lord, was intriguing.

Was it the third way?

Monty knew that Warren thought the blood canal was on top of the actual Foundation Stone in the Dome of the Rock. There was a line or two in one of his accounts of him jumping up on the stone to inspect it. But that seemed like a story. Monty knew they could not dig there. Especially after the shootings.

Juvelius also discussed the prophet Nehemiah, who, many years after the fall of Jerusalem to Nebuchadnezzar, was dispatched to the remains of the city to assess its rebuilding. Juvelius seemed to agree with biblical scholars that the parts of the Book of Nehemiah written in the first person were totally historically reliable, that the prophet was an actual person, not some kind of clay sculpture of several different authors.

When Nehemiah reached Jerusalem, he secretly left the city to check the state of the city's walls. But Juvelius did not believe that; he claimed that Nehemiah had a more clandestine mission. For one, he took a long, circuitous route that would have been unnecessary to inspect the walls. More telling was Nehemiah's own admission that "He told no man what God had put in his heart to do." Juvelius believed that Nehemiah, on his night trip, traveled through a secret underground gate that led from the city into the outer valley.

Juvelius was certain that Nehemiah knew where the hiding place of the Ark was and that his job was to confirm that it had survived the fall of Jerusalem. He rode out by the "gate of the valley" and onto the "Dragon Well" and to the "dung port" and "viewed the walls of Jerusalem." He went on to the "gate of the fountain" and up in the night to the "brook." And he got away with it: "And the rulers knew not whither I went or what I did."

Monty saw the mail on his table. It was all from the Syndicate. He sat for a minute, before opening one of the letters. There was an article clipped from the *Gentlewoman* from last July. It read:

An enterprising, and may one add, imaginative relative of Lord Morley . . . is in search of King Solomon's crown and treasure of Biblical fame. Of course "one can never tell," but it seems that they stand a good chance of "drawing a blank."

Juvelius had drawn a small map in the cipher that showed "the asylum" (the Ark) being reached two ways: from the Pool of Siloam or from the Virgin's Fountain. Was this way, Hakeldama, the third? The cipher had claimed — from its earliest form — that there were three.

Monty looked out again at the snow, falling quietly in the night. He put his hat back on because he didn't know what else to do. He was cold, tired, and alone at Christmas.

Monty stood there for a long while, stiff and ungiving, until he closed his eyes for a moment. He then summoned Macasdar, who was never far.

"I need a dragoman for tomorrow," said Monty. "To take me to Gehenna."

Macasdar smiled.

"What's so funny?"

"Nothing, effendi. Forgive me. It is just . . . Gehenna has another name."

"Which is?"

"Hell," he said. "You want to go to hell."

Thirty

MONTY PARKER

Gehenna, 1911

Monty's donkey clopped through the bushes, its head low and parallel with the path, at least where they guessed it should be. It was still snowing, and they were headed east, into the Hinnom Valley, which was adjacent to the Kidron. They were wrapped up like mummies in cloth and wool against the cold. The dragoman led the way ahead of them. Macasdar was behind. They had donkey boys, but almost no supplies to speak of. They were only going to make a quick survey.

In the snow, it was harder to see, though the landscape looked similar. They took an open road alongside a low gorge. It was certainly much quieter. Monty looked for some of Rothschild's walls; he hoped the snow and cold would at least keep the spies away. Monty knew it was perhaps not the best time to go on an afternoon trip, but the cipher's suggestion of a third way had seized his mind, along with a terrifying question:

Were they digging in the wrong place?

It was very quiet indeed. Monty's toes were already sharp with cold.

"Why is this place called hell?" asked Monty. He had asked for a dragoman with knowledge of the area. Given the amount of tourists who visited Palestine for the holy sites, this was easy to arrange. Macasdar translated.

The dragoman spoke in a slow voice. He talked for a bit, before Macasdar broke in: "This is the Valley of Hinnom," he said, "which means Gehenna, which is this gorge." He pointed down to the thin crack at the bottom of the valley. "There was an ancient cave from which smoke issued out. Some thought it went to the underworld."

"If you believe such things." Monty wondered if he didn't hear a laugh. He had seen this man around the camp before, he thought, but could not be sure. It was hard to say; he was wrapped up so tightly, though some parts necessarily appeared at times for breathing and speaking.

"You have picked a strange place to visit, effendi," said Macasdar.

They rode crossways up the grain of the

rock — Monty could feel it — and into an olive grove. There were open caves here and there, full of mystery in the falling snow. They made their way up a low ridge, to a patch of even ground. Nearby was a small ridge of stone that was riddled with rectangular caves. The dragoman stopped. The snow slashed across him.

"Here is where Molok stood."

Monty looked. The place had changed, but the ground had not. It was still here, somewhere in the past.

"It was made of copper. They heated it with coals and played horns and great drums," the dragoman said.

"Why?" asked Monty. The dragoman had already started moving forward.

Macasdar answered himself, just as he passed Monty. "So that they wouldn't hear the screams."

Not so long after, they came upon a much higher ridge. Monty spied a white building on top of it, flush against the edge. It certainly was not an ancient structure. The dragoman stopped and swept his arm across the landscape.

"The Monastery of St. Onuphrius, a desert hermit. Here the man came, the Christian, the seller." Macasdar seemed confused by his words. The dragoman pointed to the ground. Then he understood.

"His thirty pieces of silver spilled on the ground."

Monty had heard of the monastery that had been built where Judas Iscariot, the traitor to Christ, had hanged himself. The dragoman continued, pointing to the rolling ground around them. "This Hakeldama," he said, "this Field of Blood, called so because there was no place else to bury them." Macasdar explained that the silver was used to buy this accursed land for those who could not afford burial elsewhere.

They turned a corner, and Monty saw a pylon of loose stones and a ruin of what might have once been a tower, extending into the air in patches, next to a stone arch. The dragoman stopped in front of the ruin.

"The Knights Templar built this place." Monty tried to look inside. It was not even a building, more like some leftover shadow, still visible only because no one had dared test it. The scene looked like one of the pencil drawings his mother made. Realistic, but somehow a step removed, as if there was something behind it. As a boy, he would stand next to her as she drew and look at her teardrop earring.

He looked at the ruin. The roof was mostly gone, and the floor — at least what he could see of it — looked very uneven, with sticks pushing out from the snow.

"The Knights Templar ran a hospital in the city for Christian pilgrims who came to Jerusalem. When they died, they put them here."

"Buried?" asked Monty.

"No," he replied.

Here the dragoman pointed to what might have been a roof and made a motion downward. Monty looked at the sticks again. It was a charnel house. They had dropped the bodies in from the roof. And left them there.

They made their way slowly up the trail and away from the house.

The dragoman began talking again, with Macasdar catching up. When the Christians finally took Jerusalem in 1099, the Knights Templar took over the newly constructed Dome of the Rock, on the spot of the old Temple. It was there, it was said, that the Knights began excavating the forbidden space underneath the cave. People whispered that they found great relics there, such as the head of John the Baptist, the Holy Lance that pierced the side of Jesus, and even the *sangraal,* the Holy Grail. The Knights were rumored to have found the Ark as well. They were not just warriors, but smart bankers. When they were excommunicated and burned at the stake by the French, their order inspired the Freemasons, the brotherhood of secrets. They knew how to hide things.

Though Monty was not a Mason, plenty of his friends were. As for knights, Monty had been a child once and knew all the stories. There was an ancient crusader buried in St. Mary's, the church by Saltram, to the left of the chapel, in a stone tomb carved with his likeness. As Monty looked back at the dark house, he could almost see this knight and others in their armor, standing there like specters.

"A cave," said Monty, blinking. "Ask him if there is a cave by a pool." He pulled out the cipher. The paper was getting wet in the snow, but he didn't care. He started to read so that Macasdar might translate:

The entrance was not in Hakeldama or in Molok's grotto, but in a pool to the south of Jerusalem. . . . The second entrance is in a pool (spring) at a distance of 100 cabalistic steps(!) from Hakeldama.

Juvelius's calculations had put that distance at three hundred yards. The dragoman listened, then looked out over the plain and started to ride. They followed.

In the first ciphers, Juvelius vehemently claimed that a third way to the Temple from Hakeldama was not an option. But in his recent set, he relented, saying that Melander, his mentor who did advocate for a valley entrance, had been right. But Melander never knew where it was. Juvelius claimed to have found it.

They came upon a recessed plain with snow-covered steps. They were looking at a basin that had obviously once been a pool, long ago, one of so many that lay hidden within the countryside. Monty wondered if it connected somehow to their own tunnels. This could be the way to the Temple after all, the "valley side" entrance of Nehemiah's secret journey. Juvelius claimed that in addition to the Ark, it might lead to the Temple archive, a place where all the secret books and scrolls of the ancients were kept.

They started down the shallower steps toward the southeast corner. As they got closer, Monty could see that there was a cave there, set into the edge. But the roof had utterly fallen in. A huge stone slab lay in front of whatever — if anything — lay inside. He thought of getting the men to walk from the next valley and to use their ropes and arms to pull it all loose. But they did not own this land and they did not have permission to dig into it. And he knew the stone was too big to move; they would have to use the dynamite. People would notice.

There was no way in. It was then, if not at some other time, that the darkness of the place, of Gehenna as place and idea, began to overwhelm Monty. The endless legends of death and despair, all piled upon one another like stones on a cairn. All of these people had come to Jerusalem and found only death. There was God and Satan. Good and evil. There was no third way.

The way was shut. There was nothing but death here.

Monty turned away. He should not have come here. He looked out on the field.

He could hear the shells first. Then he saw, or thought he did, the soldiers fighting, those British boys fighting Brother Boer. Then, like a developing photograph, the boys became bodies and fell into heaps. Monty felt a sting in his leg. He did not move. Everything looked like an emulsion of real life, as if someone had made it come back.

He closed his eyes, as he always did to make it go away. For a moment, things were dark. The images faded. The booming went faint. He opened his eyes again.

The only person he had told about the

war was his mother. He wrote her hundreds of letters from Africa for his entire term of service, not always of towering war and death, but of the minutiae (and gift) of daily conversation. When she died, on February 10, 1908, it was only a few weeks before he first met the Syndicate. She died of acute peritonitis, and painfully. He was heartbroken. Her name was Margaret. Her friends called her Minnie.

As they started back from the closed cave, cold and silent, Monty realized something. The caved-in tunnel had to have been the one they were seeking. Why else would such impossible stories proliferate in the same few yards of valley? Because it was inherently evil in its bloody soil? Or was it because someone knew that such stories would keep anyone in their right mind away? Gehenna wasn't just a place; it was a warning.

The sky darkened as they made their way back to the Kidron, passing Molok's ridge before finally leaving the valley. Monty wondered what Macasdar might be thinking of him.

Monty was thinking of the cipher. He wondered why the Ark, the greatest treasure of the Israelites, might be associated with such a dark and horrific presence as Molok.

But he was wrong — there was no connection between the two, not really. It was a clue. He remembered his conversation with Juvelius. "Molok" was from "M'lek," which meant "king."

Like the cipher, which was a clue, but also always a deterrent, what if "M'lek" was meant to scare as "Molok," but to provide a sign to the treasure of another king, the one who built the Temple?

King Solomon.

Monty realized that the tunnel from Gehenna might have been the true path all the way through the mountain to the Ark. He realized that while they had been reading the cipher for specific directions, it must also be read symbolically. Juvelius had always insisted on that. The third way might not be a path, but a method in between, something halfway between the good of the Virgin's Fountain and the evil of Molok. Monty looked up toward the city as it came into view. The Dome was flaked in white.

Later that night, Monty could not sleep. He looked for a long time into his Bible, reading of King Solomon. In 1 Kings 11:7, he read something that was somehow both familiar and new:

Then did Solomon build a high place for

Chemosh, the abomination of Moab, in the hill that is before Jerusalem, and for Molech, the abomination of the children of Ammon.

When Solomon grew old, he became tempted by his many wives to please them. Though the Lord strongly warned him, Solomon obliged his wives by building many temples to their foreign gods, even one to terrible Molok. The Lord was not pleased and told Solomon that he would punish him by splitting up his entire kingdom through war and subterfuge. The Lord promised that, though Solomon would never see this happen, his son would bear the burden and be left with only one tribe left to rule.

Monty understood something about parents not seeing the ruin left for their sons. He looked out through the window. Monty could barely make out anything in the dark and the snow. It was a striking passage.

The Lord had warned him, yet Solomon did it anyway.

THIRTY-ONE
FATHER VINCENT

Mount Ophel, April 1911

Father Vincent stood at the entrance to the cave, flanked by Captain Parker. Inside, the workers were clearing out the room they had found carved into the ridge of the hill. The men were marveling at some blocks of stone they had found that had been dressed, meaning they had been squared and smoothed, ready for building, probably as the base of some columns. The workers soon found other items of rich character, including part of a grand table and some marble moldings. Father Vincent looked at each new find with an increasing curiosity. When the debris was finally cleared away, Father Vincent was examining a magnificent candelabra when he realized the room was quiet. He looked up to see the workers dropped to their knees and with their heads bowed. They were speaking in low tones. Father Vincent looked up.

Before them stood a remarkable throne of stone.

"What are they saying?" asked Captain Parker.

"They say they've found the throne," said Father Vincent.

"Whose throne?"

"King Solomon's."

Captain Parker got the men to their feet and they argued over how best to remove the artifact. Father Vincent agreed that it was a magnificent specimen in what was surely a luxurious room. Could it really be his throne? When the workers finally pulled the malachite chair out with their ropes, Father Vincent noticed a large, circular hole in the middle of the seat. He couldn't help but stifle a laugh, but he kept his conclusions to himself.

Father Vincent wandered back out into the sun — the works had been largely dismantled, replaced by the working fountain, which had brought much joy to the town of Silwan. The Englishmen had turned their attention to the stone ruins that could be seen poking out of the eastern slope. Even from the bottom of the valley a number of quadrangular openings could be seen in the rocks. They were caves. And though most them had been looted or destroyed,

Father Vincent was happy to look at anything they found. In truth, though he was eager to begin writing, he had enjoyed his experience with the English so much that he wanted to make it last.

Days later, Father Vincent sat near the entrance to the Virgin's Fountain, sipping water and working on his map, when he heard someone shouting to him from the crest of the hill. Father Vincent looked up and saw someone waving at him. He tucked his notebook under his arm and made his way up the trail.

When he reached the new cave this time, the look on the man's face who had called for him revealed that this was something different from what they were used to.

"They found something," the man said, with a pause.

"A tomb."

This was not completely unexpected. Part of the basis of Father Vincent's theory of why Hezekiah's Tunnel curled around the valley to avoid some possibly important tombs was that the mountains were filled with them. Mount Olive was essentially a cemetery. Even in the town of Silwan, some of the homes built into the hillside had simply taken over older caves that had once been used as tombs. There was a secret city under the ground outside Jerusalem. Because of the laws against being buried inside the city, the nearby surroundings had become a necessary necropolis.

Up on the high path, Captain Parker greeted him with a nod.

"We've found three. The first we kind of stumbled onto by accident, but we have left the others for you. We have not gone inside."

Father Vincent bowed. This is what he would miss the most. This moment of uncertainty, even in the case of some ancient death, was exciting. In this old, open space, he would learn something new.

The first cave was low and parallel to the footpath. Some of the men stood around the edge as if it opened over some unseen cliff. The demeanor of men when a tomb was found was always heavier, more contemplative. Father Vincent thought it one of the more redeeming qualities of humanity.

"It's a cave-in," said Monty. "But they are undisturbed."

Father Vincent knew that time never stood still, as much as it sometimes appeared to in caves such as these. Nor did it sympathize to protect the things they were looking for.

The first cave had indeed collapsed. It had been formed from a fissure in the limestone, the mezzy, and looked to Father Vincent like it had been open to the air long before it fell. Most of the tombs that had been found on the mountain were like this: either ravaged by time or grave robbers or locked behind immovable boulders. And even if those boulders were able to be moved, the most they could hope to find behind them was pebbles and dust.

Father Vincent made his way in, followed by Captain Parker. A few workers were already inside. Light was here, in a shaft. Father Vincent knew its slow, destructive properties. Perhaps they were too late. He looked around in the artificial dusk. There was something small piled under a rock. A small collection of dusty things. Father Vincent knew their identity immediately.

Bones.

A worker picked one up, and it crumbled to dust before them. Only its stillness had kept it solid. Only its placement had kept it real. Captain Parker ordered everyone out as Father Vincent began his investigation. As he circled around the stone, he saw an order to the things that lay there. Like the chips and edges in the tunnel, but different. There were small vectors of arrangement that combined to form meaning, like a mosaic in the dark.

"And you are certain it was undisturbed?"

Father Vincent asked.

Monty nodded. He was still in the mouth of the cave.

"These were arranged by the hands of men," Father Vincent said. "Several bodies were placed here, with some fragments of early Canaanitish pottery; some bullets for slinging; a small, shapeless bit of bronze; and a few bones of animals, which may have been offerings to the dead." Captain Parker was, once again, astounded at the man's eye.

Father Vincent knelt down. There was a larger bone here, though he did not know its origin. It was human, for sure. Without touching it, he brushed off the surrounding dust. His face became puzzled.

"Look," he said. Captain Parker cautiously walked over. There was another set of old bones. But there was something different about them.

They were red.

"Have they been burned?"

Father Vincent shook his head. "This dark coloring is spotty and flaky but deep. It is ochre. They've been stained." Monty pointed to a few of the bones underneath that were normal in color, and were animal in origin.

Father Vincent had read of occurrences all over the world of bones having been dyed red; there were theories that it was intentional. To achieve such a rich color, the flesh would have had to been cut off before staining. There was much thought and work behind its execution. It was clearly a symbolic act of some significance.

But Father Vincent had never seen such a thing in Palestine. And what could explain that only the human bones were red, and not the animal fragments?

The second tomb looked to be much more intact. Some workers were still working at the opening. Father Vincent asked them for a tool, ducked under a large outcrop of rock, and completed the clearing out of the entrance himself. Once the opening was clear, they handed him a lantern, and he stooped his way in.

"There is someone here," he said.

The low room seemed empty and quiet. Father Vincent saw a small ledge that had been cut out of the wall. On its surface was a dark, smoky stain. He approached it slowly. There were some bowls along the cave wall that looked very much like the red-stained bones he had seen in the previous tomb. He turned back to the rock ledge and knew what it was. He approached cautiously, and began to see that the black dust on the rock's surface was ash. Poking out of its thick flakes he saw a finger bone, a vertebra, and a rib. Closer inspection found even more of these skeletal pieces.

Father Vincent paused in the middle of the cave. He took note of the things in the room, what was there and what was not, and began to imagine their purpose, their direction, in both the present and the deep past. He looked at the nimbus of ash. Father Vincent drew an invisible arrow with his eye back down to the floor. There, he saw part of a skull. Father Vincent looked back to the bier. Father Vincent guessed that the dead body was placed on its side, with his knees slightly bent, toward the cave's interior. The head must have been directed toward the southwest.

Father Vincent imagined the new body, lain out on the stone. Realizing he had missed something, he slowly scanned the room until he found another small opening in the rock. He saw a few flakes of pottery and the tiny bones that suggested they were offerings to the dead. Father Vincent pictured priests or relatives killing a lamb or a bird and placing it here in the tomb with the body. The image vanished. Father Vincent chastised himself; he knew only some things about this tomb, not all of them. He dropped down and ran his thin fingers through the almost sandy dirt. There, under the offering altar, he found a single, small tooth. Captain Parker, who was watching from the entry, stared at it, even after Father Vincent placed it with the offering.

When they got to the third cave, Father Vincent could see that it had already been examined. Captain Parker led him in.

"We went through this one, mostly by accident, but there's something I left for you."

Father Vincent walked in. He immediately saw a small flash of orange from near the far wall, underneath what appeared to be a fallen chunk of rock. Father Vincent crept closer with his heart in his throat. He bent down slowly to carefully examine the space. He saw some shattered pieces inside. Nothing could survive time, not really, as he well knew. As Father Vincent turned his head to look into the opening, he gasped. There, standing almost as if they were in a museum, was a set of colorful pottery. With the exception of one of their number, they were in perfect form, having been protected by the fallen slab of rock. Father Vincent stared at them in disbelief. They had not moved for centuries.

The quiet pantry numbered nearly twelve pieces. Some were yellow or orange; one was white with a decoration painted in burnt sienna. There was an amphora with handles, a great bowl, and more. One bowl proved to be the key to the whole set. Father Vincent inspected it with incisive care. Its color was dark orange but there was a shading to it that was quite artful. A black border curled around the bowl and its interior glaze was watertight. The curious part wasn't the expertise by which it had been constructed, but that none of its attributes were local, in any time period. This was not a Palestinian bowl. But Father Vincent knew what it was.

Egyptian.

Father Vincent looked around — the whole room in fact had traces of the Egyptian to it. Who had been here? Whatever the answer was, the bowl itself dated the collection, and possibly the room.

"This is quite old," said Father Vincent, holding up the bowl to show Captain Parker. He said the next part slowly: "Over three thousand years before Christ."

The bowl was not from the City of David but from Jebus, the ancient city conquered by him. This was, Father Vincent knew, the most important find of the expedition, because it would tell much about a culture about which little was known. Father Vincent guessed that this wasn't the grave of some lost Egyptian, but of a Jebus nobleman who had developed a liking for Egyptian art. This could have been the man's home just as easily as it was his tomb. Although Father Vincent enjoyed such guesswork, all they had was the bowl. But it was enough; it told him that this place was not beholden to one era or people. He turned the bowl around in his hands. Here was a find that bled across centuries. Here was something that had lasted. This, thought Father Vincent, was the true form of the past.

Thirty-Two

CHARLES WARREN

Whitechapel, September 30, 1888
Twenty-Two Years Earlier

Charles Warren was being bumped around his stagecoach like a bruised potato, but he was grateful because it was keeping him awake. The bumpy old stones of London were at least good for that, and it was welcome for once, at this hour and in these circumstances. It was before five in the morning and everything was quiet. He saw the sign for Goulston Street. The shops were closed, the carts empty, the long swimming house quiet and still. He hoped they had beat the press.

"We're here," said the driver.

The wheels creaked when Warren got out. He had thrown on his police coat. Providing light were the streetlamps and, somewhere behind them, he supposed, the indiscernible stars.

"Show me," he said.

A policeman led the way toward a doorway about halfway in the middle of the block on the right. In the dark, it looked like one of the countless such openings along the streets of Whitechapel. The policeman showed him toward the door with an outstretched arm. There was a small crowd of police who parted for their captain.

A white trellis dressed the brick vault of the door. Warren looked up at the stone arch; it was very gentle. Not bad work at all.

"Captain Commissioner sir, over here."

These men, these boys, were jumpy. He would see the victims next; one was right around the corner. But he wanted to see this first.

"Here it is, sir."

Several policemen stood about, staring at the door and at something that appeared to be on the ground. The sky seemed to be getting darker, but it was only because it had some color to it now, a thin vein of red. Warren knew they didn't have long now. One of the cops held his club, rapping it into his other hand.

"He's not here, son," said Warren.

Another man showed him a piece of apron on the ground. It was stained and looked ripped out of some larger piece. Warren held back a sigh.

"What's that? On the surface?" asked Warren.

"Blood and shit, sir."

Warren looked up at the sky again. Dawn
was barreling down. Blast the timing.

"And the writing?"

"Right here."

Warren approached the door and stood
under its arch. He saw naught but shadow.
One of the policemen trained his light on it.
There, on the flat, thick doorjamb, were
words in English. The writing was visible
from the street.

It was an inscription.

Warren did not move. It was written in
chalk, on brick, and was ethereal and dusty,
but real. Warren, who had stared at inscriptions before, now stared at this one. It was
still but seemed almost transitory. The light
moved back and forth. The man's hand who
was holding the light was shaking.

"Is it him, sir?"

Warren squinted, as if confused. He mur-
mured something to himself. He stared at
the wall again. He took out his pencil and
wrote something down in his notebook.
Some of the men discussed what was to be
done.

After a few minutes, Warren turned and

headed back to his buggy, only turning back once before he got in.

"Wipe it clean," he said.

The policemen looked astonished.

"But sir, the photographer is on his way."

"No," Warren said. "Wipe it. Do you hear me?"

"Yes, sir."

Warren looked around. He heard some activity down the street. A detective copied the inscription down again, then Warren watched as the words were wiped down, away from the stone, as if they never were.

"Let's go see them." Warren sighed.

Later that morning, Warren was back at his heavy desk. He held his head in his hands. These sights. These horrors. He had already been asked to submit a report on the strange writing, the graffito on Goulston Street, and why he had ordered it taken down. He called on Chief Superintendent Arnold to brief him on the details. Warren handed a sheet of paper to him. Arnold, young and with a close-cropped beard, had the same confused look. He handed it back.

"Tom," said Warren slowly, "we were right. If that writing had been left there, there would have been an onslaught upon the Jews, property would have been wrecked, and lives would probably have been lost."

Warren went back to his office and read what he had transcribed from the dark wall.

> The Juwes are
> The men That
> Will not
> Be Blamed
> For nothing

One of their suspects, a few weeks back, was a local man named "Leather Apron" by the press. The *Star* was adamant that the man was Jewish, which had caused a great deal of tension in the neighborhood. When the man was finally found, along with his two alibis, the matter was dropped. But the feelings, as they always did, persisted. Warren knew that the message, regardless of who wrote it, would have acted as a match upon an already-sparking ember.

But as Warren looked at the words, they began to twist in his mind. They were of a most curious construction. Almost like a cipher or a riddle.

Whether "Juwes" was misspelled or not (someone said it might be Yiddish), its meaning was clear to anyone who read it or had it read to them. Maybe it was meant to be heard or performed.

The strangeness was really in the meaning of it all. The Jews "will not be blamed" was simple. It was "for nothing" that complicated things. This could be read in two ways: that the Jews will not be blamed for nothing (meaning they will be blameless), or they will not be blamed for literally "nothing" — meaning they will be blamed for everything. The double negative of "no" and "nothing" could cancel each other out this way, resulting in "The Jews will be blamed for" the murders and everything else.

"Blamed" in the context of where and when the writing was found could not be "for nothing." It had to mean the murders. But "blamed" has nothing to do with actual guilt. Was the writer angry that the Jews had not been blamed? Or arguing that they should be? Or was there a much more sinister way to read that last word "nothing." Such a terrible word, more like the absence or void of one, almost entirely stripped of meaning. Was he arguing that whoever is blamed — the Jews, or perhaps the man — was not worthy of blame because the crimes themselves, the murder of women, was "nothing"? Was their murder a matter so unimportant that the word itself was merely a placeholder?

Five days earlier, the Central News Agency had received a letter. Like all of them, it was initially dismissed as the nonsense of persons who have nothing but nonsense to add to their nonsense lives. But after the writing on the wall was found, the letter took on new meaning. Warren read it again.

Dear Boss

I keep on hearing the police have caught me but they won't fix me just yet. I have laughed when they look so clever and talk about being on the right track. That joke about Leather Apron gave me real fits.

How can they catch me now. I love my work and want to start again. You will soon hear of me with my funny little games. I saved some of the proper red stuff in a ginger beer bottle over the last job to write with but it went thick like glue and I cant use it. Red ink is fit enough I hope ha. ha. The next job I do I shall clip the ladys ears off and send to the police officers just for jolly wouldn't you. Keep this letter back till I do a bit more work, then give it out straight. My knife's so nice and sharp I want to get to work right away if I get a chance.

Good Luck. Yours truly

Jack the Ripper

Dont mind me giving the trade name

PS Wasnt good enough to post this before I got all the red ink off my hands curse it. No luck yet. They say I'm a doctor now. ha ha

The letter was written in a reddish, ochre-colored ink. And, in fact, part of Kate Eddowes's ear was missing when they found her. Warren could see her face frozen in his mind's eye. Small, open terrible triangles had been cut into her face. Like arrowheads.

Warren began to wonder if the letter was true. If the graffito writer was the same person and also took part of her apron, it might have been done to make the same statement he was trying to make in the letter: he was mad that the Jews were being blamed, not because he feared for their well-being, but because he wanted the spotlight alone. Warren looked at his transcription again. He was a man of languages, of translation, and he may have seen something that everyone missed.

The Juwes are
The men That

Will not
Be Blamed
For nothing

As a good translator does, Warren searched his memory for a word to substitute, one that might make more sense. The most infuriating word of the whole sequence was "nothing." But if the monster thought of these murders as trifles, as nothing, then there was another word, a saying, that perhaps might fit.

The Juwes are
The men That
Will not
Be Blamed
For ~~nothing~~
Jack

In the days that followed, Charles Warren, by all accounts public and private, seemed to become overwhelmed by the futility of his task. As letters were leaked, more arrived, one even marked "From Hell." Warren, who was out of his depth, fell back on what he knew from Palestine: science. He tried using bloodhounds in a last-ditch effort to exert reason over a situation that had become pandemonium. Conspiracies began surfacing of Russian spies and secret men.

In October, a psychic named Lees went to the police and offered his services, claiming he had a vision. He was turned away as a madman. When the bloodhound experiment failed, a chorus of public voices finally called for Warren's dismissal. Once it became public that he ordered the sponging out of the writing, it became inevitable. Someone wrote to the papers, claiming that "The sooner this is done, the better for his peace of mind, as his present position must be infinitely worse than digging for lost cities in Palestine." Warren resigned on November 8, 1888, his authority having been undermined on several fronts. The very next day, the fifth and final murder occurred, of Mary Jane Kelly, in her rented room.

As Warren left London to return to the army, a place of order and rule, the murders had stopped. But the myths about them continued to grow well beyond England's shores and even beyond reason. Warren was sent to Singapore, but the story even circulated there. It spread like plague. Some dared search for higher meaning, such as Hugh B. Chapman, a local London vicar at St. Luke's, who wrote in "The Moral of the Murders" in October, 1888 (quoting Emerson), that "The remedy of all blunders, the cure of blindness, the cure of crime, is love."

Others, such as the Brooklyn detective quoted below, were less certain:

> Mark my words, sir, we have not yet heard the last of this ultra morbid misogynist, this demon incarnate, whose unholy delight it is to dye his hands in the blood of his foully murdered victims. He has a nature which Moloch might have envied.
>
> The police are not to blame, my boy; they are doing the best they can, but all their efforts are as nothing when pitted against the superhuman cunning of this combination of Nero and Mephistopheles. He was born under a flat star, and such as he (there is not more than one in a century, thank goodness) have always turned out to be utterly and irretrievably bad.

The press lit the world on fire with daily, almost hourly stories about the murders, drenched in speculation and fancy, born of true communal fear and the whiff of commercial opportunity. The victims — Polly Nichols, Annie Chapman, Elizabeth Stride, Kate Eddowes, and Mary Jane Kelly — labeled with effortless words like "whore" and "drunk," were pushed into a mire of lies that would take more than a hundred years to begin to drain.

The creature, the anonymous evil that everyone had a theory about, was more fictional. He became his own double negative, an empty function, a vessel instead of a person. Like the graffito, if all the stories about him were true, then none of them could be.

■ ■ ■ ■

PART FOUR:
RAIDERS

■ ■ ■ ■

THIRTY-THREE

MONTY PARKER

Jerusalem, April 1911

The Arab men, dressed in their customary white robes and with covered heads, made their way across Solomon's Court, the level porch in front of the gate. There were at least ten men, maybe more. It was almost sunset, and their shadows stretched into lines, almost trying to pull them back from their forward direction. The Dome of the Rock billowed up in front of them, its curving surface catching the last golden streaks of the sun. They kept moving, and quickly. When they reached the guard at the door, another Arab, one of their number, walked up and nodded. They exchanged something in their hands, though in the twilight it was hard to tell what. The man opened the doors and let them in. They walked quickly across the threshold, some of them stilted in their gait, walking like their legs were bound.

Their feet padded first across the marble, then the carpet. The looming ceiling and silent mosaics made them feel small, but they were the only ones moving. They crisscrossed like mice through the pillars, ignoring the parallel lines that had directed so many others. The place had been closed to outside visitors for months because of the shooting of the Americans. They were finally making repairs to some of the damage caused by the bullets. One of the Arabs, taller than the others, saw a scaffold and some open pots. He kept walking, all the way around the massive stone to the trellis structure that marked the entrance where the shooter had been.

The Foundation Stone lay in the center of the room, surrounded by a rail. The stone itself was enormous, with a light silk hanging high above it like a falling leaf, stuck in midair.

The room was getting darker, taking on the color of the stone itself. The lack of sound in the room seemed to solidify the room, which was impossibly bare of people. The tall Arab in front looked back. The place was monumental. The man could only imagine how much time and money had gone into its construction. For a project of such magnitude, the man was beginning to understand that there were the facts of the enterprise, the planning and preparation, but that those things meant almost nothing compared with the vast, inestimable work itself. He also knew, now more than ever, that part of that work was adapting as one went along.

"Lock it," the man said, in a familiar English accent as he walked toward the stone. Behind him, two of the men placed a bar on the door that fell with a *thunk.*

"Torch," he said, in a low voice.

Light pooled over the surface of the stone. The man could see the cuts on its surface. These were scars, he thought.

They advanced toward the trellis and the door to the stairs.

One of the others shone his torch and pushed it downward past the floor. They could see a wide staircase descending into the darkness.

"The Well of Souls," Monty Parker said, his face lit by fire.

The men watched his shadow on the wall as he unwrapped his head coverings and put his pipe in his mouth. He turned and stood in the light. The rest of the men similarly undressed, revealing pick-axes and hammers underneath their long robes.

They looked down the stairs and began

their descent.

Monty took a breath. What they were going to do — *what they were doing* — was nothing short of heretical. In fact, it was well beyond that. He thought, perhaps, of the shooter in the corner, trying to kill the Americans. The Dome of the Rock, the Haram al-Sharif, was believed to be the center of the world. Monty didn't know if he really believed that, but at that moment, it was all he could hold on to.

The cave varied in height, from about four to seven feet. It seemed to be a natural cave of limestone, but there were parts of it — the staircase, for one — that had clearly been carved out. The walls lay across each other in jagged layers. The floor was made of square paving, some of it covered in rugs. A chandelier lamp hung down in the middle from a hole in the Rock above. Monty swept his torch in front of him. There were prayer stands in the corners of the cave, four of them, with rugs and carved-out shrines. Some of them were ornately decorated with marble. Monty moved forward with his torch. The scrollwork almost moved in the firelight; it looked quite old.

Monty turned to his men, who were doing the same, lighting the corners of this holy place with fire.

"You know what to do," he said.

The men started moving the rugs.

"Start walking."

They began walking slowly around the chamber.

"Stop," Monty said.

Someone stepped back, then forward, then back again. Monty came over and got on his knees. On the floor in front of him was a flat, shiny mosaic of pointed diamonds and triangles. He put his hand to his jaw in thought, turning his head slightly. The pattern looked somehow familiar to Monty. In the center, alone, was a blackened star.

Monty stared. It looked familiar. The cipher had mentioned that a star could direct them to the Ark. Monty thought it would be outside, high in the sky, shining and bright. Not here, in the dark of the underground. Here, where he felt alone. Here, where he no longer was.

Monty took a breath and loosened his arms. He knocked on the stone next to it, releasing a dull sound.

knknk

Monty then knocked on the star itself. He listened intently.

KNOCK KNOCK

The sound had changed. There was a hollow space beneath the stone. Monty handed off his torch. He blew the dust around the corners and, using his fingers, tried to work the stone free. It was loose.

Monty stood up, clamped down on his pipe, and grabbed a shovel.

THIRTY-FOUR

AVA ASTOR

New York City, 1911

Ava Lowle Willing Astor was in a mood. She reclined back on her chair and paged through the *Times* to take her mind off things. She pushed through the headlines to the society pages, to look for the names of people she knew and parties she had attended — and those she had ruthlessly avoided. The Sunday-morning light was streaming through her high windows. Her daughter, Alice, was around, somewhere.

"Alice!" she yelled out sharply, in no particular direction but loud. There was no answer. She was probably trying on her jewelry again. Ava made a face.

Ava was back in the devil's den of New York City, but she did not feel any better. She had been living in London, but it had been a different experience from what she had hoped for. As many parties as she went to, she was now just another divorcée in the eyes of the royal family, and this had greatly limited her range. And in London, that kind of word got around quickly. King Edward and Queen Alexandra had looked the other way when she first arrived, but once the king died, everything got more formal. She thought it a mistake when she was left off an invite list for a state ball for some German dignitary, until she heard that Consuelo Vanderbilt — who had also recently split from the Duke of Marlborough — had been similarly ignored.

The same week of the ball, Ava was driving through Hyde Park on a lovely afternoon when the car ahead of her squeaked to a stop. Ava's large black hat slid over her eyes.

"What's the trouble?" she asked a guard on the side of the road.

"Her Majesty," the guard said, his mouth barely moving. She had no idea how any sounds could escape the sliver lips of these British.

Ava looked to her left. There, near Stanhope Gate, she saw Queen Mary herself passing right by her, with her attendants in tow. She was wearing her usual sedate British gown.

Ava, on the other hand, was wearing a black satin dress that clung to her so closely that it was a miracle she was able to be seated. Ava panicked but bowed as low as she could for being seated in an automobile. When she straightened her neck, another dangerous maneuver, she saw that the queen had recognized her. Perhaps this would be their moment of reconciliation. Ava smiled demurely.

But the queen merely dropped her eyelids and kept walking. The great occasion, indeed.

Ava had first returned to the States two years earlier for her divorce in 1909, before Justice Mills in the New York Supreme Court. Though the proceedings were sealed, the press knew that there was only one ground for divorce in the state of New York, and that was adultery. The settlement gave her a lump sum of ten million dollars. When the divorce was final, Jacob threw a grand party for one hundred and fifty guests. He spent twenty-five thousand dollars on flowers alone.

To make matters even worse, a year or so ago, her son, Vincent, and his father went on a yachting jaunt to the West Indies together. They were expected to make several stops, yet neither Ava — nor anyone — heard any word from them. Days stretched into several weeks, and the press reported that there had probably been a shipwreck. When they finally returned safe and sound, Ava was furious.

For distraction, Ava plunged herself into habits old and new. She played bridge like a demon and owned the tables up and down Fifth Avenue. She then set her mind to conquering the impenetrable fortress of men's clubs that littered the metropolis. Ava, with friends, helped found the Colony Club, a social and athletic club for women. She spent many hours at the pool, glorious and blue and set in white marble. She dove into its cool water and relaxed in the Turkish baths. When she asked that more mirrors be set into the walls, the other patrons complained because no one looked like Ava.

Predictably, it did not take long until her toad of an ex-husband had taken up with some girl from — Ava drew in a breath — Brooklyn. The cherry on top was that the girl was thirty years his junior. That is when Ava took off for London again. But now she was back. Again.

"Pah," said Ava to it all, as she turned the thin page of her newspaper. The magazine section opened to a full page with a photograph of some dreary church. Ava began turning the page, but the headline held her back.

Have Englishmen Found the
Ark of the Covenant?

"Monty," she said.

Ava pulled the paper close and kept reading: "A mysterious expedition, apparently not composed of archaeologists, hunts strange treasure under the Mosque of Omar, sets the Moslems in a ferment, and may cause Diplomatic incident."

The article mentioned no names, but Ava knew. It was him.

It had to be.

That knowledge gave her not only a moment of real curiosity, but one of genuine fear for her friend, followed by her ragged, golden laugh.

THIRTY-FIVE
BERTHA VESTER

Jerusalem, April 19, 1911

Bertha Vester kept walking, her two daughters strung behind her. The shouting was rising all around her. She just wanted to get home. Marchers and protestors, their arms in the air, appeared from behind every corner. She nodded and dodged, moving faster with each step. The mob seemed to be headed toward the Ottoman consulate. She heard words that made her nearly weep with sadness.

"Death to the English!"

"Kill the governor!"

The timing for this was nearly unimaginable. The Nabi Musa festival, the annual trek of Arab believers to the Valley of Moses, had just returned. Even they, in the middle of the Dead Sea valley, had heard the news from the city. When the governor greeted them, as was the custom, they spat at him and called him "pig." Easter had just passed as well, and the city was full of beaming tourists. It was the Greek Orthodox Easter as well, in addition to Passover! Such a configuration of the major faiths was not only rare but, in this case, incendiary. This city, her city, in which she saw brotherhood and friendship every day, was coming apart over a single line of incredible news: Englishmen had pillaged the Dome of the Rock.

Bertha and her children sped down a narrow alley, cut back across the square, and made their way past the crowd. They were finally able to walk home, though Bertha did not let up her pace for even one step, much to the distress of her daughters.

"What happened?" said Jacob, as she walked in and locked the door.

"The English diggers." Bertha put tea on, more for her brother than her. She gave her daughters a treat and sat them down together. "The rumor is that they dug at the Haram . . . ," Bertha said. She turned and wiped her head. "And that they found the Ark." She shook her head. "And took it."

Jacob sat down, though he did not even look if there was a chair beneath him.

"A general strike has been called," Bertha continued. "There are at least two thousand people gathered in front of the Ottoman consulate right now, shouting for the governor! The gendarmerie was posted on every corner. I've never seen anything like it!" Bertha paced. She couldn't sit down. She just couldn't.

Over the next two days, Bertha watched from her window and listened to her many friends for news as tensions simmered then burst. Two vendors at the consulate apparently got into a fight over some sweetmeats, and shots were fired into the air, scattering thousands out of the compound. A fearful panic ensued when the peasant women and pilgrims poured out of the walls of the enclosure and ran toward the city gates.

"Massacre! Massacre!" shouted the terrified protestors. The Arab soldiers appeared from the bunkers carrying leather whips, uncoiling like snakes in the dirt.

The business places immediately closed up, as Bertha imagined every family arming themselves and barricading their homes. She heard that the Russian Compound was completely shut up. She heard even wilder rumors, that the sheik himself had been killed, that the governor had been dealt with by the mob, and so forth. She heard that officials had been sent out along the roads in every direction to assure the fleeing people that nothing was the matter. Tradespeople were urged to reopen their stores and resume business. But a few days passed, and Bertha began to breathe easier as everything began to slowly turn to normal.

For some reason, all the fuss about the Ark made Bertha remember another visitor to the Colony from when she was a child. He came from America and always introduced himself as "George A. Fuller, USA." He was a carpenter and had a beard like Santa Claus. He once crafted a pine box for Bertha's mother that he presented to her with great solemnity. But the box, painted yellow and black, was so hideous the children referred to it as "the coffin." Bertha's mother endured its presence on her table for years until she traded it for some milk when times were tight. George sighed as he watched the box leave her house, but never complained. He had come to the Colony believing that he had sinned greatly, but Bertha's father assured him that it was only in his imagination. Her father told George that God had forgiven everything. Bertha didn't know if the people of Jerusalem would forgive this. The only question left was the one everyone was asking: Where were the stolen treasures? What had really happened there at the Dome?

An Arab newspaper provided the best

answer: that "none knew, except God and the Englishmen."

THIRTY-SIX

CYRIL FOLEY

Paris, April 1911

Cyril was seated at a sidewalk café with a friend when he read the news from Jerusalem.

"Well," he said, "I suppose the opportunity was just too much for them."

Thirty-Seven
TURKISH PARLIAMENT

Constantinople, May 8, 1911

The contrast between the white marble and the hundred or so men in dark wool suits and red fezzes was striking. In the top back corner, the balcony was full of men craned over the rows of seats below them. The men in the front wore fezzes trimmed in white fur. A tight line of soldiers stood near them in front of the halberds hung on the wall, crossed and draped in red cloth, with the Turkish flag of the crescent moon and star. The holy men wore black. The man in front was speaking.

"Our report has been concluded. It was on the night of April 12 that one Mahrumi Effendi, someone who worked at the Dome of the Rock, walked by and found the gates to be unlocked. He investigated and found twelve men digging. When he told them to leave, they threatened him and told him to walk away. Mahrumi Effendi saw that the diggers had two full bags of dirt, or so he supposed." The words echoed through the Turkish parliament, leaving disbelief in their wake.

"Nine straight nights of digging!" someone yelled. The general assembly began to grumble. They seemed to agree with the outrageousness of this. Or at least most of them did.

"The man called for help," continued the speaker, "and an administrator finally came to investigate. But the Englishmen were gone. They were rumored to have taken several of the Solomon relics." The crowd got louder. So did the speaker.

"Our governor in Jerusalem, Azmi Bey, was greeted with insults and curses. It was speculated that his life was in danger. On April sixteenth, he ordered an investigation and ordered the British ship at Jaffa to be searched before they escaped." Men shouted and banged on their tables.

"Their leader, Captain Parker, was not detained."

The shouting from the floor got even louder.

"Order!"

"We have ordered the arrest of the four who allowed them in. Shaykh Khalil al-Zanaf, the official caretaker of the Haram;

two of his sons; and Macasdar, the 'translator' who was hired as their middleman.

"The British did not intervene to help. The Palestinian Jews have issued an official letter. We are being 'raided by foreigners,' they write. 'Blood has been shed, disgrace has occurred, public order has been disrupted, security no longer exists . . . Palestine is a dear land . . . Protect her in the name of God!' "

The floor sounded again, but it was hard to say if it was in agreement or denial.

"On April twenty-first, Ali Riza Bey said that his military forces would 'exert themselves night and day' in order to 'maintain public security.' " This was a serious response and was met with agreement. The speaker paused for a moment. "Our own investigation," he continued, "has revealed that Governor Azmi Bey, and others, were receiving monthly monies from Parker."

The crowd roared.

A parliamentarian, a man named Riza nur Bey, stood and shouted, his fist shaking in the air. "The government covers everything up and hides it!" he yelled.

Halil Bey, the minister of the interior, stood and said that he would be surprised if everyone in the leadership had not been in on the bribes. Parliamentarian Wenton stood and began speaking of a mysterious man who had been accused of being a spy, who had been spotted in several cunning disguises around the Haram. He had been arrested at Nablus and was, according to Wenton, a person of great interest in the case. Someone else said that the English had only left Jaffa because they had gone on vacation. The members were not persuaded.

"Heckling to order!" shouted the head of parliament, standing up once more.

Another member of the body yelled out: "This issue does not concern Islam only! It is also of concern to Christians!"

"Why was the contract kept secret?" asked someone else.

Ruhi Khalidi then addressed the crowd. An elected delegate of Jerusalem, he was the new deputy to the head of parliament. He was a thinker and lover of books.

"Sirs," he said, "to understand the foundation of the matter in question, it is necessary to discuss some history. Above all, this issue is a mystery, like a story from the *One Thousand and One Nights* or *The Count of Monte Cristo* by Alexandre Dumas. Such issues only can be observed within the grand revolutions of the great powers. When

Captain Parker, the brother of the famous Lord Morley, said there was a huge treasure worth 100 million lira in Jerusalem, well, 100 million lira is easy to speak with words, but hard to imagine. If you were to stack up a 100 million on top of each other, you would need a whole room. The largest amount of capital belongs to the Rothschilds, at 30 million. Our debts were at 115 million lira before the revolution!" He stopped, letting the numbers hit their mark. Many nodded their heads in agreement.

By June, the minister of interior reported to parliament that Governor Azmi Bey had been recalled from Jerusalem. Azmi and Sami Bey (the heads of the gendarmerie) were also dismissed; the caretakers of the Haram and Macasdar were sent to Beirut to stand trial before a tribunal. Parliament was satisfied for the moment. Someone remarked that the caretakers had been bribed by Macasdar, not the Turks. "The government and bureaucrats took no part and had no information," he said, confidently.

Thirty-Eight

MONTY PARKER

London, May 8, 1911

The door of the London office of *The Times*'s editor opened, and a mail clerk dumped the day's flurry of letters onto his already-struggling desk. There, among the usual political grumblers, harmless cranks, and self-advertisers, was a letter. The envelope had strange markings and stamps and seals with curling characters on them. The letter was from Constantinople, and even the paper itself had an exotic feel to it. Though it was October and the Jerusalem story had left the papers in favor of strikes and suffragettes, the name in the corner of the envelope had remained in the minds of some people. Copy was called. The name on the letter was The Hon. Montague B. Parker.

The Times ran the letter on May 8, 1911, the same day as the Turkish parliament was debating the incident. In the letter, Monty

Parker, the man at the center of an international manhunt — yet who had never once been charged with a crime — finally explained to the readers of *The Times* his version of what happened in Jerusalem:

Our expedition, which started in 1909, originally consisted of Mr. R. Duff, Major C. Foley, Mr. Clarence Wilson, and myself. The object of it was to find the tomb of Solomon and any Hebrew writing that existed of that period. At the end of four months the weather was so bad that we were compelled to shut down our excavations and return to England. We determined, however, to resume our work in the summer of 1910. On arriving in August 1910, we resumed our excavations, but finding that the water from the Virgin's well was very low, we decided to clean the spring out, which soon created an enormous amount of satisfaction among the villagers of Silwan, who held a big feast on the occasion of the water first flowing down the tunnel after these operations had completed. We were unable to discover any Hebrew writing, notwithstanding we had found definitely the spot where the city of David and the Jebusite city which preceded it, had existed. In [the] view of the Dominican Fathers this discovery is quite the most important that has been hitherto made in Palestine.

With regards to the rumors which have been circulated concerning work undertaken in connection with the mosque of Omar, nothing can be said until the commission appointed by the Turkish government to inquire into this question has presented its report.

Monty Parker, writing from somewhere unknown, had admitted nothing. The article was picked up by newspapers all over the world.

A week later, on May 14, 1911, *The New York Times* ran a story titled "Mysterious Bags Taken from Mosque." In it, the expedition is described as having worked for two years just "to reach that one spot." And though the article asserts that "what they really found no one knows," it notes that the expedition "told different persons that they are 'very satisfied.'" The article claims that four or five men, including Parker, Duff, and Wilson, invaded the Haram at midnight, having gained entrance by bribery, and that they lifted up a heavy stone, entered a cavern, and "took away two bags." Before they left on their white yacht from

Jaffa, they had a cup of tea. The caretaker they had bribed was in jail and suffered a further indignation: his great beard and mustache had been shaved off in public.

The same story also printed a conversation between a "very liberal" Moslem man of Jerusalem and an Englishman:

> "Suppose that some Moslems entered Westminster Abbey and deliberately carried away treasure from some secret underground vault?" asked the Moslem. "What would happen?"

> "War," said the Englishman.

THIRTY-NINE

THE FRIEND

Jerusalem, May 22, 1911

William E. Curtis was in San Francisco when he first heard what happened in Jerusalem. He was a correspondent for the *Chicago Record-Herald* and a special correspondent to the *San Francisco Star.* Curtis had been a journalist for decades and had seen almost every kind of story imaginable. He followed General Custer on a campaign against the Sioux and reported on the Coushatta massacre in Louisiana. He once met the gunslinger Jesse James, who stared down Curtis and told him he was not going to leave the room alive. When Curtis walked out, he had a career-making interview tucked under his arm.

When Curtis saw the news from Jerusalem, he wondered if the story had substance, or was just an empty bottle wrapped in a fancy label. Buried under the provocative ledes — "Disgrace of the Omar Mosque,

Treasure Diggers. Unscientific. Escape" — was more or less the same story, with some differences, mostly in the *Times* piece. Curtis got to work, and his account of the incident, titled "Moslems in a Rage," ran in the *Star* on May 22, 1911. But unlike the other articles, which mostly relied on wire reports and changed things to fit their column size, Curtis had something priceless on his side. He had a source. A firsthand one, at that.

"I have just received a very interesting and detailed account," Curtis wrote, "of the occurrence from a friend who was in Jerusalem at the time. It is the first connected and intelligent narrative that I have seen [and] it was written on April 28." He then goes on to quote the account directly:

There appeared here in 1909 a pioneer, acting mysteriously for some notable Englishmen for the acquisition of property so as to build schools or hospitals for the people in behalf of the Turkish government. . . . Soon Capt. Parker of the Royal Life Guards, brother of Lord Morley, Maj Wilson, the owner of a yacht that attended them; Mr. Duff, said to be connected by marriage to the Duke of Fife, and Mr. Foley . . . arrived with an engineer, certain overseers, and many implements for excavation. At once they set to excavating the tunnels discovered and followed for a short way by Capt. Warren. There were working at the tunnel that conveys the water from the Virgin's Fount to the pool of Siloam. There they discovered some hitherto unknown and choked-up dummy tunnels running off southward from the main tunnel, which yielded nothing.

The facts that have most impressed people are that not one of the party is an archaeologist . . . This naturally led to the conclusion that they were after treasure. They were after the Ark of the Covenant.

They had two members from Parliament from Constantinople (prominent ones) attending them as who were paid £30 a month each. They enjoyed every privilege and immunity . . . It appears that they have a secret arrangement . . . to give 50 per cent of whatever they find to the government.

The "Friend" wrote about the history of Hezekiah's Tunnel with great precision. He even marked out its exact measurements: "The tunnel, as measured, is 1200 cubits of sixteen inches in length." He wrote that it ran in "no straight line" and had "several curves and one great sweep." The account read like a recollection, not speculation:

After working for about three months, the rains came and compelled the Englishmen to stop work; so before Christmas 1909, they returned to England. The rumors about the Englishmen had started up all the Jews and presently all the land lying between their pile and the Pool of Siloam was acquired and walled up . . . It appeared that Baron Rothschild had furnished the money and was trying to get a concession . . . The government, therefore, notified the Englishmen that they must bring their work to an end within 3 years total . . . So it was when they returned in the fall of 1910 they worked through last winter, although we had an unusual amount of rain, and until their reckless course brought on the panic which has just caused them to flee and almost bring on a massacre.

On April 28, a report got abroad and spread like wildfire: English explorers had clandestinely explored the Mosque of Omar, penetrated even into the Sacred Rock and "The Well of the Spirits." The sheiks, who act as guards, and the mosque attendants and the police were in their employ. There was a report that they had carried off the Crown of David, the genii-attended ring of Solomon, the two tables of stone containing the Law and the Sword of Mahomet.

The sheikhs were put in prison and the military attendants of the Englishmen were arrested as the thieves hurried to their yacht at Jaffa. After illuminating their vessel and announcing they were going to hold a reception for the officials, the Englishmen slipped away at night. Their Turkish lawyer, who was brought from Constantinople in their service, was detained. Every bit of his luggage was turned out and searched.

A commission of nine was appointed to investigate and report. The governor was implicated as were the Turks. A confession was extorted from the son of the head sheikh, that Englishmen had worked for nine nights, coming there in fezzes to avoid detection. . . . They cleared out the rubbish in the "Well of the Spirits" for several meters and discovered a basin whose plastered interior plainly showed marks of the different levels of the liquid (blood) that had stood in it, and were only prevented by the public excitement from going still farther.

A certain Finnish government surveyor, by name Juvelius, who developed a great love and knowledge of the Talmud and Hebrew, seems to have been at the bottom of all this matter. He claims to have discovered that by reading every seventh letter in certain passages in the Talmud (much after the fashion of the Bacon-Shakespeare cipher), the key is furnished for the recovery of the hoards of treasure in Solomon's Temple.

The tension on the minds of the people of Jerusalem was so great and was so well realized by the military authorities that patrols were posted along the walls and in every street. . . . A fearful panic ensued, the peasant women and pilgrims pouring out of the walls on the enclosure and running toward the city gates crying "Massacre! Massacre!" The business places were closed up in a few minutes, every family arming itself after barricading its house.

The wildest reports were circulated — that the sheikh had been killed; that the governor had been dealt with by the mob, etc. etc. Officials were sent out to calm people. The people were urged to reopen their stores and resume business, and pretty soon everything was quite normal.

This incident will have an unfortunate effect upon other archeological investigations. The present Turkish government has been very liberal in granting permission to foreigners, but will have to be careful hereafter.

This account was the most complete summary of the expedition ever published in English and was quickly picked up by other papers based on the Curtis byline alone. Renditions of the story would be repeated many times, including by some who had actually witnessed parts of the expedition, like Bertha Vester and Cyril Foley. But this person — this Friend — whoever they were — had, unlike them, seen all of it. The new information was the most shocking, that they had indeed dug under the Well of Souls.

CHAPTER FORTY
DR. JUVELIUS

Viipuri, Finland, 1911

Dr. Juvelius read the sensational news from Jerusalem at his desk in the office next to his home. He could only imagine how widely it was being spread across the world. Juvelius knew that the rioters must have gone home by now, and that it was the press, an inexhaustible flood of misinformation, that would continue to stir up controversy, at least until people were tired of hearing about it.

Juvelius knew that the expedition had gone back to Jerusalem that previous spring to resume their work. He had been regularly informed of their progress by Mr. Parker. Mazes of tunnels were still filled with rocks and gravel, but some Hebrew antiquities had been found. Valuable finds had been made. Meanwhile, Juvelius had continued to send him ciphers. And though Mr. Parker seemed unwilling to pursue the other projects as Juvelius directed, such as the tomb of Moses and the archive, he had written to Juvelius to tell him to prepare to return. Juvelius planned to join them in a month or so. But then, right before the news from Jerusalem, a strange letter arrived from Mr. Parker. It had been sent from Port Said, and then via cable to London, then mailed to him.

Work suspended. Don't go. Closer to the letter.

Parker.

"Closer to the letter?" What did he mean? Was he referring to the cipher letter that Juvelius had sent? Were they getting closer to the Ark? Or was he referring to an actual letter, as in a character or symbol? Juvelius did not know.

Juvelius knew that the English gentlemen could never have disgraced the mosque. He knew that this recent excitement had no doubt been stirred up by something else. Secret forces had no doubt whipped up the articles in the world press. Juvelius knew that if they were in any danger, the Jerusalem governor would have warned them by express mail early enough so that they could take an ironclad train out of the city. When the rioting started, the pasha, though exposed because of their deal, probably donned a shiny suit and delayed the crowd to give the expedition more time to escape. Juvelius knew how these things went. When it was noticed that the English had escaped, the enraged people would probably attack the yacht at Jaffa. Juvelius heard that three shots were fired at them from the shore. The English escaped, though the Turks then claimed their cargo. Juvelius knew this somehow.

Juvelius wasn't worried about the newspapers, really. They were fleeting things. He knew that because he read the old books. He knew that the unscrupulousness and humbug would be dismissed by Father Vincent when he would publish his own book. Then, Juvelius thought, they would have to try again. They had survived the dangers once; they would do so again. He had been through too much to let it stop him. He was content to stay home for a little while longer, with his wife, Hanna, and their adopted daughter, Irja.

Juvelius went back to his Bible and his counting and his writing. He was also drawing a new map. He cleared his throat. He had a slight cough. But it was nothing. It was nothing.

FORTY-ONE

JOHAN MILLEN

Stockholm, Sweden, December 1915

Johan Millen looked up at the old men in the black robes. None of them looked very pleased. Some of them held books to their chests. Sturdy plaques revealed their old-fashioned names, though they were hard to read unless you stood close, and even then some of the loops and edges of the gold letters were banked with dust. Some of the men stood high in the room, others behind doors and chairs, each placed in the order of their most important discoveries or financial contribution. The portraits were ghostly at best in terms of their attentions, but to Johan Millen it was still a long way from that shabby solicitor's office in London.

Johan Millen stood at the lectern in the auditorium of the Royal Academy of Sciences in Frescati in Stockholm. It was December 3, 1915, and his living audience was not overwhelming, but Millen was not going to miss his moment. He had waited so long to talk about the expedition.

"Is this all?" Millen said, gesturing at the gold ceiling and its crystal chandeliers, illuminated by electric current. "We live now in the materialism of the past, so devastatingly developed . . . yet no one stops for a moment to reflect . . . is this all?" Millen looked at the wooden floor as if he could see past it somehow.

"I think that this belief is manifest in the most frightening of all conflict, war." Millen paused for a moment. The world had been struck in the last year by a war that felt as if it was the last of them. German forces marched on France and Belgium. There was fighting even in Asia and Africa. Millen held up a book bound in leather. "In such suffering, we turn to the Bible.

"But how do you read the Bible?" asked Millen, shrugging his shoulders. "Those who have taken up a profession to 'research' it have a right to write and publish, though the results sometimes hardly deserve the title of a historical novel." He smiled.

"The problem," he said, "is that the Bible is to some extent composed of legends or oral stories, and as such has been largely unsubstantiated by us.

"To find the truth of the Bible, one must find the 'key to the lock,' so to speak, under which the secret meaning is hidden. It is my friend, Dr. Juvelius, a Finnish scholar, who read the Bible in Hebrew for many years until he found such a key — a cipher — in the Book of Ezekiel."

Millen put both arms on the lectern. "We did take the cipher to Palestine, as you may have read in the papers, in an expedition of which I was the leader. Our plan to find the Ark was to find physical — substantiated! — proof of the contract with God." Here Millen waved his hands, at times pointing his finger to the ceiling. "All the stories about robbery will be disproved. In fact, the excavations were done not only with the most conscientious accuracy, but the workers were well treated, and no one was injured. We restored a double-clean water supply. Alms were given to the poor. We were honest and laudable.

"The reason it became such a big thing — mentioned in *The New York Times* and so forth — is that some people, who tend to unconsciously scoop stories out of murky sources, deceive gullible people to make money. A new volume by the esteemed Father Louis-Hugues Vincent will reveal our archaeological successes. Though it does not contain nearly everything we explored, it will prove our intent and results.

"History is important to help us understand the Bible. When the Israelites finally left Assyrian captivity in 606 BC, they wandered for over a year along the Caspian seas to Scythia. They settled there and never returned. The people who were left in Jerusalem took the name of Israel. But though they both worshipped the one true God, with only a few missteps, they were different peoples. The Jews had very distinctive faces. Israel, who wandered into Europe, on the other hand, were blond, tall people."

Millen paused. " 'That they never shall become a nation of their own,' says the Scripture. And why? you ask. Yes, that they crucified Christ and killed the prophets, but that isn't the answer. We have been looking to the wrong Israel.

"Zechariah tells of a sacred shepherd, a great leader who left God's city to rule his people, somewhere in Assyria, now Southern Russia. He says: 'Woe to the worthless shepherd who leaves the flock! A sword *shall be* against his arm and against his right eye; his arm shall completely wither, and his right eye shall be totally blinded.'

"His name was Odin.

"Until now, Odin has only been a figure of myth, but the Bible says he was real. Undoubtedly, Odin possessed a great number of powers. And he was a true Israelite. This is also confirmed by an old manuscript in Heralds' College in London and Sharon Turner's *History of the Anglo-Saxons.* Some of the tribes under Odin settled south of the Baltic. Odin himself continued into Scandinavia and adopted the name Æsir. This was even suggested in *Beowulf,* the oldest Anglo poem in existence. His followers spread even further, fulfilling the prophecies that Israel would find refuge in 'the land of the witch,' the 'sea-lands,' and 'the islands of the west.' They went to Ireland, England, and even America.

"And they were Israelites.

"The Assyrians however, settled in Germany. There, over time, they became inventive in the manufacture of weapons of war. Their neighbors must always be on their guard, for they are eager warriors, cruel and relentless in war. If they set up their military force, and their armored warriors march through the land they occupy, great will be the horror that they spread around them. In the days of warlike Assyria, the people fled before them; the cities fell into their hands as they marched. If we compare this assertion with today's Germans and the state of the day, very little seems to have changed.

"We see how frenetic evil grows day after day. We approach the Last War . . . mainly between the Assyrians — the Germans — and the Israelites. The prophets foresaw, among other things, the aircraft with their black guns. They saw bullets fired by the airplanes against each other, as well as cannons on wagons and how their projectiles passed through the air with a loud noise, burning over heights and through walls and windows.

"This is the time," he said.

When Millen finally stopped to take questions from the audience, he looked ahead smugly as the people erupted in disrepair with shouts of "Falsiture!" and even "Thief!" Instead, Johan Millen answered only in his head, that when someone bitingly asked what sect he belonged to, he knew that their lack of understanding was great.

■ ■ ■ ■

PART FIVE:
A BLACK STAR

■ ■ ■ ■

CHAPTER FORTY-TWO
AVA ASTOR

Ava moved back to London in September 1911. After her ex-husband John Jacob Astor remarried, he and his nineteen-year-old wife, Madeleine Force Astor, took a protracted honeymoon to Egypt and Paris with Kitty, their precious Airedale. When Madeleine discovered she was pregnant, they decided to return to America. They booked their trip home back to New York, first-class all the way, on board the *Titanic.* When it began to sink slowly into the sea, Astor lifted his wife into one of the lifeboats with the help of an officer. He then asked the man, very lightly, if he might join her because she was pregnant. The man was sorry, but women and children first. Astor bowed his head, then helped two other women onto the boat. He stood on the deck, smoking a cigarette, with the dog. A half hour later, they were gone.

When the news of the tragedy came, Ava

rushed home to New York, dragging Alice with her, to fight for her son's interests in the Astor estate. Madeleine was given the mansion and money, but only on the proviso that she never marry again. Both Vincent and Alice received substantial trust funds. When the body of John Jacob Astor was recovered from the cold Atlantic, he was carrying $2,500 in cash and his gold pocket watch. Vincent carried the watch for the rest of his life.

Ava returned to England. She became vice president of the American Women's War Relief Fund during World War I. She met Thomas Lister, the Lord Ribblesdale, an aristocrat of fiery reputation who had served under Victoria herself. Ava gave up her own divorce settlement to marry the old man in 1919, much to the chagrin of many. Ava thought she would be elevated to a life of reputation and unparalleled social life, but her grandson later remarked that all Lord Ribblesdale wanted was "to marry a beautiful woman and carry her off to his old Tudor horror of a home and read the classics to her in the evenings with his magnificent bass voice."

Ava detested it, and him. She tried to make nice with the English side of the Astors, becoming friends with Nancy Astor, who would become the first woman in Parliament. But Ava mostly spent her days in schemes trying to find a husband for Alice, who was, Ava thought, spoiled and stubborn. But Alice, who had black and blue hair, had her own ideas. She fell in love with a Russian-American prince named Serge Obolensky, who was not only unwealthy but already married. Ava was crushed. She tried to change Alice's mind, but her daughter wouldn't budge. Ava proposed a trip to perhaps distract her.

In 1923, Ava and twenty-year-old Alice voyaged to Egypt as a guest of Ava's friend George Herbert, the Earl of Carnarvon, who was funding the work of a promising archaeologist named Howard Carter. There, in the Valley of the Kings, dressed in a black fur coat and pointed white shoes, Ava visited the newly opened tomb of Tutankhamen. She posed by the stone steps as they fell downward into the sand, her hand steadying her black hat.

The earl, dressed in a khaki suit and felted hat, kissed them both and took their hands, leading them down the stairs into the tomb. They had just opened the seal to the third room — the burial chamber — only days ago, and they were going to be some of the very first people to see it. Alice walked down slowly.

With the light of an electric torch, they saw the smooth, light-colored walls. The earl told them how the first time Howard had broken through, he pushed his light through the opening and said he saw "wonderful things."

"Here we are," said Lord Carnarvon.

"Behold."

The earl was at the far wall and raised his torch.

"The king," he said, with a cough.

They had accessed the burial chamber through an old looter's passage, and everything inside remained still and undisturbed. Down there, in the dark, Ava saw a room filled with statues of strange animals, elegant vases, and everywhere — like it was part of the dust itself — the glint of pure gold. She gasped. The small room was filled by an enormous structure, perhaps nine feet tall, that reached almost to the ceiling. Gold covered its surface, except for the sides, which were colored a brilliant blue. They were inlaid with what Ava guessed had to be magical symbols that repeated themselves over and over. It was an incredible sight, but Ava felt too that it was death boxed up in the desert. She feared the thing inside and hoped they would not have to look upon its face.

Alice was looking at long pieces of wood that seemed to be boat oars. Lord Carnarvon saw her and explained.

"He needed them to make his way across the waters of the underworld."

Alice was clearly taken by the mysteries of the room. Ava watched her very closely. Alice looked at the brightly decorated people on the walls, with their dark eyes and strange poses. She knew this was magic. The earl put his hand on her shoulder and laughed.

"We will open it up soon," he said. "We need to make sure it is absolutely safe. We have tested the air for poisons already. Mr. Carter is very thorough."

Ava was glad of that.

"Mother, look."

Alice had moved to the king's feet. Directly across from them was an opening in the wall. She pointed inside to the darkness.

"A good eye," said the earl. "Just a moment." He ambled over with his light.

"I believe you will appreciate this, Lady Ribblesdale. Look." He flashed his light.

Ava adjusted her eyes and nearly jumped. There, in the dark, a great black beast with two horns was staring at her.

"Hold on," he said, adjusting his angle.

The room was bright, and not because of the light. There was even more gold. The beast looked to be a dog, sitting on a great box of some kind.

"Anubis," said Lord Carnarvon, "the jackal god." Ava looked closer: he was entirely black and lithe, swathed in a linen cloth. All of it was impossibly old. The jackal sat atop a trapezoidal wooden box covered in a thin layer of gold leaf. The box, which was around three or four feet long and two feet high, had two wooden poles projecting from the front and back with which to carry it. Ava saw Alice looking down at a brick that had an inscription on it. It read in part: *"I have set aflame the desert, I have caused the path to be mistaken."*

Whether Ava saw Monty after he returned from Palestine is unknown. The same goes for the true nature of their relationship beyond a few lines in gossipy newspaper columns. Whether she had any feelings for him is a mystery. But if she did, at that moment, in front of a golden box in the middle of ancient ground, she was surely thinking of him.

They finally ascended to the desert, full of white light and blue sky. Before they left, Alice was given a gift, possibly for her upcoming wedding, or as the momentary impulse of a powerful man. It was a necklace, from the tomb. Around a large circle of semiprecious stones were hung hundreds of tiny rams' heads set among black rocks and covered in a soft gold. She put it on. Ava stared. The necklace gave her daughter — her beautiful daughter — an aspect that was otherworldly. The earl told her they had estimated it at 3,400 years old.

Less than two months later, Lord Carnarvon died of a blood infection borne by a single mosquito bite that had become infected. He was fifty-six years old. The newspapers back home made whispers about a curse.

When they returned to London, Serge divorced his wife and married Alice in 1924. Ava grumbled through it. When Lord Ribblesdale, whose nickname had become "the Ancestor," died in 1925, Ava was alone again. She moved to New York once more.

One night, the newlyweds prepared for a fancy-dress affair. When Alice emerged from her mirror, she was wearing the necklace. It was the first time Serge had seen it.

"My God," he asked her, "what is it?"

When she told him the story, he felt like the necklace had "a power" to it. He implored her to take it off. She laughed it off, but all night he "felt the shiver of the unknown" around them.

"I am not a mystical person," Serge said, shaking his head, "preferring to stay away from such things. I believe that such things are better left alone." He looked at the necklace again.

"But the feeling is there within me."

Alice married three more times and had four children. Whenever she wore her necklace, people said she was a different person. She began to have dreams, like this one, recounted in a biography of the Astors by Lucy Kavaler:

A large, decorated mummy case would appear in the shadows of her room, and its top would open to reveal the body of a lovely, dark-haired girl who looked just like Alice. This double was dressed in rags, but her neck and arms were circled with jewelry bearing the ram's head design. Just as she was about to rise form the mummy case, a hand would reach out and push her back into the darkness.

In 1954, Ava gave a dinner party, to which she invited a psychic named Harry Stump. He was also an artist, so Alice showed him some of her things. When he touched the gold necklace, he staggered around the room and fell into a chair. Alice rushed to get him a glass of water. When she returned, he asked for a pencil and paper. He began to draw Egyptian hieroglyphs.

With her fortune, Alice helped to fund the Roundtable Foundation, headquartered at a house in Rockport, Maine, and under the direction of Dr. Andrija Puharich, a Chicago researcher interested in psychic phenomena. The foundation began running experiments in ESP and psychedelics. Puharich built Faraday cages made of copper to block electromagnetic radiation so that the psychics he tested could have stronger experiences. These cages quickly became the center of their work and were used by many, including Alice.

Alice remained active in the New York social world but poured much of her passion into her intense psychic life. Her friends became worried. "She opened Pandora's box and unleashed forces she could not control," a friend said. "She was ready to believe any claim, however suspect or implausible."

Alice died one night of a stroke at fifty-four years old. *The Egyptian Book of the Dead* lay on her nightstand. Alice, who had gone down a tunnel in the sand thirty years before, had been awakened to an endless curiosity that she would not escape. As Lucy Kavaler notes:

> Bit by bit the pressures of the lore of the past began to prey upon her, as she delved into it. She was an expert in Egyptian hieroglyphs. Who knows what secret doors might have been opened? — if indeed any such secret doors actually exist. Or do they even have to, when the mind itself may be the very largest door of all? All I know is that Alice died suddenly, unnecessarily and before her time, put upon by the pressures of this life, and cursed by the pressures of the past. God bless her, for I know in my soul that she has found at last happiness and rest.

Living in Manhattan, Ava Astor had survived her own daughter. She developed a stammer to her voice, but she was still a force of nature, and was often seen walking her pack of dogs through the city, a cloud of perfume surrounding her. She preferred the company of men mostly. Friends noted that there was a "strain of melancholy to her."

"How can I believe in heaven with what I've seen here?" Ava told a young cousin.

Ava lived to be eighty-nine and died on June 9, 1958, in her apartment on Park Avenue. She left $25,000 to her son, Vincent, and three million dollars to Alice's children.

FORTY-THREE

THE EXPEDITION MEN

Monty's men went their separate ways after the expedition ended. The last remaining connection for many of them was the nearly inescapable Great War. Cyril Ward took command of the HMS *Mischief* and survived the war, dying in 1930. Pertti Uotila fought in the Russian army and in a succession of wars and border skirmishes until his death in 1943. One of the only expedition members who escaped the violence was Clarence Wilson, who was still holding out hope to return to Palestine. In his last, mysterious letter to Monty, he wrote: "Our 'friends'? the Masons are still very busy & Ananias is not in it with them, but I think that they are getting a little tired." Soon after, Wilson suffered a mental breakdown and was institutionalized. He died in 1936.

Cyril Foley served in World War I in the trenches of France. After the war, he joined the Royal Air Corps and worked in military intelligence. His memoir, *Autumn Foliage* (1935), showcased his uncanny range of gentleman hobbies, all in his ineffable style of storytelling. When he died, still a bachelor — exactly one year to the day after the publication of his book — those who knew him were astonished, not only that he had died, but that he was capable of doing so in the first place. As one of his admirers put it, he had "a typical Englishman's way about the world, which hardly includes a proportionate reference to the couple of wars he saw through."

The year after the expedition left Palestine, Robin Duff was spotted at the Hotel Cattani in Engelberg, Switzerland, a gorgeous resort set in a small green valley in the shadow of snow-covered mountains.

"I met a big sleepy man in the Guards who has been in that mad treasure-hunt for King Solomon's treasures," wrote Rudyard Kipling in a letter to a friend dated February 8, 1912. The famous writer, nearly fifty, was amazed by the story Duff told him, of the "siphoning of the pool of Siloam."

"[He] told me that the cipher on which they worked," Kipling wrote, "and it appeared to be a perfectly accurate cipher, was discovered in the St. Petersburgh museum by one Jurisius a Finn. He had his points both as a decipherer of codes and as an explorer but he *would* rape the local virgins. Hence trouble with the Turkish authorities and the final elimination of him."

"Talk of fiction!" Kipling wrote of the story of the expedition. "Fiction isn't in it."

When the war began, Robin Duff reenlisted and was tragically killed early on in 1914, only days after leaving for the front. He left behind his wife, Lady Juliet Lowther, and a son and daughter.

Others avoided the war, though they felt its reach. Otto Von Bourg ended up in America, giving traveling lectures on his abilities that might have felt more like magic shows.

Agop Macasdar, the Armenian who was most likely a Christian, was jailed in Beirut along with Sheikh Khalil El-Danaf and his two sons for digging under the Dome of the Rock. While in prison, Macasdar wrote to the British consul general:

You should not ignore that I have been arrested for more than four months in my capacity as secretary-interpreter for the Honorable Captain Montagu B. Parker and his union in London, and this according to a contract in good standing.

My current situation has become shameful and untenable and I can no longer bear this pitiful existence, I find myself very seriously ill and I am in the last despair and the Honorable Mr. Montagu B. Parker is solely responsible for everything that can happen to me, because for more than three years that I have been under his orders I have rendered irreproachable services to him and his union. Here I am today; I am a victim of my duty, and the Honorable Mr. Montagu B. Parker shines with his silence. I also sent him the following telegram:

"I am still in prison; regret silence; are responsible for me materially, morally; shameful situation; untenable; wire back wages and expenses."

Macasdar and the others were eventually sentenced: the sheikh to twelve months; the others, to three years each. With time served, they were set free on August 16, 1911. Monty offered to pay for their traveling expenses back to Jerusalem, but they refused.

Mehmet Cavid Bey was appointed minister of finance in the Committee of Union and Progress (CUP) in Turkey. When Monty wished to return to Jerusalem in 1911, Cavid again took the position of minister of finance and nominated inspectors to approve of Monty's return. Because of his family lineage, schooling, and place of burial, Cavid is widely considered to have been a *dhome,* a cryptojew, which meant he practiced Judaism in secret in Turkey. When he used his influence to approve the Parker Expedition in 1909 (which he was paid for), he was still grieving over his wife, who had died of tuberculosis in March.

Cavid still held his position when the CUP began the genocide of ethnic Christian Armenians in 1915, though he seemed to have been deliberately left out of the decision-making process, having been sent to Germany to negotiate a railroad contract when the order was discussed and given. Cavid was later accused of plotting the assassination of President Mustafa Kemal Pasha, who many held responsible for being part of the genocide. For this crime, Cavid was convicted and hanged in 1926. Though the actual number of dead will probably never be known, the number of people who were murdered during the Armenian genocide is somewhere around 1.5 million. Turkey denies that it ever occurred.

Captain Hoppenrath returned to the Belgian Congo and his steamship. He was never made a member of the Syndicate.

Father Vincent finally wrote his account of the expedition, *Underground Jerusalem: Discoveries on the Hill of Ophel, 1909–11.* The book, which was well received, first appeared in French but was translated into English and printed by Horace Cox in 1911. Father Vincent's account is full of personality but also unabashedly scientific. He claimed that the members of the expedition "wanted their work to be presented by a witness who was not suspect and would not be biased." In his book, Father Vincent makes no mention of the Ark — there is no proof he ever knew their true plans — and concludes that the expedition was a great success. He promises a second volume that never arrives. He went on to become one of the most highly respected biblical scholars in the world. He was an honorary member of the British Academy, the Order of the British Empire, Cross of the Order of Leopold, and the prestigious French Legion of Honor. He died on December 30, 1960, and is buried in the courtyard of his order in Jerusalem.

After his lecture, Johan Millen published his own book on the expedition, *Pa Ratta Vagar* ("On the Right Track"), in 1917. The cover depicted a single eye on a red pyramid with strange beams radiating from it. In the book, Millen built on the racist theories of his lecture, in addition to providing alleged examples from the Bible predicting the machinery of the Great War. Millen's notes and papers were deposited with the Swedish Theosophical Society, to be opened at his death. When he died in 1932, the safe deposit box was bare.

Forty-Four

CHARLES WARREN

After he returned from Singapore, Warren was inducted as the first master of a new Freemason lodge, the Quatuor Coronati Lodge number 2076, in 1884. Though Warren had been a Freemason since 1859, this new lodge's focus was on rigorous scientific and historical research into the origins of Freemasonry, as well as the long-term aim of rebuilding the Temple of Solomon. Freemasonry, a fraternal society of hierarchy, secret handshakes, and charity, definitively traced its origins back at least to the Middle Ages, when a workers' organization of stonecutters and masons was formed — although some believe the group may have formed even earlier. It was rumored that some lodges asked members to believe in a Supreme Being with a secret name, or to avoid any talk of religion at all.

Warren was still in the army during the Second Boer War in 1899 and was made general of the Fifth Division of the South African Field Force. His actions at the Battle of Spion Kop, a barren hilltop in Ladysmith, were looked on with great criticism. Warren, who was nearly sixty and had little experience handling troops, made several errors throughout the battle. His division had slow mobility because of unnecessary encumbrance (including a cast-iron toilet), and he mismanaged basic reinforcement maneuvers, contributing to an overall lack of communication and eventual Boer victory. After the battle, the bodies of Englishmen destroyed by machine-gun fire lay in heaps across the grass. Nearly three hundred were killed, and over a thousand wounded. English sons were buried in mass graves in Africa. Warren was summoned back to Britain and never commanded troops in the field again. In his later years, he worked with Robert Baden-Powell to help found the Boy Scouts.

Warren always stayed active in the PEF, often publishing comments and analysis in their trade journal, the *Quarterly*. When the news of the riots in Jerusalem came, the *Quarterly* was shocked by the news of the treasure hunters. When Father Vincent's book arrived to speak to the Parker expedition's scientific value, Charles Warren, in his seventies, wrote a response.

It was not kind.

In a far-ranging and truculent article, Warren attacked Father Vincent: "The statements of Father Vincent," he writes, "do a grievous injustice to the work of the Palestine Exploration Fund in recent years." Warren listed, point by point, a series of claims made by Father Vincent in *Underground Jerusalem* that diminished Warren's own work in the tunnels and "cast [them] aside." Moreover, Warren thought that Father Vincent's maps looked suspiciously like the maps he had done for the PEF. Warren accused *le petit saint* of plagiarism. His criticism was scathing, and his grievances many.

Father Vincent wrote back.

In a subsequent issue, Vincent defended his work, finding it "inconceivable" that Warren would accuse him of such things. On the contrary, Father Vincent named Warren's findings as "heroic operations" and "precise references." "So little have I 'cast one one side,' *minimized,* or *passed over in silence* his Survey," wrote Father Vincent in response, "that my two chapters devoted to the Ophel and the Siloam conduit commenced with a tribute to his works." Father Vincent was adamant that he

427

had not *"taken from Charles Warren's drawings,"* but that he was only attracted to take up "a new survey" of the same tunnels — and did so with the work of others at his back. Father Vincent saw archaeology as work built upon slow layers, not individual competition.

Warren wrote back again, assuring readers that he had "loyally accepted his assurances that nothing had been taken" from his maps. Warren pointed out some helpful areas that Father Vincent might revisit, including the chasm at the bottom of the stairs. But overall, all was fine. "I must express my delight," wrote Warren, "that this incident would have been the means of bringing me into close acquaintance and friendship with a gentleman so distinguished as an archaeologist and so highly esteemed by all who know him."

At the end of his letter in the *Quarterly,* a small footnote read:

Sir Charles Warren wishes it to be understood that the above observations are not made as a reply to Father Vincent's defence, but in acknowledgment of his expression of goodwill.

Sir Charles Warren died in 1927. Very few

papers ran his obituary. A man named J. W. Ibbotson wrote into his local country gazette:

I could not but draw attention to his passing, as many of your readers must have known him.

Forty-Five

DR. JUVELIUS

Before he began his life's work, Valter Juvelius was a surveyor, following in the steps of his father, who was a towering figure in his life. Juvelius's mother had died when he was in his twenties, leaving his father in charge. His father drank. As a surveyor, Juvelius would go on long trips into the Finnish countryside, among the grass fields and tall pines, spending his nights alone in rustic cabins. Juvelius began to read the Bible. He felt like he was seeing something that others could not and that he must do something about it. He was accepted to the doctoral program at the Imperial Alexander University. With a family and a good job, this was a choice of tremendous risk and uncertainty.

He wrote imagistic poetry about village life and love that was published. He did translations of other poets, under the name "Valter Juva." He experienced intense depression and suffered headaches. He kept reading and writing. For his project, Juvelius tried to make sense of the chronology of the Bible. He completed his dissertation over a long and arduous journey of several years. He called it "a nightmare."

Meanwhile, he was working on a secret project. As he studied and read, he noticed a kind of invisible framework to some of the Scripture. Parts were repeated, in sequence, and seemed to provide a glimpse into a secret page just beneath the real one. He began work on a cipher to understand it. He believed that he could understand this himself, a hidden message between him and the words, between him and God.

Juvelius read books about the lost Ark by a man named Henning Melander and thought his own work might be aiming at a similar target. In 1907 Juvelius was re-acquainted with his childhood friend Pertti Uotila and began to meet others who would steer him toward people willing to fund his idea.

When he finally reached Jerusalem, Juvelius had his photograph taken at a local studio. After taking a more formal picture, he put on silks, wrapped a turban around his head (with some help), and slid two curved pistols into his belt. His face in the picture, a mixture of smugness and utter happiness, is the result of having imagined something almost unbelievable, and working to make it real.

In 1916, Juvelius wrote the book *Valkoinen kameeli* ("The White Camel"), a collection of three extended short stories written by Heikki Kenttä, a pseudonym. The middle story, "The Truth of 'The Shame of the Omar Mosque,' " is Juvelius's only firsthand account of the events — the ones depicted in this book — hunting for the Ark in Jerusalem. Although the short story is ostensibly a work of fiction, Juvelius believed that fiction conveyed truths. After all, he wrote his dissertation and indeed devoted the great work of his life to the single belief that the Bible — a collection of stories of the supernatural — could be studied *as is* for real historical truth. Whether the events of Juvelius's story contain true and factual details of the events or reflect the truth of his emotional response to the experience, they are an important piece of the story, if not a darker puzzle itself.

In 1918, Juvelius became the head of the city library in Viipuri. There, among his beloved, quiet books, he continued his work. He died on Christmas Day in 1922 after suffering from throat cancer. He was fifty-seven years old. His Bible, overstuffed with his own notes and questions to the small words within, was buried with him, placed on his chest like the shield of Moses. There was never any direct evidence of him, or any of the expedition members, being poisoned by radium.

His personal papers remained with his family until they were tracked down by a historian named David Landau, who wrote a small biographical article on Juvelius that debunked nearly all of the existing stories about him. In late August of 1996, Landau met with Tom Hilli, Juvelius's great-grandson, at a coffee shop outside Helsinki. There, on a café table among the butter and crumbs, Hilli produced the lost papers of Valter Juvelius.

David Landau described what he saw:

The documents were stored in envelopes and on each of them there was the name of the Biblical figure who's grave Juvelius drew precisely. Included were the names of the prophets, possibly all of them. Tom opened another envelope and spread its contents; here in front of us was the drawing of — Moses's catacomb. Juvelius seriously was planning to go back and continue the excavations.

"What we have in front of us is science fiction," Landau told Hilli. It could "serve as a manuscript for a new movie by Steven Spielberg!" After they were done, the great-grandson of Dr. Valter Juvelius took the papers and left. Landau was satisfied but felt there was more work to do:

> On their own merits, Juvelius' papers are no doubt worthless. Nevertheless, they should be studied more closely because they are connected to archeological excavations which were conducted in a scientific manner and produced important results.

FORTY-SIX

THE COMPETITION

In 1910, the Baron Edmond de Rothschild helped purchase valuable cemetery space on Mount Olive for the residents of Silwan. The next year, he bought up land around the Parker excavation site. He funded the work of archaeologist Raymond Weill, who in 1913 dug on Mount Ophel but accidentally destroyed two caves that he claimed were royal tombs of the House of David.

The baron was not just interested in relics; he was a leading voice in the Zionist movement to establish a Jewish homeland in Palestine that would include co-rulership with the Arabs. In a 1934 letter to the League of Nations, he stated that "the struggle to put an end to the Wandering Jew, could not have as its result, the creation of the Wandering Arab." Known as "the Famous Benefactor" in Jerusalem, the baron gave tremendous amounts of money for settlements, lands, and Jewish businesses. He died in 1934. The foundation named after him continues to support worldwide programs in philanthropy, education, and the arts.

Habib Allah, the man who shot two American women in the Well of Souls, was awaiting trial when the syndicated columnist Edward Sims Van Zile wrote Jacob Spafford in Jerusalem to see what was happening with the trial. Jacob replied with the full details of the case. When Allah was finally convicted, he was given eight years' imprisonment.

William Le Queux's *Treasures of Israel* sold widely in several editions, including an American version titled *The Great God Gold*. Timo R. Stewart uncovered that Le Queux was an attendant at one of Johan Millen's early investor meetings in London, before he met Fort or Vaughn. Le Queux appropriated the premise of the expedition — a cipher leading the way to the Ark — for use as the plot of his book. Le Queux made many claims over his years of best-selling work, including a letter that claimed Rasputin knew who committed the Whitechapel murders. His most famous book was *The Invasion of 1910* about a fictional (and successful) invasion of England by the Germans, in the tone of *War of the Worlds.* The massive fear of German spies generated by this book and others helped contribute to the formation of Great Britain's actual spy department, MI5.

The "Friend" who acted as the source for the article by William E. Curtis remains anonymous.

In March 1915, the people living outside Jerusalem watched darkness emerge from the ground. In pools of moving, clicking life, strange shapes stretched out in columns across the dirt, destroying every plant in their path.

Locusts.

The horde of millions moved. When one strayed far enough to be studied by the children, they were scared of its large eyes and two horns. The insects ate everything that was green. They claimed it as their own.

Five weeks later, they could fly.

As the plague took to the air, the black specks looked like reversed stars against the blue sky. Their thick bodies thudded off farmers. People hid and prayed. The flying clouds stripped whole areas of the cover of vegetation. Photographers from the American Colony helped document the event, the insects engulfing their cameras. The plague continued until October, when dead locusts dropped to the dry ground. By the time it was over, the locust armies had reduced much of Palestine to dirt and rock. That year's food supply was almost depleted. Though locust swarms are a recurring, natural event, many people wondered what Palestine had done to deserve such punishment.

FORTY-SEVEN

BERTHA VESTER

Bertha stopped for a moment, in the middle of the ward, and closed her eyes. For a moment there was nothing, just darkness, before she could hear the sound again. It was loud and unearthly, but it filled her entire being with happiness. There was no other noise like it, the unmistakable wail of babies. All these tiny little beings were trying to communicate something so simple — hunger, discomfort, need — and it came bursting out in the rawest song.

Bertha opened her eyes and walked down the rows of cribs as the nurses and volunteers tended to the little ones' needs. Bertha smiled at Arab babies and Jewish babies, some of them close enough to touch each other. Against the wall, a particularly pudgy infant with bushy black hair was being weighed on their brand-new scale.

Bertha felt a tear in her eye. The Anna Spafford Baby Home had been in use since

1925, growing from a small room to a full-scale professional medical care facilty and support home for new mothers. They had expanded, moved, and changed some things here and there, but essentially their mission had remained the same: to help those who could not help themselves. After a lifetime in Jerusalem following in her parents' footsteps, Bertha had finally found her true calling. Her brother Jacob, of course, had been beside her every step of the way, and was instrumental in the home's success and its ability to adapt to the individual cases that came to their doorstep.

A boy with dark hair skipped by her.

"No running!" Bertha said, stopping him gently. He looked no more than twelve. Not even her own son could break the rules in this place.

"Do you like the new ward?" she asked, putting her hands on his shoulders. The child nodded.

"When we started," said Bertha, "we were over in the embroidery school!"

The boy had heard this story from his mother so many times, but it didn't stop her. By now, everyone had heard it.

One night, many years ago, while walking outside the city to an event, Bertha ran into a Bedouin couple with a newborn boy. The baby was very sick. But they could not get into any of the hospitals. Bertha had connections and was able to find a nice warm bed for the new mother and child.

The next day, Bertha was surprised to see the father standing in her front yard, holding the same little baby. The small miracle had turned to darkness: the mother had died overnight. The baby, thank God, was doing well. But the Bedouin father, who lived in a cave in the desert, could not take care of him.

Bertha took the boy and adopted him, naming him Noel because she had found him on Christmas Eve, on her way to sing carols in Bethlehem under the night sky.

Bertha stared down at her son, still so full of promise, and could see him as he was then, a still and quiet baby, who only once in a while would sigh and squiggle, until he fell asleep.

Noel went off to find his friends. Bertha watched him go. As she left the new room, she paused by the plaque in the wall that commemorated the new wing of the Anna Spafford Childrens Home.

TO THE GLORY OF GOD
AND IN LOVING MEMORY OF
JACOB E. SPAFFORD
ADOPTED SON OF

HORATIO GATES AND ANNA SPAFFORD
IN ACKNOWLEDGMENT OF A LIFE THAT WAS AN INSPIRATION TO MANY

The American Colony had survived war, the ongoing British mandate, and rioting, but it was a day in July of 1932 when Jacob's car went flying off a swerving mountain road called the Seven Sisters that would forever diminish it. Jacob had been traveling to an archaeological dig, his lifelong hobby, in an area thought to be the site of the battle between David and Goliath.

Jacob had been her business partner and her greatest ally. She was so proud of him, her half brother, Jacob Eliahu Spafford, who had been adopted by their parents when he was young. She was proud that he had grown into such a good man and proud that he was the one, as a boy skipping school, who had discovered the Siloam inscription engraved on an ancient tablet in a dark tunnel, and had never once mentioned it to anyone, not even once.

In 1950, Bertha Vester published her memoirs, titled *Our Jerusalem.* She died, at age ninety, on June 27, 1968, in Jerusalem. She left behind two daughters, two sons, and countless more children of all kinds.

Her visiting admirers over the years included Helen Keller, Cole Porter, T. E. Lawrence, kings and dignitaries, multiple American presidents, and Marilyn Monroe. The Baby Home, now known as the Spafford Children's Center, continues to minister to the needs of thousands of patients, of all faiths, as it has done for nearly one hundred years. Bertha's adopted son Noel grew up to join the Transjordan Frontier Force and worked with the United Nations in a refugee camp in Jericho. One day, in 1953, Noel came to say goodbye to his mother. He was going to Damascus, he said. They never heard from him again.

FORTY-EIGHT

MONTY PARKER

When Monty Parker left Palestine, he traveled to Turkey, America, and Canada. Monty had mostly escaped the eyes of the continental newspapers, but he desperately wanted to return to Palestine. The Syndicate reorganized again and raised funds, and most of the crew that had allegedly been in the Dome of the Rock pledged to return with Monty. When the Turks, with help from Cavid, approved his return, the crew left for Jaffa once again. But when they arrived, they did so not as a secret cadre of Englishmen on some madcap adventure, but as some of the most infamous men to set foot in Jerusalem in the past decade.

The locals, even in Jaffa, were so incensed at their return that violence seemed imminent. Monty was told to stay on the boat. And thus the last iteration of the Parker expedition left for good on a long voyage home.

When the Great War came, Monty reenlisted with the Grenadier Guards, though some members of his family disliked his choice as being too common. Because of his injuries in South Africa, which were classified as "neurasthenia," the contemporary term for the traumatic aftereffects of the combat he had seen on the battlefield, Monty served at headquarters in France and Belgium. He saw papers with impossible numbers pass over his desk. When the war ended, he slipped back into his old life.

Monty lived with his older brother Edmund, whom he affectionately called B, at Saltram. After their father died, Edmund realized that their debt was higher than their income and had to make difficult decisions in selling off parts of the estate. After inheriting a nightmare, Edmund developed a plan to save their family home, which seemed to be working.

When World War II began, all but two — the butler and cook — of the eleven-person staff of Saltram departed. When the Luftwaffe bombed Plymouth, it was Monty and his brother who stood on the roof of Saltram and put out the fires. Monty, in his sixties, rolled up his sleeves and felt the familiar heat and heard the same loud explosions that he never hoped to again, but Monty would not let his home be taken away by the Nazis. Soon, the Americans arrived and parked their great green vehicles in Saltram Park. Monty walked around and took pictures of the smiling soldiers.

Monty's brother B passed away in 1951 at age seventy-four. Because Edmund had no children, Monty inherited both the title Earl of Morley and Saltram itself, which had bomb damage on its roof and escalating debt. With some help from politicians, including Nancy Astor, Monty arranged to let the National Trust take Saltram — all of it — to even up the heavy death-duty tax left by his brother. Though some of the outlying family members grumbled in their teacups, Monty had made the sacrifice to save Saltram, not for himself but for what it stood for.

Free of the constraints of a large household, Monty enjoyed the lifestyle of a louche, well-tailored gentleman, traveling to Greece, New Zealand, Hawaii, and points in between. He had lunches on the decks of white boats. He attended parties where women wore diamonds. With his big camera, he took photos of bathing beauties on fine sands. Pictures of him, bald, with a white mustache, appeared in the society columns of various magazines, his eyes always close to a wink. When he was home, his nephews and nieces called him "Uncle God."

Monty Parker was eighty-three years old when he died on April 28, 1962. He had just returned from a trip to Australia and the United States. His obituary mentioned that he had considerable interests in the china clay industry — and, of course, some business about Jerusalem.

He never married and had no children. His mostly spent-up estate and effects were given to Marion Elizabeth Jessie Marconi Cecil, who was identified in the probate notice as "a married woman." She was the goddaughter of Marconi, the radio pioneer. A lover of codes and ciphers, Marconi referred to her in his secret diaries as "Betty." The title went to his nephew, Jack's son, John St. Aubyn Parker, the sixth Earl of Morley.

St. Mary Church in Plympton, a fine country church dating back to 1311, is built over an old priory burial ground. Narrow and white, with a beautiful wood vault, it has, like all English churches of a certain age, its own secret things. In the chapel, tinted blue by a plate of stained glass and under a great window, there is a stone tomb of a knight. His effigy lies on top of an intricately sculpted rectangular crypt. The head of the figure is rested on his helmet. His eyes are closed but look wide open — blank — as he prays, his mouth voicing a word. On Sundays, all the children who should be listening instead stare at the box, sometimes, wondering what is inside. Or, rather, knowing. They stare at the outside of the vessel instead, built up as a kind of distraction. Or perhaps even a clue. There, right on the coffin, they can see a carving of the Father holding a crucifix, with a dove sitting on top. It is not the Holy Trinity but a representation of it — as hope, as belief — to make sense of the bones, of the darkness, within.

Monty is buried just outside the church, next to his mother and father; his brother Edmund can be found on their other side. Their Celtic-looking crosses have become chipped and worn over time, but they are strong, in their way, and picturesque in the deep green grass along the thin stone lane.

Forty-Nine
THE SECRET CUPBOARD

Throughout his public life, Monty never admitted to digging under the Dome of the Rock. It is easy to miss, because so many others did tell their versions, but Monty kept his cards close. When asked about the expedition by the press, especially in America, he would evade the question and smile.

I first heard of the expedition like so many others, in Simon Sebag Montefiore's brilliant *Jerusalem: A Biography.* In his book, he devotes several dramatic pages to the history of the Parker expedition. I was utterly fascinated, not only by what Montefiore wrote but also by the honest-to-God amazement — and hope — that someone had actually gone after the Ark. I knew there had to be more to the story.

I saw a reference in the endnotes to "Parker Family Archive" and tried to track it down to no luck. Sometime later, I wrote a letter to the Earl of Morley that was a complete shout into the void. I looked up how to address him in the proper manner. Several months later, I got a tall, rectangular envelope in the mail, with a handwritten address and a typed letter. The letter was short and was signed by hand, "Morley."

I read the letter many times before I realized there were two ways to look at it: as another dead end or as a possible clue.

In the meantime, I searched for other records of the expedition, from reports to novels; I looked for and translated and read everything I could get my hands on. It was another two years before I found an article I wanted to get translated from Hebrew. I contacted the author, who was very helpful. What she said next made me stare at my computer for a good two minutes.

The archive had been found. The bag of notes and papers that Monty carried with him every day over a hundred years ago in Jerusalem were real.

Dr. Nirit Shalev-Khalifa is a historian and curator in Jerusalem who had done an exhibit on the Parker expedition. She had been trying to find the archive since 1996. In 2012, while planning a vacation in England, she took a chance and got in touch with the Morley household. After a persuasive conversation with the maid, Dr. Shalev-

Khalifa got the email address of the earl's son; his father was very ill. She sent him a message and waited. It wasn't until the night before she was about to leave for England, when she went to close her computer — at midnight — that she saw it: an email from the earl's son. He wanted to see her.

When they met in England, it was "wonderful" said Nirit. The earl's son was very interested in hearing more about his relative. That is when Nirit saw it, lying on the table.

The box.

She knew exactly what it was.

They opened it and saw papers, photos, reports — all of Monty's original documents from the expedition. Nirit looked through it carefully. And there it was: "the treasure," she said — the cipher itself. The earl's son pointed to some words in Hebrew that she read for him. "If it's true," she said, laughing, "you'll be the richest man on earth! Or at least," she added, "you'll get a medal."

When Nirit came home, she made arrangements through her institution for a photographer to come down from Oxford. The entire box was photographed and scanned. A few years later, a man named

Graham Addison indexed and collated it all to the letter, preserving its legacy for good.

"It was nice, as a historian, to be part of history," said Nirit.

Nirit, who is warm and welcoming, listened to my own ideas and invited me to take part in a Parker conference in Jerusalem. She introduced me to other scholars, historians, and writers. All of a sudden, I was part of an expedition.

"It's a never-ending story," she said.

When I talked to the son, he was now the seventh Earl of Morley. I spoke with him and his daughter Olivia over a Zoom call. I first addressed him as "Lord Morley," after again consulting more than a few manuals of proper etiquette.

"Call me Mark," he said.

He told me that he had first seen the papers as a boy. His father, the sixth earl, John St. Aubyn Parker, was at Eton with his wife, picking Mark up from school. It was then that an old man, the Parker family lawyer, came up to them with his face white as a sheet.

"We found these papers," the man said, his voice cracking with nerves. He produced a box from under his arm. "These should be kept quiet. They might cause an international incident!" Mark looked up at all these people who were taller than him and thought it all sounded incredibly interesting. He had met Monty once, he remembered. His granduncle had slipped him a toy at some family gathering. It was a little brown mouse, carved out of wood.

"We want the story out there for history," Mark said. "It's a real blue-sky adventure." When I told them I had found a strange, symbolic connection to Jack the Ripper, his wife laughed off-screen, and we all had to agree. Locked in our homes during a pandemic, separated by an ocean, it was a good way to spend a morning, making a connection to the past through the present. The archive, like the Ark, was never where it was supposed to be. I can imagine there is some kind of lesson in that.

I thanked the Parkers for letting the story continue. Over the next days, I began going through Monty's archives myself. Among the ciphers and reports, I found exactly what I had been searching for as the truth of this story. Not if he *found* it, but if he *did* it — did he really try that last gambit and dig under the Dome of the Rock? There is so much uncertainty in the other accounts that this became the most important question for me. Mostly because he never says so.

But in Monty's archives, I found the answer.

The letter was from Monty to Constantinople, dated November 2, 1911. When I finally read it, it did not fall lightly out of an old, worn book, crumbled with age. The soundtrack didn't swell behind me. Nor did I have to read it in a mirror or apply a secret reagent. But as I slowly opened the PDF on my computer screen in Cleveland, it sure felt like all these things happened. There, on a perfect scan of an old piece of paper, was Monty's only confession.

During my last stay in Jerusalem, it was claimed that I smuggled into the revered Omar Mosque to do searches and that I even took some objects.

My entry into the revered mosque has been duly authorized by the authorities and I have never bribed anyone for this purpose.

The object of my research in the so-called revered mosque is purely scientific with the sole aim of discovering whether there is not a tunnel under the mosque leading to Silwan.

As for the objects found, there are some potiches discovered in my excavations at Silwan which are currently in a cupboard placed in a gallery, and the said cupboard was sealed jointly by the inspectors and by me.

Therefore, I assure you that I have taken away nothing and I hope that you will not listen to unfounded tales manipulated by intriguing outrageous people.

The people and the faithful of Jerusalem, not knowing the authorization I had and ignoring the scientific purpose of my research in the said sanctuary, wrongly accused me of desecration.

Believe, honorable deputies, I worshiped mosques as well as churches and other holy places.

Upon entering the revered mosque in question I never thought of committing a wrongdoing; but unfortunately, unwittingly, I had offended very respectable feelings, I deeply regret this and I beg you to accept my sincere apologies.

My duty and the duty of all honest people is not to have the innocent wrongfully convicted; therefore I urge to be heard before the judgment by a Letter of Request officially appointed.

Having explained the situation to you clearly, I hope that you, Honorable Members, will help me to save these poor innocent fathers of families. I also hope that you will help my friend Hanna Bey to calm the spirits for the continuation of the works to take place without further complications and under the supervision of the Authorities, according to my contract with the Government.

Please accept, Honorable Deputies, my most respectful tributes.

Capt. Montague B. Parker

Even in this, Monty's only admission, there is still some sway from the slippery adventurer. For though he does not mention the Ark, he admits to being there to search for a tunnel that would reach down into the valley. Was he confessing to unburden his soul or as part of an agreement where he would take at least a bit of responsibility (if only in a file somewhere) to free the prisoners in Beirut? If we are following Monty's own words here — and we shouldn't always, for obvious reasons — we can at least know one thing: he did dig under the Dome of the Rock.

There is no evidence — and I looked — of a gold box somewhere in Saltram or a massive influx of cash to Captain Parker in a buried account notice. Juvelius claimed there were ten full boxes taken from the yacht that were seized by the Turks and remained in Malta, unopened. This is an easy scene to imagine. When this was brought up later in the Turkish parliament, one of the ministers noted dryly that the boxes contained only "tools, clays, and stones."

There was one last clue in Monty's confession that struck me: the curious "cupboard" he refers to. In no other account was there a reference to a hiding place. I kept looking.

On December 19, 1919, the brand-new Jerusalem Headquarters of Antiquities, housed in Way House and consisting of only a few shelves, tasked with preserving the history of the region, received a typewritten telegram from the military governor of Jerusalem on green and yellow paper in thin, faint type. It was stamped and penciled and official looking. Since it was so new, the headquarters did not get a lot of mail. The subject line read: "Silwan, Confiscation of Antiquities from D. Parker's Excavation." The telegram stated:

I beg to report that Ibrahim Eff. Stambuli states that Mr. Montagu Parker, who was excavating in Silwan before the war, left in his charge two cupboards containing antiquities and deposited in his house in Silwan. The two cupboards of antiquities, which were sealed by the Turkish Government and Mr. Parker, still remain intact.

The captain inspector of antiquities responded five days later with a response typed on a small placard with holes, meant to be filed as a record.

> The two sealed cupboards you have called my attention [to] will be visited shortly. If the seals are unbroken, they had better remain so.

After some more back-and-forth between government entities, the matter seemed to be lost to the bureaucracy until a July 17, 1920, telegram from the adviser on antiquities finally offered news.

He had been to the site. The telegram read:

> The two cupboards were inspected by me 28.4.20 and their seals were found intact. One cupboard contained the property of Captain Montague Parker and is deposited in the house of Hussein Musa, Mukhtar of Silwan. Owing to his absence from Jerusalem, he requests that they may be taken under Government Control and opened.

Two years passed before anyone responded.

It was a tumultuous time in Jerusalem, but there were probably legal issues as they tried to get in touch with Captain Parker before breaking the seal and opening the containers. On May 2, 1922, the director of antiquities wrote directly to the governor of Jerusalem:

Certain antiquities discovered in excavations previous to the War by Capt. Parker and his colleagues are housed under seal in the Parker Mission House on Ophel. I desire to take possession of these antiquities. On behalf of the Government as under Turkish Law no private person could stand legally possessed of discoveries in excavation, and in the meanwhile there is great danger of these antiquities being damaged or removed. Will you kindly grant the necessary authority, and indicate the steps to be taken?

A response came the very next day:

This period of 12 months has long since elapsed, and I infer from your report that a list of the antiquities has not been furnished to our dept.

An official order was asked for and given, and on May 10, 1922, it stated:

The site in question has been inspected by Captain Mackay, Chief Inspector of Antiques. He reported them sealed and safe and didn't open. Since that date these antiquities have remained undisturbed, no list of them has been forwarded to this Department, as required by the Antiquities Ordinance.

Harry Charles Luke, the acting governor of Jerusalem, responded with a firm command:

I do order that the said antiquities be seized and placed in the custody of the Director of the Department of Antiquities.

On May 29, 1922, the department summarized what happened next, two years after the initial discovery of these mysterious items:

On May 23rd and 24th, this Department formally seized and conficated the following antiquities:

460

> Antiquities discovered by the Parker Expedition 1909–1911 which had been deposited in a sealed cupboard at Silwan.

> The antiquities were removed without opposition or disturbance and are now deposited in the Museum premises.

They had seized the items but made no mention of what they had found.

On June 15, 1922, the acting governor wrote again:

> With reference to your letter, it would be of interest to this Governorate to learn if anything of ~~interest~~ out importance was found among the antiquities in respect of which I sent you orders of seizure.

On June 20, 1922, eleven years after the riot, the director of antiquities finally revealed what he had tried to hide behind in a sealed cupboard in Silwan:

> The bulk of the antiquities seized by this Department consisted of very important primitive remains discovered by the Parker Expedition of 1909–1911. These

remains were almost entirely ceramic.

Most of the objects seized have now been placed in the Palestine Museum and I should be very glad to receive a visit from any member of the Governorate who is interested in these matters. The specimen of greatest interest is a fragmentary bowl of polished red and black ware, whose analogies with the pre-historic Egyptian.

A few months later, on November 20, 1922, the museum received another letter:

I am desirous of disposing of the collection we have stored up in Jerusalem as the result of our excavations. I should indeed be very glad if I in this could count on your exceptional expert advice, and how and where to sell it.

Yours faithfully
Johan Millen

The museum, and the government, were not pleased. The attorney general responded to the museum in an internal letter:

Article 9 of Ottoman Antiquities says if a person fails to inform the Government of a find of antiquities, he shall be liable to a fine of up to PT 1000 and the antiquities shall be confiscated.

W. J. Phythian-Adams of the Department of Antiquities then responded directly to Millen:

In regards the last paragraph of your letter, I have to inform you that all antiquities found by excavators before the war pass automatically into the hands of the present Administration. Your name has recently been reported to me in connection with the work of the "Parker Expedition." If the antiquities to which you refer are those which were found by that party, I have to inform you that they have now been removed to the Palestine Museum where the bulk of them are on exhibition.

The last note in the file is dated July 13, 1938:

For list of Antiquities confiscated from Silwan see File 1052 (3199/ATQ/1052).

Across the left of the small card was drawn a long arrow pointing down.

I could not find any evidence of file 1052 in the official records, so I wrote to Fawzi

Ibrahim, the curator of the Rockefeller Archaeological Museum in Jerusalem.

Dear Mr. Ibrahim,

I hope this message finds you well. I am a writer in the States who is working on a book about the Parker expedition. I'm looking to find out what happened to a bowl (or the remains of one) that was part of the collection of the old Imperial Museum of Antiquities. If I'm reading the history right (thanks to your work here), some/most of that collection ended up in the Rockefeller. Am I right in this?

The only information I have is the initial information when the bowl was claimed by the government for the museum in 1922 after being found in a locker in someone's home.

Best,
Dr. Brad Ricca

I included a copy of that last card. I received a reply soon after.

Dear Brad,
The Bowl fragment is exhibiting in the museum.
It is "Khirbet Kerak Ware" style-early

464

Bronze Age Diameter: 13.5 cm

Best

Fawzi Ibrahim

Curator of the Rockefeller

Archaeological Museum

Though the final contents of the secret cupboard did not include the Ark, everyone on that chain of correspondence — every last one — wondered if it did. For those few minutes, as I read through those old cards and telegrams that told a story from the past through one serial cliff-hanger to another, the slim glimmer of possibility that the Ark itself might have been at the end of it — that was the good part. That was the adventure. That is why the story never ends.

The bowl, though not named, is arguably the greatest archaeological legacy of the Parker expedition. It is proof of an entire group of people who worshipped strange gods and had different stories from the ones we know. Though they were conquered and disappeared, we have physical proof of their existence and culture. We have a vessel for further understanding them. So though it is not the Ark, or the Holy Grail, it is still a Thing to Hold a Space, and is thus like them: an impossibly old artifact that we can, in a way, use to communicate with an imagined past. It is a space of uncertainty and thus an invitation to a story. As Father Vincent writes near the end of his account, the work of science revealed "the long evolution of human life in these hills." Whether you believe that God is real or a story — a supernatural being or a copper mountain somewhere in Canaan that once inspired a gratitude or awe — it is the uncertainty of it all, and even the fear, that is the very definition of adventure, and perhaps the beginning of faith.

Decades after the bowl was recovered, famed archaeologists Ronny Reich and Eli Shukron were in Hezekiah's Tunnel, where they found three things: metal pails, a pickax, and a pipe. With some work, they identified the items as being from the Parker expedition. Did they just forget them? Or were they left there in a hurry as they escaped? The pails are still there, stuck in the cement for eternity so that people can see them when they walk by the newly refurbished and renovated Hezekiah's Tunnel, where tourists and the curious can take off their shoes and wade through cool water down the entire tunnel.

In the end, the bowl, the tunnel, and even the pipe ended up as more empty vessels to be filled by the imagination, to be looked at and thought about — what they meant, what they mean — in the context of larger questions about the infinite — and its opposite. Maybe Monty finally learned this, which is why he left the bowl behind and didn't fight to keep it. Maybe he learned that it belonged in a museum after all.

Epilogue

Monty Parker straightens his back and, with some hesitation, steps forward, leading with the toe of his left foot. Mrs. Astor lays her hands lightly against his and steps back with her right foot. Monty steps to his right and closes his left, before stepping back in a smooth, swaying motion. He pushes back with his left, then closes with his other foot in a nice box step. She matches him, like a shadow in 3/4 time, counting in her head 1–2–3, 1–2–3, repeating.

They waltz around the drawing room at Saltram, under old paintings with gold frames. The paintings are still, but they move as the couple does. Portraits of dark-haired relatives with blanched faces go fleeting by. The couple moves, round and round, past the old books in their creased leather, and the candlesticks, and the stiff mantel. They dance, moving through space, their faces close. It has been a long time.

The sun is shining through the high windows, caught by the chandelier. The moment is an elegant one, ripe with fulfillment, the crowning touch of a shared history in an old, grand room. As the music begins to close, Monty twirls her around in a tight, invisible circle.

The music stops and the small group of admiring people clap their approval. Monty bows to her, and she does the same, a great smile on her face.

The woman in the corner unplugs her smartphone from the speaker. Monty turns and tries to smooth out his striped sport coat. The couple separates; other guests are dancing and having tea and biscuits. Monty might walk to the great room, the one that has a massive staircase rising and turning around the walls with multiple landings and that is completely open, completely hollow, underneath. It is breathtaking. As he wanders the room, looking at the art and furniture, he sees portraits of Parkers great and small. He makes the turn toward the dining room, smelling something delicious. He sees an arresting painting of several explorers shipwrecked upon a beach. The men in the picture point toward the shore, where an arrowhead-like symbol and a circled triangle have been carved into the ground. Monty looks at the placard. The painting is called *Aristippus and His Companions After Being Shipwrecked Seeing Mathematical Diagrams and Realizing the Land Was Inhabited,* by Antonio Zucchi (1726–1796).

Aristippus was a Greek philosopher who, when shipwrecked on Rhodes, felt his fear turn to hope when he saw geometrical figures drawn upon the shore. He felt safe because he knew that they were the measured signs of man, that there was reason on the island, and that it would rescue him.

Monty moves into the library, with its walls of books and thick rug. On a small table, he sees a black homemade book, long and rectangular and old. He opens it to find all kinds of pencil drawings and even some watercolors. They are quite accomplished, of men and ladies, places and things. There is one of a city on a hill, surrounded by a wall with a dome peeking over the edge of it. There is another drawing covered with brightly colored mosaics, centered around dark diamonds and stars. There is even a meticulous illustration of some ancient Egyptians pulling a cart. There is a drawing of a stone fountain, sublime and low. There is one of a fierce dragon and another with two cherubs, with layered, wonderful wings.

Monty touches one of the pages, though

he knows he probably should not. He is surprised that many of the drawings are on tracing paper. He imagines the artist placing them over some perfect masterpiece and trying to capture its beauty and order in a collection of careful lines. He sees someone trying to take something perfect from the past and bring forth a new version of it — an imperfect one — into the present again.

Monty looks around the high room again, filled with beautiful, paintings and fresh-cut flowers. And though the real Monty Parker is long dead, this version, as played by a nice volunteer named Chris Langmead, might wonder whose heaven this might be.

Saltram remains a magnificent Georgian-style mansion in Devonshire, though it is no longer occupied by the House of Morley. Now held by the National Trust, Saltram has been transformed into a living museum, accessible to all as guides and docents take daytrippers along its plush gardens, stunning rooms, and a small shop at the end. Though the Parker line no longer lives here, their past is still a fundamental cornerstone of the house's story, alongside the incredible collection of Joshua Reynolds paintings and the stunning Chinese wallpaper. Guests stare at the portrait of John Parker, the first Earl of Morley, with his white curls and paunchy cheeks, and tilt their heads and squint, trying to see Mr. Darcy himself, Jane Austen's famous character in *Pride and Prejudice,* who was supposedly based on him. And, of course, they learn the thrilling story of Montague Parker — an explorer — at engaging teatime talks and at day camps for children, who listen in wide-eyed silence before they scamper off on scavenger hunts to collect their own treasures. They sprint by many of Monty's photographs from his military years, bound in black paper books, shown under glass.

Many decades after the expedition ended, a failure by most accounts, a boy named Philip made a painful face.

"Ow!" he said. His tooth hurt. Not the kind that might go away, but the kind that meant he had to go to the dentist. After giving it a few days, just in case, he gave up and went in.

When he arrived, the old dentist smiled, helped him into the chair, and tipped it back, the stainless steel gleaming under the lights. Once Philip was ready, mouth and eyes wide open, the dentist told the same story he did every time. He told him about the Ark.

For some reason, the dentist was obsessed

with the subject. He told Philip how it had to be handled very carefully and how it had powers that could wipe out entire armies! And how you could never, ever, look into it. It had been sought after by great adventurers, but had never been found. The dentist would make noises and gestures in his small office as he told the story. The mirrors and brushes seemed to disappear. Philip never forgot it.

By 1974, Philip was grown up, writing and directing his own stories for film. He invited a friend to come over one day to his home in southern California. This friend was thin and wore a sweater. He had a dark beard and his name was George. They went for a walk, and George told Philip all about this idea he had for a movie about an archaeologist from the 1930s who would go on all kinds of adventures looking for supernatural treasure. He was really excited about it. He had his character all mapped out, but there was one problem. He didn't know what his guy was going to go after. What was he trying to *find*? George shrugged.

Philip remembered his old dentist in Chicago.

"The Ark of the Covenant," Philip Kaufman said to George Lucas. And that was it, or at least the start of it. When George told his friend Steven Spielberg, they had their expedition.

In 1981, I was ten years old and sitting in a movie theater in a suburb of Cleveland. My dad and little brother were with me. It seemed like we had waited an eternity to see *Raiders.* It was summer outside, but the inside of the theater was so dark that when I shut my eyes, then opened them again, it all looked the same. Then, a beam of light appeared from the projector behind us and hit the massive rectangular screen, flooding it with brightness. When the mountain appeared, with the stars circled around it, we were no longer alone. As we sat there, we didn't know that parts of the story might have been real, might have been true, but we somehow felt they could be. I think that's why, even after it ended, and for years later, we held on to that old story, told best in the dark, in a place that seemed like our eyes were still shut.

NOTES

The historical record of the Parker expedition is a collection of often incomplete sources of varying provenance spread out across time, space, and languages. It includes letters, reports, books, a complicated mathematical code, Scripture, hand-drawn maps, notes, legends, memoirs, conspiracy theories, scientific reports, government records, and thinly disguised fiction. For a story about a supernatural object like the Ark, this range of information seems wholly appropriate and reflects the uncertainty of the adventure itself.

I have tried to piece these fragments together into a larger, more coherent characterization of the facts. Where cracks remained, I have filled them in with incidental content — dialogue or even scenes — as adhesive to help convey the facts. Everything appears because they experienced it, wrote about it, or read about it. Rather than a history, this is a history of the story. Chapters are grouped into parts that are based on the point of view of the person or source used. Here in the notes, I have tried to be as transparent as possible about my use of these sources. That being said, I do not presume to tell you who — or what — to believe.

The Parker archive is perhaps the most significant source of primary information about the expedition. It was amassed by Parker and kept by him during the dig and includes original documents, translations, and the cipher itself, amid a variety of letters, reports, and other things. I believe that the materials were kept with the Parker family lawyer, Martineau, and his offices, though they seem to have been trotted out a few times over the years. I used their digital form for this book. As such, and for simplicity's sake, I cite everything only as *Parker Archive.* The archive has been meticulously indexed by Graham Addison so that anyone interested in more specific aspects of the archive can find them.

References to biblical verse cite the 1769 Cambridge edition of the King James Bible available at *King James Bible Online,* 2021, kingjamesbibleonline.org.

Chapter One

The tunnel: Charles Warren and Charles Wilson, *The Recovery of Jerusalem: A Narrative of Exploration and Discovery in the City and the Holy Land* (New York: D. Appleton, 1871), 489–502, 237–57. I have followed Warren's own description, even though it does not always align with other versions. The map I used is from Aryeh Shimron, "Response: Warren's Shaft," *Biblical Archaeology Review* 30, no. 4 (2004): 14–15. For topography, see Stuart Thornton, "Water Works," *National Geographic,* September 19, 2013, nationalgeographic .org/article/water-works. The debate over the origin and use of the tunnel is ongoing.

Palestine: During the time frame of this story, "Palestine" refers to the entire region.

Jacob Eliahu: Our Jerusalem, 95–98; Stig Norin, "The Age of the Siloam Inscription and Hezekiah's Tunnel," *Vetus Testamentum* 48, no. 1 (1998): 37–48.

Mr. Schick: C. Schick, "Phoenician Inscription in the Pool of Siloam," *Palestine Exploration Fund Quarterly Statement,* 1880, 238–39; E. W. G. Masterman, "The Important Work of Dr. Conrad Schick,

Biblical World 20, no. 2 (August 1902), 146–48. Dr. Conrad Schick was the noted German architect and archaeologist who designed buildings in Jerusalem and created small-scale models of the Temple Mount.

Behold: A. H. Sayce, "The Ancient Hebrew Inscription Discovered at the Pool of Siloam in Jerusalem," *Palestine Exploration Quarterly* 13, no. 3, 149.

Chapter Two

The man in the white captain's hat: Of all the people in this story, Monty Parker is the most like a cipher himself in the historical record. To reflect this, I have characterized him somewhat as a medium between the reader and the cipher, as he was the one reading them. I have imagined his interior life quite a bit but have tried to do so only around general questions shared by him and the reader. In some ways, I have characterized Monty as a response to the theory that Indiana Jones doesn't affect the outcome of *Raiders of the Lost Ark,* but functions as a bystander. I don't agree with this, but I tried it as an experimental model for Monty, given the scarcity of first-person accounts from him.

I eventually settled on Roger Ebert's point that in the film, Indy's "the fulcrum, not the lever," which seems a fair fit to Monty's own role. At first, I desperately sought to avoid any links to *Raiders,* but I came to the conclusion that the movie will unavoidably color a vast majority of any reading experience about the Ark, more so than possibly even religion. The nods throughout are homage, but also an acceptance of the way fictional interpretations can not only color but help to understand quasi-historical events. All such moments occur only when I found actual similarities in the story. See Roger Ebert, *"Raiders of the Lost Ark,"* April 30, 2000, rogerebert.com.

Princelet Street: Autumn, 111–12; *Valter,* ch. 5. Martineau had official barrister offices in the Raymond Buildings at Gray's Inn, but that didn't seem to be a believable place for them to discuss their "proposition." They had a later listing for an office on Princelet Street in the East End, so I set their meeting there. The timing of what happened and who did what when is reflective of the historical record.

him with a thud: "Records of Princes (later Princelet) Street Synagogue, Spitalfields,

1883–1973," W/PRI National Archives, UK.

known as the Beehive: "Has the Times Done This?" *Daily Telegraph,* October 3, 1888, 3.

mohel: Philip Walker, *Jewish East End of London Photo Gallery & Commentary,* jewisheastend.com/princelet. His name was Reverend A. Tertis.

"You need a soldier" UK, British Army Records and Lists, 1882–1962, Provo, UT, ancestry.com, 2015.

The cipher: Parker Archive. The cipher exists in the Parker Archive in several forms: the original Swedish by Juvelius, a version translated by Millen into English, a version professionally translated into English by Venn & Sons, and the newer ciphers done by Juvelius and Millen.

Chapter Three

Royal Ascot: "Royal Ascot," *Morning Post,* June 17, 1908, 9; Ascot Gold Cup, *Singleton Argus,* June 20, 1908, 4; "Royal Ascot," *Sportsman,* June 18, 1908, 5; "The Ascot Cup," *Illustrated Sporting and Dramatic News,* June 19, 1909.

Monty and Ava: "London Day by Day,"

Sheffield Daily Telegraph, March 21, 1925, 8.

were indefatigable: Chas. P. Norcross, "Mrs. Astor May Lose Royal Favor," *San Francisco Examiner,* Nov. 14, 1909, 1.

Ava Lowle Willing Astor: Lucy Kavaler, *The Astors: A Family Chronicle of Pomp and Power* (New York: Dodd, Mead & Co., 1966).

was nearly thirty: "Born Montague Parker on October 13, 1878 in Westonbrit House, Tetbury, in Gloucestire England to the Right Honorable Albert Edmund Parker, Lord Borington the Third Earl of Morley and Margaret Holford Parker, the Countess Morley"; his middle name "Brownlow" seems to first appear when he is baptized on November 13, 1878; Gloucestershire, England, Church of England Baptisms, 1813–1913, Provo, UT, ancestry.com. Thanks to Olivia Parker for the birth certificate information.

Nothing remotely "perhaps": ibid.

His mother drew horses: Margaret Holford, *Drawings. Album of drawings and watercolour sketches by Margaret Parker (née Holford), 3rd Countess Morley. Includes: landscapes made at home and during holidays on the continent; scenes of domestic life; sketches worked as exercises, etc.,* NT

3041433, Saltram, Devon, 1871.

Lord Curzon: "Lord Curzon or the Dashing Capt. Montague Parker?" *Knoxville Sentinel,* January 8, 1910, 17.

Chapter Four

chops, St. Hilaire: supper menu, *Waldorf-Astoria Hotel,* October 11, 1905. New York Public Library Menu Collection, menus.nypl.org/menus/21406.

"we're full up": Autumn, 112; *Parker Archive.* On the official list of donors, many subscribers were family and close friends. Thanks to Graham Addison.

help as well: Valter, ch. 5. Juvelius showed only portions of the cipher in their first meeting, so I am guessing that he showed them the example first.

Hesekiel's chiffer: A full comprehension of the cipher would require a knowledge of ancient Hebrew, Swedish, and arguably Valter Juvelius himself. I considered hiring an expert to satisfy the first two, but the cipher's dual status in the story as both a doubtful and hopeful thing fits more accurately with the aims and perspective of this book. Stewart makes the terrific point that the cipher as experienced by Juvelius was incredibly unwieldy, as Hebrew added thousands of words to the equation. For a brilliant example of how to read the cipher, see *Valter,* ch. 4.

"delight return!": Parker Archive.

Melander: Valter. Henning Melander, as Stewart relates in detail, is a fascinating figure, but was not directly associated with the expedition. Melander was convinced that Juvelius stole the cipher idea from him and even published some of the Juvelius ciphers as revenge. Melander wrote a book accusing the Parker expedition of being Masonic agents. See Henning Melander, *Frimurarnas hemlighet och Israels förbundsark* (Stockholm: Sv. kristl. Arkforskningförb, 1916).

"J.M.P.V.F.": Parker Archive. The official documents were drawn up and approved on October 28, 1908.

In Jerusalem: It is unclear who hired whom and when, but this is the timeline I have worked out that satisfies the most sources. Monty, as leader, most likely made these decisions, although invitations to join seem to have been extended through a friendly network of ex-soldiers, friends, and people known to each other by reputation.

Chapter Five

Jerusalem: C. R. Conder, *The City of Jerusalem,* London: John Murray, 1909, 15.

"least two Gethsemanes": Parker Archive.

"base of knowledge": ibid.

the faithful to prayer: Conder, 21.

"Lake of Fire": John Milton, *Complete Poems and Major Prose,* New York: Macmillan, 1957, 218, (280).

Praise the Lord: Parker Archive.

Ye are digged: Isaiah 51:1.

Nebuchadnezzar: 2 Kings 24–25:22; Simon Sebag Montefiore, *Jerusalem: The Biography* (New York: Knopf, 2011), 37–43.

unmentioned in the lists: 2 Chronicles 36:7, 18; 2 Kings 24:13.

Chapter Six

June, 1909: Autumn, 111.

"why he did it": ibid., 35–37. For those readers unfamiliar with the sport, I recommend "The Basics of Cricket, Explained," *Chicago Tribune,* February 15, 2015; Neil Nitin, *How's That? Let's Play Cricket,* self-published, 2020.

and the West Indies: Autumn, 22–44; "Cyril Foley," ESPNCricInfo.com. Cyril was part of the very first reverse sweep in first-class cricket. See "The Very First Reverse Sweep or That There Tim Takes a Bit of Beating," *Down at Third Man,* downatthirdman.wordpress.com.

"fantastic proposition for you": Autumn, 111.

"call the police": Cyril Foley, "In Search of the Lost Ark of the Covenant," *Sunday Express,* October 9, 1926, 16.

Chapter Seven

"authority must disappear": Millen, Johan. *På rätta vägar: Davids forntida stad upptäckt: Israels tio stammar återfunna (äro icke judarna)* (Stockholm: A.-B. Hasse W. Tullberg, 1917), 70.

Description of the Ark: 1 Chronicles 28:18, 1 Kings 8:7, and Exodus 25:22. A replica of the Ark was displayed a year earlier in a London exhibit on Palestine; see Valter, ch. 3. The most accurate (and prolific) visual image of the Ark is the version by James Tissot in two paintings, *The Ark Passes Over the Jordan* (1908) and *Ark of the Covenant: Moses and Joshua Bowing Before the Ark* (1900). Tissot emphasizes the sweeping, aggressive wings of the cherubim that appear almost Egyptian. His skills with color also gave the Ark a gleam that lasted all the way to the version seen in *Raiders of the Lost Ark.*

"in some form or another": Exodus 25:10.

A man named Uzzah: Millen, 70; 2 Samuel 6:3–8.

"front of the procession": 2 Samuel 6:14.

Urim and Thummim: Millen, 70–72. Urim and Thummim is mentioned in the Bible in Exodus 28:30, Leviticus 8:8, Numbers 27:21, and Deuteronomy 33:8.

Chapter Eight

Thursday, July 22, 1909: Autumn, 113.

some of their expenses: Valter, ch. 6. I have chosen not to focus on the business side of the expedition. For more, see *Valter* and *Parker Archive* for most of the original business records.

Otto von Bourg: "When the War Will End," *Ashbourne News Telegraph,* March 4, 1904, 8; "Missing Body Traced Through Clairvoyance," *Light,* February 16, 1901, 79–81.

Lee: Autumn, 113; *Valter,* ch. 9. Stewart names him "James Lee" but also considers the option that his name could have been misconstrued as someone else, possibly Millen.

for three years: Parker Archives, Louis Fishman, "The 1911 Haram Al-Sharif Incident: Palestinian Notables Versus the Ottoman Administration," *Journal of Palestine Studies* 34, no. 3 (2005), 6–22.

"the great Juvelius": Autumn, 114.

Water Lily: ibid.; "Cowes Week," *Times,* August 1, 1910, 11; "Adventurous Cruise," *New Zealand Herald,* April 11, 1932, 10. There is an anonymous erotic novel titled *Cruise of the Water-Lily* (1908), but it is hard to say if it refers to Wilson's vessel.

"just before sunup": Autumn, 114.

medical officer: United States, Office of Naval Intelligence, *Port Directory of the Principal Foreign Ports,* 5th ed. (Washington, D.C.: Government Printing Office, 1928), 584.

"No shaking hands": Autumn, 114–15.

"I went to Cambridge!": Autumn, 5–22.

Jaffa: "Syria," *Tablet,* May 5, 1888, 729; "Jaffa," *Jewish Virtual Library,* www.jewish virtuallibrary.org/jaffa.

the cleanest in Jerusalem: ibid., 116.

Chapter Nine

upside-down mutton: Bethica Das Bethica Das Sharjah, "Upside Down Mutton Biryani," cookpad.com.

not building hospitals: Our Jerusalem, 225.

"gather the bits": ibid., 226.

"he will not": ibid.

"the boys rode on the donkeys": ibid.

Frederick: ibid., 203–05.

Mrs. Bertha Vester: ibid., 226. It is not certain that it was Monty with whom she met; she says she meets "some of them."

some other children: American Colony, Photo Department, photographer, *Studio Portraits of Members of the American Colony Jerusalem, Friends, and Associates,* Palestine Jerusalem, [between 1870 and 1935], loc.gov/item/2007675263/.

"He is an archaeologist": Our Jerusalem, 226. There are two versions of how Father Vincent met with the expedition. This is Bertha Vester's; the next chapter will be the competing version in Vincent's own words.

Chapter Ten

Father Vincent: Hugues-Vincent, *Underground Jerusalem: Discoveries on the Hill of Ophel (1909–11).* London: H. Cox, *Field* office, 1911. *Underground.* This is the primary scientific text of the expedition.

a pulley and rope: Autumn, 116–17.

captain's hat with a pipe: My association of these items with Parker is rooted somewhat in fact (several photographs) and somewhat in homage.

Palestine Exploration Fund: For more information on the PEF, their website (pef .org.uk) has archived the *Quarterly,* a vitally important resource for understanding the history of biblical archaeology and its unique personalities. Archive.org also has some of these issues.

then lost to all: I am very conscious that this is a book about a treasure hunter, and a somewhat romanticized one, at that. The history of the stealing of relics, of land, of culture and identity in the entire region is significant and important. See Katharina Galor, "Jerusalem: Archaeologists Versus Residents?" *Review of Middle East Studies* 51, no. 2, 2017, 203–13.

Katharina Galor and Gideon Avni, eds., *Unearthing Jerusalem: 150 Years of Archaeological Research in the Holy City* (Winona Lake, IN: Eisenbrauns, 2011); Raphael Greenberg, "One Hundred and Fifty Years of Archaeology and Controversy in Jerusalem," *Routledge Handbook on Jerusalem* (London: Routledge, 2020); John James Moscrop, *Measuring Jerusalem, The Palestine Exploration Fund and the British Interests in the Holy Land* (New York: Leicester University Press, 2000). Thanks to Professor of Anthropology Dana Keithly for her help in this research.

"we can go down together": Underground, 1–3.

Father Vincent: W. F. Albright, "In Memory of Louis Hugues Vincent," *Bulletin of the American Schools of Oriental Research*, no. 164 (1961): 2–4.

Chapter Eleven

on who was asking: Autumn, 117.

easier to clear out: ibid., 116.

"as to be unforgettable": ibid.

did not look pleased: ibid.

their own reputations: ibid. The only thing I have consolidated in this book is the location where they rented a house. They moved around a bit in the beginning, and I felt it would be more confusing than helpful to detail their movements, given the rotating narrators. I am presenting their base as an unnamed amalgam most like the Augusta Victoria Hospice, where they stayed for the majority of their time, from 1910 on. For specific documentation and rental agreements, see *Parker Archive*.

"more amused than angry": Autumn, 30. The Western Wall is currently open to all but separates men and women with a parti-

tion. See Amanda Borschel-Dan, "When Men and Women Prayed Together at the Western Wall," *Times of Israel,* June 29, 2017.

"nothing to the Jewish historians": Autumn, 117–18.

bigger on the inside: Aryeh Shimron, "Response: Warren's Shaft," *Biblical Archaeology Review* 30, no. 4 (2004): 14–15.

Dragon's Well: Nehemiah 2:13.

made the ascent in 1867: Charles Warren and C. R. Conder, *The Survey of Western Palestine-Jerusalem* (London: Palestine Exploration Fund, 1884), 366–68.

"no second-class bat, either": Autumn, 120–23.

that very same gutter: 1 Chronicles 2:6; *Autumn,* 120.

"and so can you": Autumn, 122.

"I thought of Juliet": ibid., 123.

"are we not?": ibid.

finally being rescued: "The Loss of the Victoria," *Morning Post,* July 3, 1893, 7; "The Loss of H.M.S. Victoria," *London Evening Standard,* July 4, 1893, 3.

Chapter Twelve

"Um ed-Derej": Lewis Bayles Paton, "Jerusalem in Bible Times," *Biblical World,* Uni-

versity of Chicago Press (January-June 1907), 168.

Jerusalem limestone: Judy Siegel-Itzkovich, "Limestone Bedrock Persuaded King David to Choose J'lem as his Capital," *Jerusalem Times,* October 25, 2009.

son's swaddling clothes: This is a local legend and is not found in the Bible. There are two other places that lay claim to his same story: the Fountain of the Virgin in Nazareth and a similar fountain in Grand Cairo in Egypt.

"the Virgin's Fountain": Underground, 3. Father Vincent often refers to it as the "Virgin's Well," but nearly everyone else uses "Fountain" (as does Vincent on his map), so I have normalized it to that.

"God save King Solomon": 1 Kings 1:33–39.

began sketching: Underground, 69.

"a slight slope here": ibid.

called him the Master Architect: ibid., 26. Father Vincent calls him the Architect, the Master, or the Master of the Work at different times. The term might be problematic to current readers because it calls to mind the Great Designer, Watchmaker, and so forth, but Father Vincent uses the term in strict secular terms to refer to the human being who oversaw the carving of the tunnels.

Chapter Thirteen

Dr. Juvelius: Valkoinen. A work of Finnish fiction, the characters within are only barely disguised analogues of expedition members, as Juvelius uses various literary devices to shift between realist and imaginary modes.

against climate fever: James Copland, "Inflammatory Fever," *A Dictionary of Practical Medicine,* vol. 1 (New York: Harper, 1855), 1144.

"always so blazing hot": Juvelius doesn't identify Hoppenrath's wife by name in the text. Her name was Jeanne Marie Charlier; they married in Sweden in 1906.

of his friend's work: For more on Uotila, see *Valter,* ch. 5.

"steel between the ribs!": Valkoinen.

right then and there: ibid.

take no more time: Valter, ch. 5.

"Are you drunk?": Valkoinen, ch. 1. According to Stewart, Juvelius had a history of family alcoholism and suffered from depression and physical pain.

the rabbi: Valkoinen. In the text, he is identified as "Rabbi Jonathan ben Jochaita." I could not determine if it was a real name, so I left him anonymous.

Chapter Fourteen

big camera: Olivia Parker, email to author, January 12, 2021; Michael Pace, message to author, December 22, 2020. We tried to identify Monty's "big camera" from several photos. Olivia Parker knew the photo size was three and a half by three and a half. Pace suggested an "Al-Vista." For a moment, we entertained the thought that he might have had a movie camera, but we could not find any proof. Monty was a photographer for much of his adult life, especially during the First Boer War, where he took many photos of construction, demolition, and assorted scenery. I was looking for any photos of Modder River, the British-run concentration camp where many Grenadier Guards were stationed. There are binders of his photography held at the Imperial War Museum in London and at Saltram. Thanks to Olivia Parker for her help and information about some of these photos.

John Venn & Sons: Parker Archive.

"Signed V. H. Juvelius": ibid.

"could not be passed over": Ezekiel 47:1–6.

Threshold! / Be silent!: Parker Archive.

written it in 1907: ibid.

"the star": ibid.

"the holy place": ibid.

Monty sometimes thought of his older brother: "Captain Parker Holds Secret of Treasure,"

Washington Post, November 22, 1912, 6.

"was confirmed and reliable . . . measure / the entrance! / IT!": Parker Archive. ibid.

Chapter Fifteen

"Look . . . They are here!": Valkoinen.

three-story building in white: Postcard of Jericho, circa 1910.

Jericho: "Jericho, Whose Walls Fell," *Oakland Tribune,* March 7, 1909, 3; Harold J. Shepstone, "Excavations at Jericho, Palestine," *Scientific American,* June 5, 1909, 426.

"not leave alive anything that breathes": Michael Freeman, "Religion, Nationalism and Genocide: Ancient Judaism Revisited," *European Journal of Sociology* 35, no. 2 (1994): 259–82; Daniel L. Hawk, "Christianizing Joshua: Making Sense of the Bible's Book of Conquest," *Journal of Theological Interpretation* 5, no. 1 (2011): 121–32; Michael Walzer, "The Idea of Holy War in Ancient Israel," *Journal of Religious Ethics* 20, no. 2 (1992): 215–28.

"upon a heap": Joshua 3:13.

"were passed clean over Jordan": Joshua 3:17.

"do not get my meaning": Valkoinen.

"We are close now": ibid.

"Ayun Mûsâ!": Dorot Jewish Division, The New York Public Library, "Ayun Musa. The Wells of Moses, Wilderness of Tyh," New York Public Library Digital Collections.

When Moses died: Deuteronomy 34. The quotes are from the pseudo-epigraphical "Testament of Moses." I have used a contemporary translation by Louis Ginzberg, *The Legends of the Jews,* vol. 3 (Philadelphia: Jewish Publication Society of America), 1911, 463–81. See also Rimon Kasher, "The Mythological Figure of Moses in Light of Some Unpublished Midrashic Fragments," *Jewish Quarterly Review* 88, no. 1/2 (1997): 19–42; Joseph P. Schultz, "Angelic Opposition to the Ascension of Moses and the Revelation of the Law," *Jewish Quarterly Review* 61, no. 4 (1971): 282–307; D. M. Berry and S. Eden, "How Did Moses Die?" *Jewish Bible Quarterly* 46, no. 2 (2018), 104. The pseudo-epigraphical books are readily available online at earlyjewishwritings.com.

tomb of Moses: Brent J. MacDonald, "Moses' Spring," bibleistrue.com/qna/pqna57 .htm.

"the unspoken name": Valkoinen. Also known as the Tetragrammaton. See Thomas Tyler, "The Origin of the Tetragrammaton," *Jewish Quarterly Review* 13, no. 4 (1901), 581–94; Alyssa Roat, "What is the Tetragrammaton?" christianity.com; "Tetregrammaton," jewishencyclopedia.com.

"The entrance is noisy": Parker Archive.

Chapter Sixteen

"would come back soon": Underground, 7.

Father Raphaël Savignac: Raphaël Savignac was the gifted photographer of the École Biblique. See ebaf.edu/the-photographic-collection/history-of-the-funds.

Parker had only two rules: Underground, 1.

his relentless curiosity: W. F. Albright, "In Memory of Louis Hugues Vincent," *Bulletin of the American Schools of Oriental Research,* no. 164 (1961): 2–4.

"hounds of God": From the Latin *Domini canes.* Saint Dominic's mother, so the story goes, had a vision of a black-and-white dog holding a torch that set fire to the earth wherever it went, the flame of the Gospel. These dogs appear in some religious imagery, including as a dalmatian

in a stained-glass window in the Church of St. Catherine of Siena, New York City.

excavation grew great companions: Underground, 1.

looked like an arrowhead: ibid., 29.

a tablet: ibid., 9.

had missed something: ibid., 17.

"any subterranean mysteries at all": ibid.

two Turks: Fishman. "1911." The two watchers were Abdulaziz Mecdi Efendi and Habip Bey, both members of the Turkish parliament. They were each paid 200 Turkish pounds per month to supervise. According to Fishman, Mecdi said, "I was going to take leave anyway, and this matter would both benefit the state and allow me time off. I could travel and supervise this work at the same time."

"Just don't do it again": ibid., 7. The head in question is, I think, pictured in *Underground,* 63.

Chapter Seventeen

the heat's ferocity: "Temperature of the Air at Jerusalem," *Quarterly Journal of the Royal Meteorological Society* 25, no. 109 (1899), 67–69; "When to Go," *Frommers Israel,* frommers.com/destinations/israel/planning-a-trip/when-to-go.

"unspoken name you mentioned": Valkoinen. See also Samuel S. Cohon, "The Name of God, A Study in Rabbinic Theology," *Hebrew Union College Annual* 23, no. 1 (1950): 579–604.

"which she later ate!": Valkoinen.

"Juvelius regarded the wise man": ibid. I do not know if this meeting happened or is symbolic of Juvelius's fears, beliefs, and state of mind.

"bust of Moses": ibid.

"following them": ibid.

Chapter Eighteen

different amounts of pay: Autumn, 124.

Ramadan: Rachel Ross, "What Is Ramadan?" *LiveScience,* May 16, 2018, livescience.com/61815-what-is-ramadan.

Hussein Bey al-Husayni: Mayor from 1909 to 1917. See also Abigail Jacobson, "A City Living through Crisis: Jerusalem during World War I," *British Journal of Middle Eastern Studies* 36, no. 1 (2009): 73–92.

the courthouse: Autumn, 124.

"should be set free": ibid., 125.

posed for a photograph: ibid., 124–25. This photo is important since it not only shows most of the expedition at once, but everyone is named by Cyril.

Their procession: "Jerusalem," Perry-Castañeda Library Map Collection, Historical Maps of the Middle East at the University of Texas at Austin Library, legacy.lib.utexas.edu/maps/historical/history_middle_east.

finest in the world: Autumn, 126.

Chapter Nineteen

All of the material in this strange chapter is a faithful retelling of the events from *Valkoinen.*

Chapter Twenty

This chapter is also adapted from *Valkoinen.*

quin: I think they are talking about a "summer quin," a drink made with quinquina, a variety of apéritif wine. Many cocktails originally contained quinine to guard against malaria. Bond's famous martini is made with Kina Lillet, a French aperitif wine.

new epilogue about the incident: At different times, Juvelius hints that this report will contain new cipher readings, a map to Moses's grave, and a plan to retrieve the Temple archive, a hidden repository of knowledge and Jewish magic.

Baron Edmond de Rothschild: There are countless books, articles, websites, movies, and pamphlets filled with anti-Semitic conspiracy theories about the Rothschilds. I choose not to cite them here and would rather let Juvelius's (and others') words speak for themselves. For more analysis, see Sam N. Lehman-Wilzig, "The House of Rothschild: Prototype of the Transnational Organization," *Jewish Social Studies* 40, no. 3–4 (1978): 251–70; Niall Ferguson and L. J. Rather, "Disraeli, Freud, and Jewish Conspiracy Theories," *Journal of the History of Ideas* 47, no. 1 (1986): 111–31; Bernard Harrison, *Blaming the Jews: Politics and Delusion* (Bloomington: Indiana, 2020).

farther on to home: Valter, ch. 7.

Chapter Twenty-One

bombed these shafts: Charles Warren, *Underground Jerusalem* (London: Richard Bentley, 1876), 316: "In those days, they could pull down, but they could not blow up; we can destroy from the bottom, but they could only work their destruction from the top: and so it was that as the blocks of stones were detached and hurled into the

Valley . . . until a time arrived when the rubbish reached the height of the ruined building, and then destruction could go no further: the foundations remain intact and we are able to examine them at this day"; see also Francis Donaldson, *Practical Shaft Sinking* (New York: McGraw-Hill, 1912). Thanks to Dana Keithly for her help unpacking the maddening phrase "sank a shaft."

O, Y, and Q: Warren, *Underground Jerusalem,* 420–22.

designed and built Solomon's Temple: Paul Leslie Garber, "Reconstructing Solomon's Temple," *Biblical Archaeologist* 14, no. 1 (1951): 2–24; Ernest G. Wright, "Solomon's Temple Resurrected," *Biblical Archaeologist* 4, no. 2 (1941): 17–31.

construction of the structure: Warren, *Underground Jerusalem,* 421.

El Melek: ibid., 71.

Chapter Twenty-Two

yoreh: Rabbi Uzi Kalchaim zt"l, "The First Rain," Shvat 5768, yeshiva.co/midrash/6799: "The word 'yoreh' means to teach. According to the Talmud, the 'yoreh' (first rain) teaches us to prepare for the winter, to plaster our roofs, to seal up any holes through which rain might possibly leak. This is our first warning of winter's arrival." See also Deuteronomy 11:14.

after the wet Jerusalem winter: Autumn, 127.

throw them off the trail: Parker Archive.

"the heap of stones": ibid.

"Something = the ark!": ibid.

"Behold the confusion!": ibid.

Molok: Charles George Herbermann, *Catholic Encyclopedia* (New York: Encyclopedia Press, 1907). Also known as Molock, Moloch, or Molech, I have used the spelling from the Juvelius cipher, "Molok." He was mentioned in many sources, mostly in sermons, and in Milton's *Paradise Lost.* He also appears in Gustave Flaubert's historical novel *Salammbô* (1862), which was popular in England. Taking place in ancient Carthage, the story involves the theft of a holy veil known as the Zaïmph, and has many similarities to stories of the Ark. More recently, Molok has been used by the far right in America as a politicized symbol to describe the actions of the left. See also Timothy K. Beal, *Religion and Its Monsters* (New York: Routledge, 2002), 153–55; George C. Heider, *Cult of Molek: A Reassessment* (Sheffield, England: Sheffield University Press, 2009); mfr.fandom.com/wiki/Moloch. For atmosphere, I also used Mike Mignola, *Hellboy: In the Chapel of Moloch* 1, no. 1, October 2008. And from Allen Ginsberg, "Howl," San Francisco, City Lights Books, *Howl and Other Poems,* 1956: "Moloch! Solitude! Filth! Ugliness! Ashcans and unobtainable dollars! Children screaming under the stairways! Boys sobbing in armies! Old men weeping in the parks!"

smoke raised from below: Charles Foster, "Molech," *Bible Pictures and What They Teach Us* (Philadelphia: Charles Foster Publishing Co., 1897), 74; freegroups.net/photos/album/Bible-Pictures--1897-W-A-Foster/.

"pass through the fire to Molech": 2 Kings 23:10.

For children: John Day, *Molech: A God of Human Sacrifice in the Old Testament University of Cambridge Oriental Publications* 41, 1989, 87–89.

Chapter Twenty-Three

The information in this chapter is from several sources, including E. J. Lynett, "Story of Shooting," *Times-Tribune,* April 2, 1910, 1; "American Women Shot by Fanatic," *Vancouver Daily World,* March

15, 1910, 18; "Afghan Fanatic Fires on Tourists," *Republic,* March 10, 1910, 1; "Turkey Apologizes for Shooting," *Evansville Press,* March 15, 1910, 3; "Acts in Shooting of American Tourists," *Buffalo Courier,* March 11, 1910, 1; William James Adams, "Human Sacrifice and the Book of Abraham," *Brigham Young University Studies* 9, no. 4 (1969): 473–80.

The Reverend: "Rev. Chas. H. Bohner in the Holy Land," *Allentown Leader,* March 25, 1910, 1; "Lecture on the Holy Land," *Allentown Leader,* June 8, 1910, 12. His wife's name was Carrie.

pairs of flimsy slippers: Lynett, 1.

once-in-a-lifetime trip: ibid.

comprising one perfect dimension: The Haram is not a mosque, nor is it the Mosque of Omar, but it was called both with great frequency in the press of the early 1900s. See Frank G. Carpenter, "Site of Solomon's Temple," *Boston Globe,* November 27, 1910, 61; "Mosque of Omar on Holiest Spot," *Chicago Tribune,* November 27, 1910, 10. My own descriptions rely on period photographs and Jerry M. Landay, *Dome of the Rock* (New York: Newsweek, 1972); G. S. P. Freeman-Grenville, *The Beauty of Jerusalem* (London: East-West

Publications, 1983), 69.

Foundation Stone: Lynett, 1; George Lambert, *Around the Globe and Through Bible Lands* (Elkhart, Ind.: Mennonite Publishing, 1896), 216–17.

"I'm a librarian": "Miss Maurice," *St. Louis Globe-Democrat,* March 11, 1910, 1. She was a librarian in "New York."

Well of Souls: Lambert, 216; William Simpson, *The Jonah Legend* (London: G. Richards, 1899), 116–18; Charles Clermont-Ganneau, "The Kubbet es Sakhra," *Archaeological Researches in Palestine During the Years 1873–1874,* vol. 1 (London: Committee of the Palestine Exploration Fund, 1899), 179–227.

A shot thundered out: Lynett, 1. It was important to me to make this scene realistic, not cinematic: Deborah Cotton, "What It Really Feels Like to Get Shot," *Thrilllist,* 2017, www.thrillist.com/health/nation/what-does-it-feel-like-to-get-shot; Lois Beckett and Jamiles Lartey, "Stories of Loss, Love and Hope: Six Firsthand Accounts," *Guardian,* November 14, 2017; Lisa Hamp, "I Survived a Mass Shooting," *Washington Post,* February 15, 2018. Jim Schaefer, "Inside the El Paso Shooting," *El Paso Times,* August 10, 2019.

if he had any: Lynett, 1.

few weeks' time: "Victim Is Terre Haute Society Girl," *St. Louis Globe-Democrat,* March 11, 1910, 1. The sunny diagnoses of the victims in the newspapers stand in stark contrast to what experts know about shooting survivors. See Amy Novotney, "What Happens to the Survivors," *Journal of the American Psychological Association* 49, no. 8 (2018), 36.

God alone, without partner: Marcus Milwright, "Initial Description of the Mosaic Inscriptions," *The Dome of the Rock and Its Umayyad Mosaic Inscriptions* (Edinburgh: Edinburgh University Press, 2016), 49–82.

Chapter Twenty-Four

He was quite sick: Charles Warren, *Underground Jerusalem,* 528.
work in this area: ibid., 523–24.
mourn for them: ibid., 530.
through into a passage: ibid., 582.
"standing on a roof": ibid.
the time of the Temple's destruction: ibid.

Chapter Twenty-Five

new machinery: Vincent, *Underground,* 2.
reveled in it: ibid., 17.

to meet somewhere in between: ibid., 20.

like a black rectangular door: ibid.; Patti Smith, "Land: Horses/Land of a Thousand Dances/La Mer (De)," *Horses,* Arista, 1975.

"a detailed plan of it": Underground, 18.

detailed photographs of the tunnel: ibid., 43–65.

easier to correct later: ibid., 22–24.

eleventh century BC: ibid., 51–52.

"washed, and came seeing": John 9:1–12.

"A tomb": Underground, 21.

Chapter Twenty-Six

view from the roof: Our Jerusalem, 203.

Mr. Moses: ibid., 146–49.

Miss Poole: ibid., 132–33.

made manifest in him: 46. Chapters 1 and 2 of *Our Jerusalem* tell this very moving story. See also Jane Fletcher Geniesse, *American Priestess* (New York: Nan A. Talese, 2008).

"shall we be too": Our Jerusalem, 47.

three years old: ibid., 57, 65.

Chapter Twenty-Seven

middle of the dirt road: Charles Warren, "The Moabite Stone," *Palestine Exploration*

Quarterly 2, no. 5 (1869): 169–83.

Moabite Stone: Charles Warren, *Underground Jerusalem,* 536–37. See also James King, *Moab's Patriarchal Stone* (London: Palestine Exploration Fund, 1878); Robert Francis Harper, "The Moabite Stone," *Biblical World* 7, no. 1 (1896): 60–64; Warren and Wilson, *Recovery,* 489–502.

Charles Clermont-Ganneau: "The Late M. Charles Clermont-Ganneau," *Palestine Exploration Quarterly* 55, no. 3 (1923), 137–39.

"but they failed": Warren, *Underground Jerusalem,* 540.

"will fall upon their crops": Warren, "Moabite Stone," 162.

make a squeeze of the stone: ibid.; Warren, *Underground Jerusalem,* 540–42; Warren and Wilson, *Recovery,* 498–501.

with a spear in his leg: Warren and Wilson, *Recovery,* 390–93.

letter: Warren and Wilson, *Recovery,* 170–71.

None of it was true: Warren, *Underground Jerusalem,* 543–44.

"and I took it, for Chemosh": Warren and Wilson, *Recovery,* 170–71, 503–04; Thomas Parker, "Recent Explorations in Palestine," *Christian Ambassador,* vol. 10 (Lon-

don: G. Lamb, 1872), 63–64.

"Chemosh upon the wall": 2 Kings 3:27.

"and the publicity given": Warren and Wilson, *Recovery,* 496.

"moral order is preserved": ibid., 510.

Louvre: The Mesha Stele, Louvre Museum, Paris, louvre.fr/en/oeuvre-notices/mesha stele.

"ten, or maybe twenty years": Warren, *Underground Jerusalem,* 605.

Chapter Twenty-Eight

"most kind and hospitable": Autumn, 28. In his preface, Foley says that his book "does not profess to record anything of historical interest, with the possible exception of the Jameson Raid."

"we completely broke down": ibid., 29–30.

Any minute now: ibid., 119.

"But can you beat it": ibid., 46–47.

"wristwatch stopped": ibid., 61.

"taken food from a child:": ibid., 64–67; Ishay Govender-Ypma, "Mealie Pap Is a South African Breakfast for All," *MyRecipes,* April 2, 2018, myrecipes.com/extracrispy/mealie-pap-south-africa.

"munching an apple": Autumn, 67.

"and we looked the part": ibid., 71–73.

"would need a lot of men": ibid., 76.

"Does it matter?": Valter, ch. 5. Parker was diagnosed with neurasthenia, largely understood as shell shock, or PTSD; *Valter,* ch. 4; M. A. Crocq and L. Crocq. "From Shell Shock and War Neurosis to Posttraumatic Stress Disorder: A History of Psychotraumatology," *Dialogues in Clinical Neuroscience* 2, no. 1 (2000): 47–55; Caroline Alexander, "The Shock of War," *Smithsonian Magazine,* September 1910.

silt of three thousand years: Autumn, 119.

"I fought Dracula": bit.ly/3a0d2s5.

"Not even by the Hittites!": Autumn, 128.

Chapter Twenty-Nine

snow was falling over Jerusalem: "A White Christmas in Jerusalem," *Evening News,* December 23, 1910, 1.

soup kitchen downstairs: Valter, ch. 7.

"mysterious": "Pool of Siloam," *New York Times,* December 12, 1909, C4; "Strange Treasure Hunt," *Irish News and Belfast Morning News,* May 14, 1910, 3; "King Solomon's Treasure," *Dundee Evening Telegraph,* July 8, 1910, 4.

Le Queux: "Fiction," *Banbury Advertiser,* August 4, 1910, 6.

"among his best work": "Treasures of Israel,"

Dublin Daily Express, February 24, 1910, 7.

Le Queux: Valter, ch. 5. This successful novel hinged on a professor from a university in "northern Europe" who cracked the cipher. Stewart's treatment of his work is exhaustive. A later fictionalization of the expedition is Elizabeth Peters, *A River in the Sky* (New York: Harper, 2010). A *New York Times* bestseller, the book finds Peters's beloved protagonist Amelia Peters following "would-be archaeologist Major George Morley" as he hunts for the Ark in 1910.

French archaeologist: Galor, Katharina, *Finding Jerusalem: Archaeology between Science and Ideology* (Oakland: University of California Press, 2017), 119–122.

"entrance, seek!: Parker Archive.

"also was found": ibid.

Warren thought the blood canal: Charles Warren, *Underground Jerusalem,* 404–05.

"went or what I did": Nehemiah 2:1–20

"drawing a blank": "Cosy Corner Chat," *Gentlewoman,* July 23, 1910, 17.

small map: Parker Archive.

"go to hell": J. Lusthaus, "A History of Hell: The Jewish Origins of the Idea of Gehenna in the Synoptic Gospels," *Journal for the*

Academic Study of Religion 21, no. 2, (2009), 175–87; Alice K. Turner, *The History of Hell* (New York: Harvest Books, 1995); Elaine Pagels, *The Origin of Satan: How Christians Demonized Jews, Pagans, and Heretics* (New York: Vintage, 1996).

Chapter Thirty

Gehenna: I do not know for certain if Monty went to Gehenna, but it was nearby, and he certainly interacted with it conceptually in trying to understand the cipher. My model for their tour, whether real or imagined, is from Mark Twain, *The Innocents Abroad; or, The New Pilgrims' Progress* (Connecticut: American Publishing, 1869), 582–83. When Twain visited Palestine, he also visited the American Colony. See also Lloyd R. Bailey, "Enigmatic Bible Passages: Gehenna: The Topography of Hell," *Biblical Archaeologist* 49, no. 3 (1986): 187–91.

"went to the underworld": Underground, 17.

"Here is where Molok stood": Twain, 583.

"St. Onuphrius, a desert hermit": "Venerable Onuphrius the Great," oca.org/saints/lives.

not afford burial elsewhere: Matthew 27:3–10; Leen Ritmeyer and Kathleen Ritmeyer, "Potter's Field or High Priest's

Tomb?" *Biblical Archaeology Review* 20, no. 6 (1994): 22–78; Danny Herman, "Akeldama, the Field of Blood," dannythe digger.com/jerusalem/akeldama.

was a charnel house: "Akeldama (Field of Blood)," seetheholyland.net/tag/charnel house/.

Knights Templar: Dan Jones, *The Templars: The Rise and Spectacular Fall of God's Holy Warriors* (New York: Penguin, 2018); Michael Baigent, Richard Leigh, and Henry Lincoln, *Holy Blood, Holy Grail* (New York: Delacorte, 1982).

Freemasons: There is no physical or anecdotal evidence that Monty was a Mason, so I chose to present it instead from an outsider's (his) view. In an email on January 12, 2021, Olivia Parker wrote, "As far as I know, no Parkers were Masons (I haven't been taught the secret handshake yet anyway)." See also Michael Baigent and Richard Leigh, *The Temple and the Lodge* (New York: Arcade, 2020); Graham Addison, email to author, October 23, 2020. According to Graham, Cyril Ward was a Mason.

knights: Graham Naylor, "St. Mary's Church, Plympton," *A Church Crawler's Journal,* September 11, 2016, someoldde vonchurches.wordpress.com. There were knights who held the Morley and Parker name, but not related to Monty. In January 1908, when the new session of Parliament opened, a strange man walked into the chamber wearing rich robes trimmed in ermine. He sat down in the House of Lords just before the Royal Procession entered. The Yeoman Usher of the Black Rod confronted him and called over the Garter King of Arms, who asked for his credentials. "I am the Lord de Morley," the man said with a sneer. His name was James Thorne Rowe. He then produced a writ of summons issued by Edward I in 1299. They ordered him to leave. When he would not, they conducted him out in full view of the other astonished lords. Soon after, Rowe filed an official claim that he was descended from Sir John Parker, the eldest of Henry Parker, who died as the Tenth Baron de Morley in 1556. The royal officials checked their thick books and agreed that he indeed had a claim. But when it was found that Sir John had been born out of wedlock, his claim was permanently denied. Rowe was right that the Barony of Morley title had fallen into abeyance when Henry Parker died in 1556. It was resuscitated in 1815 in a different form when John Parker, the Second

Baron of Boringdon (and no relation to that first Henry Parker!) was conferred the title of Lord Morley, even though he was not of the same Parkers or Morleys. This practice was fairly common, according to peerage enthusiasts. Even the original Morleys had complications with their lineage. At the siege of Calais in 1346, two knights — Nicholas, Lord Brunel, and Robert, Lord de Morley — walked on the field bearing arms of the exact same color — an unthinkable transgression. One of Brunel's knights immediately challenged Morley to a duel, but the king intervened and had the matter handed over to the Court of Chivalry. During the proceedings, it was revealed that Morley had previously served as an esquire to a Brunel, and when his knight died he assumed the arms with his dying blessing. Robert de Morley did not like his chances in court, so he whispered to the king that if his arms were taken, he could no longer in good faith fight for His Majesty. It was a very risky move, but it was successful, as Robert kept his arms instead of losing his head. They agreed that Robert could keep them until his death. When he died while on crusade in Prussia, Robert's heart was sent home to England. Somehow, his arms stayed in use for several generations, until they changed and no one cared anymore. The current crest of the House of Morley, in use since 1815, is a stag's head on black, with two great antlers. Their motto is simple but hopeful: *Fideli certa merces,* or, "Reward is sure to the faithful." See David Stone, "The Very Early Members of the Morley Family," Dereham and District Team Ministry, 2011, derehamand districtteam.org.uk; John O. Morley, "The Origins of the Morleys in England and their Early Appearance in Wales," *Annals of Geneaological Research* 9, no. 1 (2013), 1–61.

"steps(!) from Hakeldama": Parker Archive.

three hundred yards: ibid.

utterly fallen in: ibid. Juvelius says in the cipher that the way is blocked, though he is unclear which cave he is referring to. There is other contemporary evidence of tunnels being inaccessible there. See James Hastings, ed., *A Dictionary of Christ and the Gospels,* vol. 1, part 2 (Honolulu: University Press of the Pacific, 1906, 2004 reprint), 852; W. E. Manley, "Letters to my Friends in Connecticut," *Manford's Magazine* 29, no. 12 (1885), 675.

his mother: Olivia Parker, email to author, November 15, 2020; Ceri Johnson, *Sal-*

tram (Great Britain: National Trust, 1998), 54–55.

"children of Ammon": 1 Kings 11:7.

Chapter Thirty-One

"King Solomon's": Underground, 29. Father Vincent's story of the grand and ancient toilet is corroborated by Juvelius in *Valkoinen,* though the timelines disagree by over a year.

A necessary necropolis: Etan Nechin, "Dying in Jerusalem," *Boston Review,* April 6, 2020.

The first cave: Underground, 24–25.

the second tomb: ibid., 25.

the third cave: ibid.

colorful pottery: ibid., 27–29.

Chapter Thirty-Two

The primary sources for this chapter are Warren's own letter, contemporaneous newspaper articles, and some of the official evidence. Whenever possible, I cite the online database casebook.org because of its ease of navigation and its policy of avoiding displaying the photos of the victims without warning or pause, as so many of the others commonly do. The secondary resources on this topic are too numerous to list or mention, though I found some helpful things in Nigel Graddon, *Jack the Ripper's New Testament* (Kempton, IL: Adventures Unlimited, 2019); Alan Moore and Eddie Campbell, *From Hell* (Marietta, GA: Top Shelf, 2004); Richard Whittington-Egan, *Jack the Ripper: The Definitive Casebook* (Amberley Publishing, 2015). The most helpful model for trying to write about this subject at all was Hallie Rubenhold, *The Five* (Boston: Mariner Books, 2019), which I wish I had read first.

Goulston Street: For images, see casebook.org/victorian_london/sitepics.w-goul.

"the writing": "Murders in the East-End," *London Evening Standard,* October 2, 1888, 3; "The Whitechapel Tragedy. Chalk-Writing the Wall," *Eastern Daily Press,* September 12, 1889, 8; "The Writing on the Wall," October 12, 1888, 3; "Letter from Sir Charles Warren," *London Evening Standard,* October 4, 1888, 3; "The Whitechapel Murder," *London Daily News,* September 14, 1888, 6; "The East-End Murders," *Lloyd's Weekly Newspaper,* October 14, 1888, 3.

"would probably have been lost": Charles Warren, "Warren's Report to the Home Secretary," November 6, 1888, casebook .org/official_documents/warrenlt.

"for nothing": "Copy of attachment to a Police report from Chief Commissioner Sir Charles Warren of the Metropolitan Police, to the Home Office," November 6, 1888. Home Office archive, HO 144.221.A49301C.8c, commons.wiki media.org/wiki/File:Juives.jpg.

might be Yiddish: Bruce Robinson, *They All Love Jack* (New York: Harper, 2015). For any readers interested in a detailed Masonic reading through Warren and his experiences in Palestine, this is the book to read.

"Dear Boss": "Letter received on September 27th, 1888," casebook.org/ripper_letters.

Kate Eddowes's: "The Whitechapel Mystery," *Illustrated Police News,* October 13, 1888.

that perhaps might fit: "Jack," *Oxford English Dictionary Online,* 2nd ed., 1989, oed.com/oed2/00122699. Etymologically "Jack" comes from the word for a "generic," "common" man. The definition I am considering is "To things of smaller than the normal size . . . a very small amount;

the least bit; a whit . . . [as in] jack-bowl, jack-brick, jack-fish." This later becomes Americanized in the idiom "you don't know jack," meaning you don't know anything / you know nothing. And "jack-ass."

Russian spies and secret men: William Le Queux, *Things I Know about Kings, Celebrities, and Crooks* (London: Eveleigh Nash and Grayson, 1923), 258–72; "Jack the Ripper," *Nottingham Evening Post,* October 25, 1923, 1.

turned away as a madman: "Tracing Jack the Ripper," *Northampton Chronicle and Echo,* January 13, 1931, 3; Jennifer D. Pegg, "Robert James Lees & Visions from Hell," casebook.org/dissertations/rip peroo-lees. I tried, for far too long, to determine whether Robert James Lees could have been the mysterious James Lees identified with the expedition. Since I could not make an even transitory connection (I could not locate his 1888 diary), the story ends here, though the question is open.

the bloodhound experiment: "Charles Warren and the Bloodhounds," *Yorkshire Post,* November 13, 1888, 6; Angela Buckley, "Dog Detectives," *Victorian Supersleuth Investigates,* January 25, 2019, victorian-supersleuth.com/dog-detectives.

"for lost cities in Palestine": "Our London," *Dundee Courier,* October 11, 1888, 3.

on several fronts: "Resignation of Sir Charles Warren," *Morning Post,* November 13, 1888, 5; "Sir Charles Warren's Resignation," *Globe,* November 13, 1888, 4.

in her rented room: There are rumors that the crime scene contained something on the walls that looked like writing. I finally looked at the photograph, just to make sure. Trust me, there is nothing there. Don't look at it.

"of crime is love": "The Moral of the Murders," *The Star,* October 5, 1888, 1; Ralph Waldo Emerson, "Worship," 1860, emersoncentral.com/texts/the-conduct-of-life/worship/.

"to be utterly and irretrievably bad": "Points about Policemen," *Brooklyn Daily Eagle,* December 9, 1888, 15.

Polly Nichols, Annie Chapman, Elizabeth Stride, Kate Eddowes, and Mary Jane Kelly: Hallie Rubenhold, *The Five* (Boston: Mariner Books, 2019).

Chapter Thirty-Three

at least ten men: William E. Curtis, "Moslems in a Rage," *Evening Star,* May 22,

1911; the records analyzed in Fishman, "1911."

Dome of the Rock: description from Jerry M. Landay, *Dome of the Rock* (New York: Newsweek, 1972).

A blackened star: William Simpson, *Cave Under the Dome of the Rock, Jerusalem,* pencil and watercolor, 1870; Daniel Estrina, "Replacing Carpet at Jerusalem Shrine Reveals Religious Rift," AP News, April 21, 2015; Kylen Chase Campbell, "(When) History Is Rocky," *Roots to Now,* roots2now.wordpress.com/tag/dome-of-the-rock; Rabbi Leibel Reznick, "Secret Chambers of the Temple Mount," *Jewish Action,* spring 1997, jewishaction.com/jewish-world/israel/secret-chambers-temple-mount; "Well of Souls," Madain Project, madainproject.com; Rivka Gonen, *Contested Holiness: Jewish, Muslim, and Christian Perspectives on the Temple* (Jersey City, KTAV Publishing, 2003), 23.

Chapter Thirty-Four

Ava Lowle Willing Astor: Ava Astor did not leave behind many primary sources. The best source I found is Kavaler. Though gossipy (as it should be), she talked to many family members, though the obvious caveats apply. See also Justin Kaplan, *When the Astors Owned New York* (New York: Penguin, 2007).

Alice: She was seven years old at the time.

"Her Majesty": "Snubs Mrs. Astor," *Sunday Star,* May 21, 1991, 1. Consuelo Vanderbilt was also linked to the expedition as a secret financier, but there is no evidence of her help in the official reports. Same with the Armour meatpacking family of Chicago. Thanks to Graham Addison for his fine research in this area.

ten million dollars: Kavaler, 165.

twenty-five thousand dollars on flowers: ibid., 166.

her son, Vincent: "Vincent Astor as Head of His Family," *New York Times,* April 17, 1912, 13.

the Colony Club: ibid., 164; "Woman's World," *Daily Globe,* November 18, 1908, 6; Madame X., "Colony Club the Holy of Holies for the 'Smart' Women Set," *Chicago Tribune,* April 30, 1911, 21.

"may cause Diplomatic incident": "Have Englishmen Found the Ark of the Covenant?" *New York Times,* May 7, 1911, 50.

Chapter Thirty-Five

The mob: See Fishman, "1911"; Ark of the Covenant Stolen from Mosque?" *Indianapolis News,* May 3, 1911, 1; "Where's the Ark?" *Ottawa Citizen,* May 4, 1911, 1; "Lost Relics Stir Riot," *Washington Post,* May 4, 1911, 5; "Secrets of the Temple," *Globe,* September 20, 1911, 1; "Stole Ark of the Covenant," *Boston Globe,* May 3, 1911, 5; "The Excavations at Jerusalem," *The Times,* May 10, 1911. Directly above this article was a story about a woman explorer who had just returned from Africa.

"Kill the governor!": "Alleged Sacrilege at Jerusalem," *Guardian,* May 5, 1911, 6.

in addition to Passover: Louis Fishman, interview with author, January 19, 2021. Louis noted in conversation with me that it was also Passover, which is why he thinks there was not a more immediate reaction from the Jewish population. Louis was the first to find a record of the expedition in the Ottoman Archives, which gave the story a greater weight than it had previously had among many historians. He argues that the riot was indicative of an emerging Palestinian nationalism. For context, see also Louis A. Fishman, *Jews and Palestinians in the Late Ottoman Era, 1908–1914: Claiming the Homeland* (Edinburgh: Edinburgh University Press, 2019).

"The English diggers": Our Jerusalem, 227–30. Though Bertha was a resident of Jerusalem and does add details to the account, she did not start keeping diaries until later. Most of her account borrows heavily from the syndicated article "Moslems in a Rage," by Curtis. Or vice versa.

"A general strike has been called": Fishman, "1911," 7.

"Massacre! Massacre!": Curtis, "Moslems in a Rage"; *Our Jerusalem,* 229.

resume business: Our Jerusalem, 229.

"George A. Fuller": ibid., 138–39.

"except God and the Englishmen": "Fear Diggers Took Ark of the Covenant," *New York Times,* May 4, 1911, 6.

Chapter Thirty-Six

"too much for them": Autumn, 127.

Chapter Thirty-Seven

the Turkish parliament: Ottoman Parliament in December 1908 (Second Constitutional Era of the Ottoman Empire), December 1908, mideastimage.com/cities/istanbul.

"was hired as the middleman": Fishman, "1911," 12.

"in the name of God": ibid., 14.

"and hides it": ibid., 16.

"a mysterious man": ibid., 17.

"Stand trial before a tribunal": ibid., 18.

Chapter Thirty-Eight

"has presented its report": "Ancient Jerusalem," *Times,* May 8, 1911, 8.

said the Englishman: "Mysterious Bags Taken From Mosque," *New York Times,* May 14, 1911, 3.

Chapter Thirty-Nine

William E. Curtis: "Curtis Found Jesse James," *New York Times,* October 7, 1911, 11; Benjamin A. Coates, "The Pan-American Lobbyist: William Eleroy Curtis and U.S. Empire, 1884–1899," *Diplomatic History* 38, no. 1 (2014): 22–48. In the William Eleroy Curtis Papers Repository 1877–1912, Western Reserve Historical Society, MS3276, Cleveland, OH, there is a curious listing: "Photographs (4) of a mummy's eye (see letter of H. W. Wiley dated February 28, 1903) undated." Due to the pandemic, I was sadly unable to view these photographs. Thanks to Ann Sindelar for her help.

"to be careful hereafter": Curtis, "Moslems in a Rage."

Bertha Vester and Cyril Foley: Their versions of the Curtis article, at times word for word, appear in *Our Jerusalem* and *Autumn.* This is a testament to how complete the account was, even to people who knew those involved. Or it may suggest something else.

Chapter Forty

Juvelius read the sensational news: Valkoinen.

spread across the world: "Sacred Ark of Covenant Lost in Holy City," *Mexican Herald,* May 4, 1911; "Holy Land Treasures," *Eastern Province Herald,* May 11, 1911; "Seeks Solomon's Temple," *Washington Post,* May 4, 1911, 5.

"Closer to the letter": Valkoinen.

Turks then claimed their cargo: ibid.

Chapter Forty-One

Millen stood at the lectern: Millen, Johan, *På rätta vägar: Davids forntida stad upptäckt: Israels tio stammar återfunna (äro icke ju-*

darna) (Stockholm: A.-B. Hasse W. Tull-berg, 1917). The book is not a transcript of the lecture but was an extension of it.

"Is this all?": ibid., 8.

"A historical novel": ibid., 5.

"leader": I found no evidence that Millen went to Palestine with the expedition or visited them at any time.

"honest and laudable": Millen, 21.

"blond, tall people": ibid., 79.

"Odin": ibid., 85.

the people erupted: Some accounts put Henning Melander at this lecture. Melander's ideas about the Ark were taken up by the political activist Theodor Herzl, who brought it before Kaiser Wilhelm II, who was supposedly interested. Any project they may have conceived together to seek the Ark as a German concern died with Herzl in 1904.

Chapter Forty-Two

the Titanic: "Noted Men on The Lost Titanic," *New York Times,* April 16, 1912, 4; "How Col. Astor Died," *New York Times,* April 19, 1912, 7; *New York Times,* April 17, 1912.

gold pocket watch: David Belcher, "Tracing a Precious Relic of the Titanic," *New York*

Times, November 28, 2013; Vincent Astor as Head of His Family," *New York Times,* April 17, 1912, 13.

"his magnificent bass voice": Kavaler, 169.

voyaged to Egypt: "Mainly About People," *Sphinx* 30, no. 489, December 16, 1922, 17; "Mainly About People," *Sphinx* 30, no. 520, July 21, 1923, 12; Kavaler, 262–63.

steadying her black hat: Tomb of Tutankhamun, Valley of the Kings, Egypt, 1923, Historica Graphica Collection, Heritage Images, Science Photo Library.

glint of pure gold: Howard Carter, "November 26, 1922," *Diary, Part 1,* Griffith Institute, griffith.ox.ac.uk/gri/4sea1not.

Anubis shrine: I. E. S. Edwards, *Tutankhamun: His Tomb and Its Treasures* (New York: The Metropolitan Museum of Art, 1976), 153. Alice Grenfell, "Egyptian Mythology and the Bible," *The Monist* 16, no. 2 (1906): 169–200; tutankhamuns world101.weebly.com/anubis-shrine.

"the path to be mistaken": Howard Carter, "Excavation Journal 5th Season, September 22nd 1926 to May 3rd 1927," Griffith Institute, griffith.ox.ac.uk/discoveringtut/journals-and-diaries/season-5/journal; Maria Rosa Guasch Jané, "About the Orien-

tation of the Magical Bricks in Tut-ankhamun's Burial Chamber," *Journal of the American Research Center in Egypt* 48 (2012): 111–18.

necklace: Kavaler, 262.

"is there within me": Serge Oblensky, *One Man in His Time* (Lucknow, India: Lucknow Books), 461.

"back into the darkness": ibid., 262.

Roundtable Foundation: Annie Jacobsen, *Phenomena: The Secret History of the U.S. Government's Investigations into Extrasenory Perception and Psychokinesis* (New York: Little, Brown & Co., 2017), 28–60.

"suspect or implausable": ibid., 274.

Alice died: Kavaler, 274.

"strain of melancholy": ibid., 170.

"with what I've seen here?": ibid., 170.

Ava lived to be eighty-nine:: "Lady Ribblesdale Dead. First Wife of John Jacob Astor IV. Mother of Vincent Astor," *New York Times,* June 11, 1958, 35.

Chapter Forty-Three

Cyril Ward: "Death of Capt. The Hon. Cyril Ward," *Western Daily Press,* January 17, 1930, 9.

Pertti Uotila: Otto Favén, "Homeland," *Kansan uutiset,* July 12, 2014, kansanuutiset.fi/

artikkeli/3199033-internationalen-neljas-kaantaja.

"getting a little tired": *Parker Archive.* Thanks to Graham Addison.

"he saw through": "Eventful Years," *Belfast Telegraph,* March 10, 1936, 7. Vincent McCaffrey, who reviewed his book on his website in 2009, said, "He is alive today for anyone with the time to read."

"final elimination of him": Rudyard Kipling, "Letter to Colonel Feilden," February 8, 1912, *Letters of Rudyard Kipling 1911–19,* vol. 4, (Iowa City: University of Iowa Press, 1999), 84–85.

"Fiction isn't in it": ibid., "Letter to C.R.L. Fletcher," 85–86.

Robin Duff: "Reported Death in Battle of Sir Robert Duff," *Rippon Observer,* October 22, 1914, 5.

Otto Von Bourg: "Von Bourg," *Minneapolis Star,* September 30, 1929, 18.

most likely a Christian: The overwhelming majority of Armenians were Christian.

"back wages and expenses": *Parker Archive.*

Cavid Bey: H. O. Ozavci, email to author, November 9, 2020. According to Ozavci, there is no proof of this, but only because it is the type of information that is typically not recorded. It is only "the family lineage, the schools he attended, the

532

mosques he followed and the cemetery he was buried in" that make it a widely accepted fact for those who study him. See also Ozan Ozavci, "Honour and Shame: The Diaries of a Unionist and the 'Armenian Question,' " *The End of the Ottomans: The Genocide of 1915 and the Politics of Turkish Nationalism* (London: I.B. Tauris, 2019). Sources on the Armenian genocide are numerous and important. In the spirit of this book, I recommend Daniel Melnick, *The Ash Tree* (Fresno, CA: West of West, 2012).

eye on a red pyramid: Matthew Wilson, "The Eye of Providence: The Symbol with a Secret Meaning?" *BBC Culture,* November 13, 2020, bbc.com.

safe deposit box: Kalevi Mikkonen, "Dr. Juvelius and the Quest for the Ark of the Covenant," *Finnish Ufological Society,* no. 1 (1993), 1.1/93.

Chapter Forty-Four

Quatuor Coronati Lodge: "Founders of the Lodge," *Quatuor Coronati,* quatuor coronati.com/about-qc-lodge/founders/. See also Colin Neil Macdonald, *Warren!: The Bond of Brotherhood* (Singapore: self-published, 2007).

Spion Kop: "A Tale of the Boer War," *Guardian,* January 26, 1905; Winston Churchill, "Five Days Action at Spion Kop," *Morning Post,* February 17, 1900, 8; "Battle of Spion Kop," *British Battles,* hbritish battles.com/great-boer-war/battle-of-spion-kop; Defender, *Sir Charles Warren and Spion Kop: A Vindication* (London: Smith, Elder, & Co., 1902).

Warren attacked Father Vincent: Hugues Vincent and Charles Warren, "Recent Excavations on the Hill of Ophel," *Palestine Exploration Quarterly* 44, no. 3 (1902): 131–35.

Warren died in 1927: "Death of Famous General," *Shepton Mallet Journal,* January 28, 1927, 7; "Letters to the Editor," *Sheffield Daily Telegraph,* February 1, 1927, 6.

Chapter Forty-Five

dissertation: Juvelius defended his dissertation, *Jodarnes Tiderakhing* ("The Time of the Jews") on November 10, 1906, in public before the Department of Historical and Linguistics of the Faculty of Philosophy of Imperial Alexander University. See also "The Hat and Sword," University of Oulu, oulu.fi/conferment ceremony/the_hat_and_sword.

In Finnish tradition, a scholar who successfully defends their dissertation is given a top hat and a sword. This custom is still recognized, though all Ph.D. graduates will appreciate the proviso that "a young doctor needs to order his/her sword by him/herself."

Finnish fiction: Finnish modes in fiction lean more toward make-believe than made up. This seems to take the form of personal and confessional modes — along with the often-ready presence of magic as it intersects with the physical world. See Anneli Asplund, "Fact and Fiction: Aspects of Finnish Narrative Historical Songs," *Lares* 51, no. 4 (1985): 647–58. The rich tradition of Scandinavian true crime also may fit this model. See Andrew Nestingen, *Crime and Fantasy in Scandinavia: Fiction, Film and Social Change* (Seattle; London: University of Washington Press), 2008.

He died on Christmas Day: Valter, Introduction.

"movie by Steven Spielberg": David Landau, "Information on Valter Henrik Juvelius in Finnish Sources," September 1996, modeemi.fi/~david/juvelius/juv. Landau's personal website was the first real work using primary sources on Juvelius in English, and transformed nearly all of

what had come before. In *Valter,* Stewart examines some of the other branches of the Juvelius papers as they were found and distributed. There is a website titled "Help Crack the Juvelius Code" that produces some of Juvelius's papers from this batch, collated by Erling Haagensen.

"produced important results": Landau, "Information."

Chapter Forty-Six

Rothschild . . . Raymond Weill: Galor, Katharina, "Institutionalization," *Finding Jerusalem: Archaeology between Science and Ideology* (Oakland: University of California Press, 2017), 34; Raymond Weill, *La Cite de David* (Paris: P. Geuthner, 1921); Gerald M. Fitzgerald, "The City of David and The Excavations of 1913–1914," *Palestine Exploration Quarterly* 54, no. 1 (1922), 8–22; "Tombs of the Jewish Kings," *Aberdeen Press and Journal,* November 21, 1910, 8.

"the Wandering Arab": Elizabeth Antebi, "Baron Edmond de Rothschild (1845–1934): From *HaNadiv* (The Benefactor) to *HaNassi* (The Prince)," *Jewish Studies at the Turn of the Twentieth Century: Judaism from the Renaissance to Modern Times*

(Germany: Brill, 1999), 251.

the foundation named after him: See edmond derothschildfoundations.org for the foundation's current work.

Habib Allah: "Personal and Pertinent," *Scranton Times,* September 12, 1910, 6.

William Le Quex: His book *The Great God Gold,* was also published as *Treasures of Israel* (Boston: Gorham Press, 1910); Roger T. Stearn, "The Mysterious Mr. Le Queux," *Critical Survey* 32, nos. 1–2 (2020), 17–58; David A. T. Stafford, "Spies and Gentlemen: The Birth of the British Spy Novel, 1893–1914," *Victorian Studies* 24, no. 4 (1981): 489–509; 283 N. St. Barbe Sladen, *The Real Le Queux* (London: Nicholson, 1938).

The "Friend": I thought that the friend might be a local competitor or a Jerusalem professor who wrote to the American press, but the information is so close to some of the primary accounts of the expedition that it seems highly unlikely. Nearly everything the friend said was true in that it could be corroborated across several different sources. No other account in this book can boast that. The report's comprehensiveness points to someone in the raiding party, though I cannot say who with complete certainty.

Locusts: "River of Locusts," *Westminster Gazette,* November 8, 1915, 9; *The Locust Plague of 1915,* American Colony in Jerusalem, 1870 to 2006, Library of Congress, loc.gov/item/mamcol.058/; "Plague of Locusts Timelapse," Wild Africa, BBC Earth, August 21, 2009, youtube.com; Exodus 10.

Chapter Forty-Seven

Baby Home: Our Jerusalem, 329; Elias Antar, "The Story of Bertha Vester," *Saudi Aramco World* 18, no. 4 (July/August 1967), 24–33; Spafford Center, spafford center.org/about-us/history.
Bertha took the boy: Our Jerusalem, 327–328.
the plaque: Jacob Spafford tablet in Baby Home, American Colony in Jerusalem, 1870 to 2006, Library of Congress, loc .gov/pictures/resource/matpc.22448/.
Jacob Eliahu Spafford: Our Jerusalem, 230.
never heard from him again: Dan Fisher, "Legacy of a Latter-Day Madonna and Child," *Los Angeles Times,* December 25, 1986.

Chapter Forty-Eight

he traveled: "Captain Parker Holds Secret of Treasure," *Washington Post,* November 22, 1912, 6.

even in Jaffa: Montefiore, 520.

When the Great war came: Mark and Olivia Parker, interview with author, August 26, 2020.

he affectionately called B: Olivia Parker, email to author, February 25, 2021. B stood for Borington, his title before becoming earl.

their debt: Johnson, 56.

the Luftwaffe bombed: ibid., 57.

B passed away in 1951: "The Earl of Morley," *Belfast News-Letter,* October 11, 1951, 4; Johnson, 65. His brother Jack died in 1955, his sister Mary Theresa St. Aubyn in 1932.

even up the heavy death-duty tax: Johnson, 57; Kavaler, 213.

Monty enjoyed the lifestyle: Mark and Olivia Parker, interview with author, August 26, 2020.

"Uncle God": Johnson, 57.

Monty was eighty-three: "Earl Dies Soon After Return," *Cornish Guardian,* May 3, 1962, 7.

Marion Elizabeth Jessie Marconi Cecil:

"Brownlow, The Right Honourable Montagu, Fifth Earl of Morley," *The Gazette,* November 30, 1962, thegazette.co.uk/London/issue/42846/page/9447/data.pdf; Marc Raboy, *Marconi: The Man Who Networked the World* (Oxford: Oxford University Press, 2016), 322, 527.

St. Mary Church: Graham Naylor, "St. Mary's Church, Plympton," *A Church Crawler's Journal,* September 11, 2016, someolddevonchurches.wordpress.com.

thin stone lane: Olivia Parker, email to author, August 30, 2020.

Chapter Forty-Nine

evade the question and smile: "Captain Parker Holds Secret of Treasure," *Washington Post,* November 22, 1912, 6. The only article in which Monty comes close to saying anything is "The British Excavators in Jerusalem," *Manchester Guardian,* May 10, 1911, 6, in which he makes mention of "old treasures," but because the first half reads so similar to the *Times* interview, this second part rings a little suspect. Either way, he does not mention the Ark. The only other physical clue, though it is not from him, is Gustaf Dalman, "The Search for the Temple Treasure at Jerusalem," *Palestine Exploration Quarterly* 44, no. 1, 35–39, who notes in a visit to the Dome of the Rock soon after that it looked as if the mosaic tile with the black star had been repaired.

"Parker Family Archive": See Montefiore.

"Morley": Earl of Morley, letter to author, September 16, 2017.

Dr. Nirit Shalev-Khalifa: Nirit Shalev-Khalifa, audio message to author, February 23, 2021.

Monty's original documents: Mark and Olivia Parker, interview with author, August 26, 2020.

"Call me Mark": ibid.

"my most respectful tributes": Parker Archive.

ten full boxes: Valkoinen.

"tools, clays, and stones": ibid.

correspondence about the cupboard: Israel Antiquities Authority, Silwan-Confiscation of Antiquities, Montague B. Parker's Excavation ATQ_1870a (27 / 27).

"in someone's home": Author, email to Fawzi Ibrahim, November 8, 2020.

"diameter: 13.5 cm": Fawzi Ibrahim, email to author, November 9, 2020.

"life in these hills": Underground, 31.

copper mountain: "Jewish God Yahweh," *Haaretz,* April 11, 2018, haaretz.com; Adam Gonnerman, "Yahweh's Forge," *Me-*

dium, July 15, 2019, medium.com; Nissim Amzallag and Ariel David, "Furnace Remelting as the Expression of YHWH's Holiness: Evidence from the Meaning of Qann קַנָּא) in the Divine Context," *Journal of Biblical Literature* 134, no. 2 (2015): 233–52.

metal pails: Ronny Reich and Eli Shukron, "Light at the End of the Tunnel," *Biblical Archaeology Review* 25, no. 1 (1999): 22–72.

Epilogue

Saltram as a museum: Mary, "Saltram Comes to Life," *Devon Daily,* June 11, 2013, thedevondaily.co.uk. "Lady Astor" is supposed to be "Nancy Astor." There is a priceless photo of "Monty" and "Lady Astor" that can be easily found on Pinterest. Thanks to Dave Lucas for help describing Monty's spectacular sport coat.

Saltram: See Johnson. The film *Sense and Sensibility* (1995) was filmed at Saltram.

Astrippus and His Companions: Antonio Zucchi, *Aristippus and His Companions After Being Shipwrecked Seeing Mathematical Diagrams and Realising the Land Was Inhabited,* NT 872168, Saltram, Devon

(Accredited Museum), 1768, nationaltrust collections.org.uk/object/872168.1. Thanks to Louise Ayres for the invaluable help in establishing where the painting was in Saltram and that it was there for the duration of Monty's life there.

pencil drawings: Margaret Holford, Countess of Morley, *Art / Drawings and watercolours* 22208, Saltram, Devon (Accredited Museum), 1855–1908, nationaltrust collections.org.uk.

the dentist: J. W. Rinzler, *The Complete Making of Indiana Jones* (New York: Del Rey, 2008), 14–18.

BIBLIOGRAPHY

Key Sources Cited in This Book

Foley, Cyril P. *Autumn Foliage.* London: Methuen & Co., 1935.

The Holy Bible, King James Version. Cambridge Edition, 1769. *King James Bible Online,* 2021. kingjamesbibleonline.org.

Juvelius, Valter (as Heikki Kenttä), *Valkoinen kameeli ja muita kertomuksia itämailta,* Helsinki, Finland: Otava Publishing Co., 1916. Unpublished translation, n.p.

Kavaler, Lucy. *The Astors: A Family Chronicle of Pomp and Power.* New York: Dodd, Mead & Co., 1966.

Millen, Johan. *På rätta vägar: Davids forntida stad upptäckt: Israels tio stammar återfunna (äro icke judarna).* Stockholm: A.-B. Hasse W. Tullberg, 1917.

Parker Archive, Yad Ben-Zvi Archives, Captain Montague B. Parker Archive.

Stewart, Timo R. *Valter Juvelius ja kadon-*

neen arkin metsästys. Helsinki, Finland: Otava Publishing Co., 2020.

Vester, Bertha Spafford. *Our Jerusalem: An American Family in the Holy City, 1881–1949.* New York: Doubleday, 1950.

Vincent, Hugues. *Underground Jerusalem: Discoveries on the Hill of Ophel, 1909–11.* London: H. Cox, "Field" Office, 1911.

Warren, Charles. *Underground Jerusalem.* London: Richard Bentley, 1876.

Warren, Charles, and Charles Wilson. *The Recovery of Jerusalem: A Narrative of Exploration and Discovery in the City and the Holy Land.* New York: D. Appleton, 1871.

Research Sources

Backholer, Paul. *The Ark of the Covenant.* Byth Media, 2018.

Baigent, Michael, Richard Leigh, and Henry Lincoln. *Holy Blood, Holy Grail.* New York: Delacorte, 1982.

Buron, Melissa E. *James Tissot.* New York: Prestel, 2019.

Carew, Mairead. *Tara and the Ark of the Covenant.* Dublin: Royal Irish Academy, 2003.

Coetzer, Owen. *The Anglo-Boer War.* London: Arms and Armour Press, 1996.

Dalman, Gustaf. "The Search for the Temple Treasure at Jerusalem." *Palestine Exploration Quarterly* 44, no. 1 (1912): 35–39.

Fishman, Louis. *Jews and Palestinians in the Late Ottoman Era, 1908–1914: Claiming the Homeland.* Edinburgh: Edinburgh University Press, 2021.

Horovitz, Ahron. *Discovering the City of David.* Jerusalem: Koren, 2015.

Israel Antiquities Authority. *Jerusalem: Biblical Archaeology.* Jerusalem: Carta, 2017.

Johnson, Ceri. *Saltram.* Great Britain: National Trust, 1998.

King, Charles. *Midnight at the Pera Palace.* New York: W. W. Norton & Co., 2015.

Kingsley, Sean. *God's Gold.* New York: HarperCollins, 2007.

Landay, Jerry M. *Dome of the Rock.* New York: Newsweek, 1972.

Masterman, E. W. G. "Recent Excavations in Jerusalem." *Biblical World* 39, no. 5 (1912): 295–306.

Millgram, Abraham E. *Jerusalem Curiosities.* Philadelphia: Jewish Education Society, 1990.

Montefiore, Simon Sebag. *Jerusalem: The Biography,* New York: Knopf, 2011.

Moore, Alan, and Eddie Campbell. *From

Hell. Marietta, GA: Top Shelf, 2004.

National Geographic Society (U.S.), Cartographic Division. "The Holy Land." *National Geographic Magazine.* Washington, D.C.: Cartographic Dept., December 1963.

Price, Randall. *In Search of the Temple Treasures.* Eugene, OR: Harvest House, 1994.

Rinzler, J. W. *The Complete Making of Indiana Jones.* New York: Del Rey, 2008.

Robinson, Bruce. *They All Love Jack.* New York: Harper, 2015.

Rubenhold, Hallie. *The Five.* Boston: Mariner Books, 2019.

Silberman, Neil Asher. *Digging for God and Country.* New York: Random House, 1982.

Sladen, N. St. Barbe. *The Real Le Queux.* London: Nicholson, 1938.

Von Daniken, Erich. *Chariots of the Gods.* New York: Berkley, 1999.

ACKNOWLEDGMENTS

Thank you — first of all, most of all — to you out there who are reading and thinking and listening. I wrote this book during a tough time for all, and for so many of you, unimaginable. I thought of you while writing this book. I hope these words find you in a better place.

I've been waiting to write this book for almost forty years. Thanks to Scott Mendel, my agent, ally, and friend of over ten years, When I first told him about this idea years ago, he instantly recognized not only the audacity of the story itself, but what it meant to me. And though we knew there were going to be many hurdles in its development, he said, "You are going to write this book." It took me many years to figure out how to do so, but he was right, and his faith and encouragement in helping me write stories about things that matter to me is priceless.

Thanks to my editor, Michael Homler, on our fourth book together. Did he pitch this book with the aid of an action figure and the John Williams soundtrack crescendoing in the background? Of course he did. Thanks for your support, my friend — on this book, which you played a key part in, and in more important, far more difficult pursuits — as we both were home for a year with our small kids doing our best.

Thanks to the teachers and friends who informed parts of this book in real life and in my memory: Dr. John Romano, Dr. Britton J. Harwood, Dr. Gary Lee Stonum, Dr. Beverly Saylor, Dr. Patricia Princehouse, Dr. Peter McCall, Mike Sangiacomo, Dr. Tim Beal, and Rev. Clover Reuter Beal.

Thank you to all the librarians and archivists who were able to help me — and especially to those who couldn't because their beloved books were locked away due to the pandemic. Thanks especially to Ann Sindelar and Madelin Evans. And to Louise Ayres and Zoe Sherman for their great help at the magnificent Saltram.

Thank you to Jeff Trexler, who embodies the words of a mutual friend: "There is a right and a wrong in the universe and the distinction should not be hard to make." Your friendship, your help, and your propensity to help others inspire me.

To Mac's Backs (macsbacks.com), the Ohioana Library Association, the Cleveland Arts Prize, and Susan Grimm for their support.

Thanks to my St. Martin's Press family: Cassidy Graham, Hector DeJean, John Morrone, and Danielle Prielipp, who is a creative inspiration every time we talk. And a special thanks to Diana Frost for her care and powerful expertise. I am grateful to Dr. Angela Gibson for her terrific eye. I also dedicate this book to Sue Llewellyn, for her rich life in books.

Thanks to the various experts I consulted on things: Michael Pace of shotbypace .photography, Dana Keithly, David Landau, and Aura Nurmi. Sincere thanks to Charlotte McDurnan, John Richardson (a gentleman and a scholar). Also to Sherri Jackson, Felicity Cobbing, and Ivona Lloyd-Jones. And to Father (and Dr.) Jean-Michel de Tarragon of the École Biblique in Jerusalem for his help and generosity.

Thanks to my unforgettable Spring 2020 Graphic Narratives class at Case Western Reserve University. And to my new friends on Broxton, the best Halloween street of all.

To my colleagues in the ongoing expedition of the Parker story, I am honored to be part of your company: Dr. Nirit Shalev-Khalifa, for her utter generosity to someone new, and also a great tip of the hat as she was the one to finally bring the Parker archive to the world; Graham Addison, for his encyclopedic knowledge and absolutely brilliant organization of the archive itself; Dr. Ozan Ozavci, for his help on Cavid Bey, and to Dr. Louis Fishman, not only for his first, revelatory discovery in the Ottoman Archives, but for helping me to find my way through a time and place I was unaccustomed to. There are more stories to tell from all of these explorers and I cannot wait to hear them.

A special thanks to the Parkers, Lord and Lady Morley; aka Mark and his lovely wife. Mark's generosity in sharing the archive unconditionally has given us a gift that is beyond any treasure: a good story. And great thanks — and much respect — to Olivia Parker, a crusader and friend. Olivia was a great help to me and it was always a very welcome email conversation to talk Monty, all the way from the other side of the globe. As I sat at home and did research, she was the adventurer. Not only will her story be powerful, but if anyone can find the Ark, it's her.

To all my friends who understood *Raiders* from day one on Gershwin Drive and later on in the Nerd Herd. Special thanks to Chris Kelly, for always representing. And to Chris Strompolos, Eric Zala, and Jayson Lamb, who inspired me to actually do something about my favorite movie.

Love to my family: Nancy, Chris, Steph, and Sally, for helping us out, always, even if from six feet away. When this is over, we are all going to Disney World. For my Aunt Shirley, who inspires me. For Steve and Elaine and the rest of the family. On the New York side: Theresa, Richard, Bobby, Aunt Liz, and Alexa in Paris. Everyone: you know who you are — instead of some line in a book, I can't wait to see you in real life.

For my boys — James, Brandon, and Alex — who are going to see *Raiders* soon. You guys are everything to me; never forget that. And for Caroline, who is the one person I don't have to think up some incredibly over-the-top dramatic line about, because she already knows. This was the year I quit my day job to take care of the boys while she taught high school math behind a face shield. My hero. Love you — love all of you.

And thanks to my parents, who took me to movies of all kinds and let me read what I wanted. They let me find as much wonder as I could possibly imagine, from *Little House on the Prairie* to *Fangoria.* Not as mindless escape, not really, but as a means of understanding the world — not only as it is, but what it might be.

ABOUT THE AUTHOR

Brad Ricca is the author of the Edgar Award-nominated *Mrs. Sherlock Holmes, Olive the Lionheart,* and *Super Boys,* winner of the Ohioana Book Award for Nonfiction. He won the St. Lawrence Book Award for *American Mastodon.* Ricca lives and works in Cleveland.